Orthodox Reviva

MW01716878

Orthodoxy has achieved a large-scale revival in Russia following the collapse of Communism. However, paradoxically, although there is a high level of identification with Orthodoxy, there is in fact a low level of church attendance. This book, based on in-depth ethnographic fieldwork, explores the social background and moral attitudes of the "little flock" of believers who actively participate in religious life. It reveals that the complex moral beliefs of the faithful have a disproportionately high impact on Russian society overall; that among the faithful there is a strong emphasis on striving for personal perfection; but that also there are strong collective ideas concerning religious nationalism and the synergy between the secular and the religious.

Milena Benovska is a Professor in the Department of Ethnology and Balkan Studies at the South-West University of Blagoevgrad, Bulgaria.

Routledge Religion, Society and Government in Eastern Europe and the Former Soviet States

Series Editor

Lucian Leustean is Reader in Politics and International Relations at Aston University, Birmingham, United Kingdom.

This Series seeks to publish high quality monographs and edited volumes on religion, society and government in Eastern Europe and the former Soviet States by focusing primarily on three main themes: the history of churches and religions (including, but not exclusively, Christianity, Islam, Judaism and Buddhism) in relation to governing structures, social groupings and political power; the impact of intellectual ideas on religious structures and values; and the role of religions and faith-based communities in fostering national identities from the nineteenth century until today.

The Series aims to advance the latest research on these themes by exploring the multi-facets of religious mobilisation at local, national and supranational levels. It particularly welcomes studies which offer an interdisciplinary approach by drawing on the fields of history, politics, international relations, religious studies, theology, law, sociology and anthropology.

Orthodox Religion and Politics in Contemporary Eastern Europe
On Multiple Secularisms and Entanglements
Edited by Tobias Köllner

Forced Migration and Human Security in the Eastern Orthodox World
Edited by Lucian N. Leustean

Religion during the Russian-Ukrainian Conflict
Edited by Elizabeth A. Clark and Dmytro Vovk

Russian Orthodoxy, Nationalism and the Soviet State during the Gorbachev Years, 1985–91
Sophie Kotzer

Orthodox Revivalism in Russia
Driving Forces and Moral Quests
Milena Benovska

For more information about this series, please visit: www.routledge.com

Orthodox Revivalism in Russia

Driving Forces and Moral Quests

Milena Benovska

Routledge
Taylor & Francis Group
LONDON AND NEW YORK

First published 2021
by Routledge
2 Park Square, Milton Park, Abingdon, Oxon OX14 4RN

and by Routledge
605 Third Avenue, New York, NY 10017

First issued in paperback 2022

Routledge is an imprint of the Taylor & Francis Group, an informa business

Publisher's Note
The publisher has gone to great lengths to ensure the quality of this reprint but points out that some imperfections in the original copies may be apparent.

British Library Cataloguing-in-Publication Data
A catalogue record for this book is available from the British Library

Library of Congress Cataloging-in-Publication Data
A catalog record for this book has been requested

ISBN: 978-0-367-56385-1 (pbk)
ISBN: 978-0-367-47420-1 (hbk)
ISBN: 978-1-003-03547-3 (ebk)

DOI: 10.4324/9781003035473

Typeset in Times New Roman
by Apex CoVantage, LLC

To Ivan (1950–2013)

Contents

Acknowledgments

The intention to write this book dates back to 2006, when I got the opportunity to develop an associated project with the research group "Religion and Morality in European Russia" (2006–2008) of the Max Planck Institute of Social Anthropology in Halle/Saale. My appreciation goes first and mostly to this Institute. I would like to express my gratitude to its director, Prof. Chris Hann, and to members of the research group: Tünde Komáromi, Tobias Köllner, Agata Ładykowska, Detelina Tocheva, and Jarrett Zigon, for productive discussions, exchange of ideas, and useful comments on my research papers. I am also grateful to the administrative team of this Institute; last but not least, to its excellent librarians.

The anthropologist Jennifer Cash, who did English language editing, deserves my special appreciation. Due to her work, my manuscript was significantly improved and became more readable.

A number of institutions and individuals backed up my fieldwork in the city of Kaluga in 2006 and 2007 (total of three months). European University in St. Petersburg helped me to conduct my pilot study in 2006 and provided administrative documents required to obtain a Russian visa. I am grateful to Prof. Albert Baiburin and to Elena Kokorina, both from the Faculty of Anthropology at the European University, and again to the devoted team of university librarians.

The sociologist Prof. Viacheslav Popkov from Kaluga helped to arrange my stay in this city during the hot summer of 2007. I owe special appreciation to my research assistant Natalija Makarova: Without her energetic assistance, I would not have managed to organize my research during the short time I had. My gratitude goes also to the parish priests E.K. and A.B. from Kaluga, for their time and their "blessing" (i.e. permission) to carry out research observations among their parishes.

After long years of struggle with academic precarity in my native country of Bulgaria, personal losses, and a failure to organize another field trip to Kaluga I considered indispensable, in 2018, I received a research grant from German research foundation DAAD. It gave me the opportunity to complete the present book, spending two precious months in 2018 at the Max Planck Institute of Social Anthropology in Halle/Saale and profiting from its library resources and the friendly environment. I express my gratitude to both institutions.

I am grateful to the publishing team of Routledge, especially to series editor Lucian Leustean and Peter Sowden, for their helpful suggestions and comments.

I thank my family for their patience and understanding during the periods of research spent away from home.

Finally, my warmest appreciation goes to those Orthodox believers from Kaluga who shared their time, friendship, and hospitality with me. This book is about them.

Introduction

In the final days of August 2007, I was preparing my departure from Kaluga, a regional capital city in Central Russia. While I was buying small gifts for my family in a nearby supermarket, I noticed that I was being watched. I recognized one of my interlocutors, a regular worshiper in a parish where I had conducted fieldwork. The man critically scrutinized my purchases and offered to teach me how to recognize the commodities marked by barcodes that, he thought, were hiding the deadly dangerous number 666, the "number of the Beast" (i.e. Satan). The man was one of the so-called *vocerkovlënnye* (enchurched), making him among the most zealous of Orthodox believers. His concern about the dangers hidden in the barcodes reflects a fragment of the discourses typical of the most zealous believers. That he approached me so confidently in a place as public and commercial as a supermarket showed the depth of the socio-cultural change associated with the resumption of religious life after 1988.

How is it possible that there has been such a transformation of Russian society: From the damage of repressive Soviet atheistic politics lasting 70 years to the transformation, since last Soviet years, of Orthodox Christianity into an important factor in both the Russian public sphere and everyday life? This is the first and among the most important research questions I address in the chapters that follow.

This book is based on research conducted mostly among those Orthodox believers who – not infrequently – call themselves "little flock" [*maloe stado*]. The name refers to a passage in the Gospel of Luke: "*Fear not, little flock; for it is your Father's good pleasure to give you the kingdom*" (Luke 12: 32). In modern Russia, as those who adopt this name point out, only a relatively small number of people devote themselves entirely to living according to the Orthodox canon. This book is dedicated to the study of this "little flock" and its importance to the development of contemporary Russian Orthodox Christianity. The purpose of the study is to show the underlying forces of contemporary Orthodox life in Russia, beyond paradoxes and appearances.

Theoretical approaches

The 1980s were a decade marked by the unprecedented return of religion to the public world as a global process. The lesson of the political power of religious practices was again and convincingly recalled. The triumph of "disenchanted" rational modernity (in the sense of Max Weber) proved prematurely announced against the backdrop of radical religious movements that gave strong political messages. The disintegration of socialism between 1989 and 1991 gave impetus to the postsocialist revival of religious life, which, despite its controversial and disputable nature, has been a manifestation of both massive postsocialist social changes and an aspect of the global rise of religiosity since the 1980s (Borowik and Tomka, 2001, p. 8; Hann, 2006b; Casanova, 1994; Berger, 1999; Cannell, 2006, p. 30). Modernity and religiosity were no longer perceived as incompatible and mutually exclusive (Hervieu-Léger, 1999a, p. 16). Inevitably, all this changed the "landscape" of the academic debate about the essence and role of religion.

To set the scene of this study, I will follow some main trends in the contemporary discussion of religion, but without following chronological order and without seeking for exhaustiveness. Two of the most influential voices in the new landscape are those of José Casanova and Peter Berger and their derived theoretical models of "deprivatization of religion" and "desecularization of the world". Although these theories are familiar, it is worth recalling them because of their importance. According to Casanova (1994, p. 5), the most distinctive feature of the new role of religions in the world is their return from the private to the public sphere:

> By deprivatization I mean the fact that religious traditions throughout the world are refusing to accept the marginal and privatized role which theories of modernity as well as theories of secularization had reserved for them. Social movements have appeared which either are religious in nature or challenging in the very name of religion the legitimacy and autonomy of the primary secular spheres, the state and the market economy.

Approximately at the same time, Peter Berger conceptualized the rediscovery of religion as a "desecularization of the world" (Berger, 1999). Berger, who had previously contributed significantly to the development and legitimacy of secularization theories (e.g. Berger, 1967) called for a radical rethinking of the earlier theories and perhaps even their rejection. The intellectual courage of this gesture of self-denial actually reinforces the authority of the thesis of desecularization.

Casanova, unlike Berger, does not dispute the justification of secularization theories themselves: "the core of the theory of secularization, the thesis of differentiation and emancipation of the secular spheres from religious institutions and norms, remains valid" (Casanova, 1994, p. 6). For others, (Western) Europe is regarded as the only continent to which secularization theories are valid, and in this sense, it is "the exception that proves the rule". Thus, Danièle Hervieu-Léger and Grace Davie, observing France and Britain respectively, confirm the view of the sustainability (within a specific framework) of religion in the lives of these countries. Religion in Western Europe is still viable as a phenomenon of social memory (Davie, 1999; Hervieu-Léger, 1999a; Davie, 2000), although marked by the distinctly atomized search for spirituality that shifts the individual's participation in the institutional religious life.

The complexity of Western European religious landscapes in late modernity and the careful analyses of social data are reflected in Grace Davie's witty and popular theory of "believing without belonging" (Davie, 1999). Half-empty churches testify to alienation from collective religious life, yet the interest in various forms of spirituality speaks to the vitality of religious practices (ibid.). It appears that in countries with a distinctly secular political structure, like France, "religion is everywhere" in unexpected forms, and "everyone has the choice to maintain practices and beliefs that suit him". The frequency of individual conversions and the mass appeal of pilgrimage practices are one of the most important manifestations of Western European religious life at the end of the twentieth century and the beginning of the twenty-first century (Hervieu-Léger, 1999b).

Among anthropologists, theoretical debate over the last 30 years continues to challenge the relevance of the very concept of religion (see most recently, *Current Anthropology* 2014; *Anthropological Forum* 2017, issues 34, 35). The main question continues to be whether or not it is possible to reach a universal definition of religion. The beginning of the debate (in its intensive phase) can be traced to the 1970s when Clifford Geertz insisted on the necessity of "an analysis of the system of meanings embodied in the symbols which make up the religion proper, and, second, the relating of these systems to social-structural and psychological processes" (Geertz, 1973, pp. 87–125). According to a judgment, the result of this debate is "a tectonic movement" (Orsi, 2017, p. 54) in the research of religion.

In his influential criticism of Geertz, Talal Asad is skeptical about the opportunity to find "a universal definition of religion, not only because its constituent elements and relationship are historically specific, but because that definition is itself the historical product of discursive processes". Instead, Asad (1993, pp. 27–54, 60) insists on the need to link the notion of religion to power and history; a similar approach taken up earlier by Maurice Bloch (1989, pp. 44–88) and Michel Foucault (1980, pp. 103, 157).

Although not many anthropologists share (at least not entirely) the criticism of Geertz, nor accept all of Asad's arguments, his analysis remains an unchanging reference point. At least as Simon Coleman does, Talal Asad can be described as a representative of the "historically contingent approach" in constructing religion as an object of anthropological analysis. Certainly, this approach is well established and widely represented in the anthropology of Christianity. But Asad should never be taken alone; as Coleman points out, there is another valuable stream of scholarship that deals with the Christian roots of anthropology as a discipline (Cannell, 2006, pp. 1–45; Tomlinson and Engelke, 2006, p. 3). On different grounds, this stream also does not accept the attempts to give a universal definition of religion "as such" (Coleman, 2017, p. 87).

Other authors stress that the debate cannot and should not be resolved in either direction. Though they support sensitivity to the theoretical complexity and untangling the contradictions inherent in the concept of "religion", they warn against producing an "infertile nihilism" that would deny the concept of religion, and along with it the reality that it proposes to encompass. They warn against treading the same discursive paths that sent the concepts of "culture", "history", and "science" into a "black hole" at the end of the twentieth century. To use the concept of religion reflexively and critically is not the same as the refusal of it (Orsi, 2017, pp. 55–56).

A second orientation in the anthropological theorizing of religion is based on psychology. Simon Coleman describes it as a "cognitive orientation" according to which "predisposition or latent ability to religion that is embedded in our thought-thinking apparatus from birth and is the result or the side effect of human evolution".[1] The third orientation, which Coleman claims "did not receive the necessary recognition", is characterized by interdisciplinary hybridization: A cross between philosophy, anthropology, and theology (Coleman, 2017, pp. 89–90).

As it appears, however, the attempts to deconstruct the very notion of "religion" become one of the "fermenting agents" that catalyzes the flourishing and abundant output in the field of the anthropology of religion and, in particular, of the anthropology of Christianity. The latter, according to some influential voices, is "more or less a child of the new millennium" (Robbins, 2014, p. 158). Joel Robbins dated the "birth" of this "child" (if we develop the metaphor) between 2003 and 2006, when three edited volumes appeared – a significant milestone in the research field. Two of them carry the same title *Anthropology of Christianity*: One edited by Joel Robbins himself and the other by Fenella Cannell); the third one is titled *The Limits of Meaning* (Robbins, 2003; Cannell, 2006; Engelke and Tomlinson, 2006). According to the authors of the three volumes, the anthropology of Christianity at that time was new, since until then anthropologists had ignored the study of Christianity. Whether or not this is true, since 2010 publications in anthropology of Christianity have become so numerous that it is difficult to identify a single "approach" (Robbins, 2014, p. 158; Barker, 2008, pp. 377–381).

Though Robbins points to a new concern with "Christianity" as such, others note that the anthropological interest in Christianity is not a novelty. Instead, they see the remarkable developments since the turn of the millennium as a continuation of trends that began as early as the 1960s, with well-known research by influential authors, such as Edith and Victor Turner and Jean and John Comaroff, at the top of a long list (see Hann, 2007, pp. 394–402; Chua, 2012, pp. 12–18). Indeed, recent contributions to the anthropology of Christianity have a somewhat unbalanced and reductionist character: They suffer from a "deep-seated problem of idealism" regarding Christianity (Comaroff, 2010, p. 529; see also, Englund, 2007, pp. 481–482), in part related to being engaged predominantly with the study of Pentecostal and Charismatic movements. Thus, they sometimes represent a "Christian" culture detached from other social contexts (Chua, 2012, pp. 16–18; Hann, 2014, pp. 182–183; Orsi, 2017, p. 64; Englund, 2007, pp. 481–483).

Still, the new anthropology of Christianity has distinctive features compared to previous intellectual trajectories in which Christianity was implicated. This anthropology is a reflexive project. Those who undertake it seek to give new directions to anthropological theory; to move the study of Christianity closer to the center of anthropological knowledge; to respond to the changes in the world (the ambitious public role of religion and the emergence of "world Christianity"); and of changes in anthropology itself. The new anthropology of Christianity sheds light on radical social change; it points to social "rifts" in long-standing interest of anthropology in cultural continuity (Harris, 2006, p. 72; Robbins, 2007, pp. 5–38; Robbins, 2014, pp. 158–162, 167). Whether or not practitioners have yet succeeded is not clear, and the new studies have yet to answer directly the criticisms levelled at them.

In the coming chapters, I do not attempt to answer how new the "new" anthropology of religion is. However, I do address one of the main criticisms directed at the scholarship. Certainly, the main protagonists of the anthropology of Christianity are almost exclusively interested in Pentecostal and Charismatic movements. They see these offshoots of Protestantism as the bearers of great religious change in the contemporary world and as messengers of "world Christianity". Not only does such an approach ignore the still-strong role of Catholicism in the world, but it misses Orthodoxy altogether. I am not the first author to see evidence of an unbalanced approach in terms of this lack. Regarding the omission of Orthodoxy from the "new" anthropology of Christianity, for example, Robert Orsi, ironically and rhetorically asks:

> Can Orthodoxy with its inherent complexity and geographic dispersal offer researchers another prospect of creating non-modern theories of religion? In particular, [comes to mind] the practical theology of the icons, the worship of the saints and of places of their burial, the place of prayer in everyday life, the patterns of power, obedience and discipline, the history of contacts with Muslims and Jews, and the diverse experience of relations with different states
> (Orsi, 2017, p. 65, my translation from Russian)

If only the "silence" on the 200 million mass of Orthodox Christians were the only deficiency of the new approach, it might easily be excused and simply rectified. But this "silence" is almost certainly linked to the insurmountable negative stereotypes of Orthodoxy (Kennworthy, 2008, p. 23), built into additional layers by the accumulation of Cold War political and cultural stereotypes on both sides.

Omission of Orthodoxy means that the full range of Christian ideas, along with the inner heterogeneity and complexity of Christianity, are lost. Additionally, omitting Orthodoxy means foregoing a rich opportunity to explore another model of modernity, based on the combination of Orthodox cultures and the socialist social orders (Hann and Goltz, 2010b, pp. 1–29; Köllner, 2012, p. 16; Hann, 2014). Moreover, the global significance to Christianity of the revival of Christian practices in postsocialist countries, and especially in Russia, after decades of severe repression and thousands of murders, should not be underestimated.

Despite the lack of interest for Orthodoxy within the "new" anthropology of Christianity, a number of anthropologists, including Western ones, have been engaged in the study of Orthodox Christianity in the postsocialist world over the last two decades. The end of socialism and postsocialist developments provided a clear incentive for the study of Orthodoxy (as well as, of course, other religious traditions, old and new). As official atheism had been an inseparable part of politics, social orders, and the cultures of socialism, the resurgence and rise of religious life after its end are a fundamental aspect of postsocialist change. The studies that have been taken up are almost all based on solid ethnographic case studies; they concern a wide range of social practices unfolding in the orbit of religious experience; and they treat the problems of how religious ideologies and institutions are interwoven with politics, morality, economy, solidarity, charity, memory, and nationalism. I identify some of the most relevant to my own research.

Part of the research on religion in postsocialist space finds similarities and confirms the development of global trends. It is worth mentioning the importance of conversion (Pelkmans, 2009; Wanner, 2009, pp. 163–182; Engelhart, 2005; Benovska-Sabkova et al., 2010, pp. 23–43); the strengthening of the public aspects of religion (Hann, 2006b; Wanner, 2018, pp. 88–95); and mass participation in pilgrimage practices (Vulchinova, 1999; Naletova, 2010, pp. 240–266; Kormina, 2004, pp. 27–40, 2010, pp. 267–286, 2012, pp. 195–227, 2018, pp. 143–162; Köllner, 2012, pp. 141–169).

A particular feature of postsocialist religious landscapes is the growing ethnonationalism that marks the rise of religiosity (including Orthodoxy) in Central Eastern Europe and Russia (Buzalka, 2007, pp. 9–12; Naumescu, 2007, pp. 27–56; Wanner and Steinberg, 2008, pp. 2, 22; Hann and Goltz, 2010b, p. 10; Köllner, 2012, pp. 169–173). The coexistence of religious revivalism and ethnonationalism is partly related to the ability of religion to express the revival of old identities (as well as the invention of new ones). Observations by anthropologists show how certain religious communities that almost ceased to exist in socialism, or survived only underground, are now resurrecting. These include Old Believers in Russia and Romania (Rogers, 2009; Naumescu, 2018, pp. 29–54)[2] as well as Greco-Catholics (Uniats) (Naumescu, 2007; Buzalka, 2007; Mahieu and Naumescu, 2008; Hann, 2014, pp. 186–189).

To turn specifically to the study of contemporary Orthodoxy in Russia, various disciplines, including anthropology have been in close communication. Still, broadly speaking, two basic approaches to the anthropological study of Orthodoxy can be outlined: The first involves a general survey of Orthodoxy with a "close-up" or national-level view; the second involves a problem-oriented approach to social practices on a religious basis. In the Russian postsocialist context, the first approach often focuses on topics such as: The rise of religiosity, secularization or desecularization, the democratization (or not) of contemporary Russian Orthodoxy, the relationship of religion to modernity and the national identity, religious ideology, the nature of religious power, and the relationship between church and state. Sociologists, political scientists and philosophers engage with this approach more often than anthropologists do. I consider their research in my study, but do not include deep attention to them for the moment. Nevertheless, this first approach sets a powerful and general framework for studying Orthodox Christianity in modern Russia. An influential voice in this research area is that of Alexander Agadjanian (Agadjanian, 2001, pp. 473–488; 2003, pp. 327–346; 2013, pp. 75–94; 2010, pp. 97–113, 2011, pp. 16–26, 2017, pp. 39–60; Agadjanian and Rousselet, 2006, pp. 8–32).

The approach I define as problem-oriented has resulted in a variety of anthropological contributions based on ethnographic work. These allow an in-depth look at the specific spheres of Orthodox practices and ideologies – mainly in Russia, but also in other Orthodox traditions. An undoubtedly non-exhaustive list should not omit some of the most productive models of research penetration into Orthodox sociality, ideology, and culture. Here we have to take insightful analyses of the "materiality" and "sensuousness" emblematic of Orthodoxy, including acoustics and identity politics in Orthodox singing and mediaized music, sacral visual images (e.g. icons), and communication with and through them (Hanganu, 2010, pp. 33–55; Engelhardt, 2010, pp. 101–123, 2018, pp. 58–81; Luehrmann, 2010, pp. 36–78; Mahieu, 2010, pp. 79–100; Bandak, 2014; Keane, 2014; Heo, 2018, pp. 83–102). So, too, the subject of sensitivity in Orthodox Christianity, presented through the prism of prayer practices, has enabled a group of authors to address the question of the essence of Orthodoxy and its various expressive forms (Luehrmann, 2018).

Ethnographies and analyses of modern monastic Orthodoxy have been carried out with full professional dedication: The asceticism, values, labor, social, and aesthetic practices of monastic Orthodoxy (Forbess, 2005; Forbess, 2010, pp. 131–154; Naumescu, 2010, p. 176; Poujeau, 2010, pp. 177–192; Dubovka, 2015a, pp. 322–344, 2015b, pp. 63–81, 2017, pp. 33–64, 2018, pp. 192–213; Medvedeva, 2016b, pp. 92–108, 2016a, pp. 59–72). Moreover, Daria Dubovka and Ksenia Medvedeva lived and worked in Russian monasteries as *trudniki* during their research.[3]

The process of canonization of "new martyrs", mainly from the Soviet era, is an important and vigorously debated aspect of the post-Soviet rise of religiosity and Orthodoxy in particular (Christensen, 2018). Therefore, it is unsurprising that the contemporary worship of Orthodox saints has attracted lasting interest by a group of Russian anthropologists. They show how the respect for (new) martyrs as exemplary images – a source of charisma but also morality – is constructed through communication and interaction between the clergy and laity. The authors also manage to address the internal tensions between the "folk customs" and the position of the clergy to the latter or the "regimes of Orthodox religiosity" for the intertwining of faith, morality, and politics (Shtyrkov, 2001, pp. 130–155; Kormina and Shtyrkov, 2008, pp. 154–184; Kormina and Shtyrkov, 2011, pp. 168–191; Filičeva, 2006, pp. 171–183; Kormina, 2010, pp. 1–28; Kormina, 2011, pp. 189–211).

The significant political and economic changes since the end of the Soviet era, accompanied by tensions and anxiety in Russian society (especially in the 1990s), are also expressed through the religious language of millenaristic expectations, social movements, and narratives, including in the Orthodox environment. This socio-cultural phenomenon has been analyzed in a number of publications (Tarabukina, 2000; Panchenko, 2001, pp. 10–26; Akhmetova, 2004, pp. 238–249, 2006, pp. 238–249, 2010). In a similar sense, but also in relation to the more general tendencies towards the rise of ethnonationalism in the context of religious renewal in postsocialist societies, the manifestations of religious nationalism should be understood (Shtyrkov, 2011a, pp. 232–244).

Processes of theoretical renewal and reflexive change accompany anthropological contributions to the study of the different dimensions of modern Russian Orthodoxy: Ideologies, practices and institutions. Rethinking the notion of "popular Christianity" as "an ideologically and methodologically indefensible term" (Shtyrkov, 2006, p. 7, see also Panchenko, 2004 [2002], pp. 64–80) is subject to conceptual criticism. A sign of renewal in the terminology toolkit is at least the mention of "popular Christianity" in quotes (compare, for example, Panchenko, 1998, 1999, 2006b, pp. 189–193, 2012, pp. 321–340). The academic reputation of the discipline of the anthropology of religion is also enshrined institutionally by the foundation of the Center for Anthropology of Religion at the European University in St. Petersburg in 2010.[4]

The study of contemporary religion in Russia should consider contemporary Orthodoxy through the prism of the social practices that are integral to it and to the social communities that are the foundation of Orthodox life. The publication of two collections of articles gives a clear sign of this effort to study the intimate mechanisms of the social fabric and to shorten the distance between scholars and the people studied – their partners in the production of knowledge – although this effort is not limited to these two books. The editions are in Russian, the result of a Russian-French collaboration carried out by Alexander Agadjanian and Kathie Rousselet (2006, 2011).

Ksenia Sergazina (2006, p. 124) reached the conclusion that a number of newly "invented" Orthodox practices arose, paradoxically, in a collective searching for "authentic" religiosity. Others have reached the same conclusion (Kormina, Panchenko and Shtyrkov, 2015). In this second case, comparative study of post-Soviet religion in Russia, Ukraine, and Armenia offers an unusual explanatory model for the "religious revival" in post-Soviet space. By critically rethinking the theories about the return to religion through the prism of "rift" – the sudden and unexpected social change in the collapse of the Soviet Union – Kormina and Shtyrkov, in turn, privileged a different theoretical model that emphasized the continuity (Kormina and Shtyrkov, 2015, pp. 7–45). I will go back to this important question in the next chapter of the book.

Studies that bridge the topics of religion and morality in postsocialist space are appearing too. If the anthropology of morality can be established with Howell's (1997) founding contribution, the post-Soviet space has been particularly attractive for some theory-builders (e.g. Heintz, 2009b; Zigon, 2008a). One of the contributions to this area is the collection of articles on *Religion, Morality and Community in Post-Soviet Societies* (Steinberg and Wanner, 2008). Through separate ethnographic case studies and historical analyses, the authors present several dilemmas in the collective searching for a new moral order after the collapse of socialism. Religiosity here appears as a resource of variable importance for finding "appropriate and viable moral practices", both collectively and personally (Wanner and Stenberg, 2008, p. 4). Most anthropologists that take up the question of "morality and religion" at all have continued their efforts in this direction (Rogers, 2009; Wanner, 2011, pp. 214–225, 2018; Zigon, 2010, 2011c, 2011a; Caldwell, 2011, pp. 48–66).

These questions, as well as others related to them, were addressed by the research group with which I was associated. This group studied specific aspects of the relationship between religion – Orthodox Christianity – and morality in contemporary European Russia, but we also carried out our work in the broader frame of postsocialism.[5] Studying the nature of Orthodox values and moral practices among today's Russian entrepreneurs, Tobias Köllner also reveals the moral judgments of the believers in Vladimir, a city with a significant role in the history of Russian statehood. In line with the contradictory logic of the Orthodox attitude towards wealth and money, Köllner (2011, pp. 191–213, 2012) shows how Orthodox moral judgments favor the "donations" made by parishioners through self-reliance in the restoration of Orthodox churches to impersonal monetary donations. In contrast, an ambivalent attitude is manifest towards the large donations of wealthy entrepreneurs. These donations give ground to the metaphoric expression as "built with gold", but the collective moral preference is still for churches "built with tears". The author also reveals the hidden mechanisms and logic of exchange in the context of the post-Soviet relations between state power and the economy: "at times the idea to give donations to the Church seemed to be a feasible way to prevent pressure from the state's side" (Köllner, 2011, p. 198).

Religious education in Russia's secular schools placed another set of problems before us. The introduction of *Fundamentals of Orthodox Culture* as a school course certainly functions as a legitimation of the religious above all secular powers, but it also provides a vision for the moral re-education of post-Soviet Russian society (Köllner, 2016, pp. 366–386). The ethnographic work by Agata Ładykowska among women teachers in Southern Russia (Rostov-on-Don) who teach courses on Orthodox culture discovers that these women are important actors in the Russian "religious revival". Her careful analysis of the moral conceptual dictionary adopted in this environment shows subtle semantic distinctions, testifying to enhanced reflection. The ambiguity of terms such as morality and ethics allows not only the construction of a new moral personality in the post-Soviet context, but also the preservation of the continuity of personal moral trajectories as well as collective moral values inherited from the Soviet era (Ładykowska, 2011, pp. 27–47). Moreover, Ładykowska, together with Detelina Tocheva, reached the important conclusion that the teaching of Orthodox culture by women teachers also serves to modify the structure of religious authority in the otherwise patriarchal structure of the Orthodox Church's institutions (Ładykowska and Tocheva, 2013, pp. 55–74).

Detelina Tocheva's research focuses on issues opposite the value orientations pursued by Tobias Köllner's entrepreneurs. Based in a smaller city in Northwestern Russia, Tocheva discusses social practices related to poverty, charity, and forms of solidarity (including alms-giving) in the Orthodox environment (Tocheva, 2017). Spontaneous and altruistic donation in the everyday context ("grassroots charity") does not have a religious purpose, even when it takes place in the temple; however, an "imagined horizontal community of those in need" is formed in this way (Tocheva, 2011, p. 87).

While exploring "religious and secular concepts of evil" (including problems such as conversions and ghostly possessions), Tünde Komáromi (2010, pp. 103–106) is also interested in more general questions about Orthodox religion in Russia. In a dialogue with Alexander Agadjanian (2011a, pp. 16–26), she distinguishes the following types: Remote religiosity, passionate religiosity, and balanced religiosity (Komáromi, 2011, pp. 94–96).

Jarrett Zigon (2008a, 2008b, 2010, 2011a), also belonged to the research group. Zigon examines the moral concepts and social practices of the Russian Orthodox Church integrated into drug rehabilitation programs in St. Petersburg, following his previous fieldwork in Moscow among HIV-positive people. His theoretical views are summarized in the introduction to the collection *Multiple Moralities and Religions in Post-Soviet Russia* (2011a), cited earlier according to individual contributor. Zigon places a strong emphasis on the concept of "moral rift". It is the key to understanding the distinction between "morality, done and articulated or unconsciously or discursively, and ethics as a conscious attempt to be moral in a moment of dilemma or questioning" (Zigon, 2011a, p. 8). As in his earlier publications, Zigon defines morality in three different aspects: Institutional, that of public discourse; and as embodied predisposition. Such a definition leads to the logical conclusion that there are a multiplicity of moral discourses and practices in every society – a view that is, indeed, generally accepted by anthropologists working in contemporary Russia.

Contemporary Russian Orthodoxy continues to evolve, often following contradictory trajectories. Accordingly, researchers continue to look for the appropriate theoretical models from which they can best offer a critical and reflective understanding of these processes. Recent publications (e.g. Wanner, 2018, pp. 88–95 or Kormina, Panchenko and Shtyrkov, 2017, pp. 127–166) make a strong claim that research, exploration, and discoveries are far from exhausted. Later in this book, I will return to these theoretical problems once again and critique the concepts on which I rely. The first chapter is the right place for review.

Field research. Kaluga: The place and the people

The following pages present my fieldwork as the empirical basis of this study and as an integral part of the research process. They outline: (a) a brief introduction to the city of Kaluga and its historical, economic, social, and cultural characteristics as they relate to the field study; and (b) fieldwork analysis. This presentation is not an expression of the "narcissistic reflexivity of postmodern anthropology" (Bourdieu, 2003, p. 281), but of the intention to ensure the transparency of the research procedures. The latter gives an opportunity for the validity of the observations and conclusions to be critically evaluated and, ultimately, verified. The field study in Russia was conducted in Kaluga for three months. A pilot study was conducted in September 2006, which aimed at becoming familiar with local contexts, specifying research strategies, and identifying specific locations for the next year's ethnographic observations. In 2007, fieldwork lasted for two months, from the end of June until the end of August.

At the end of June 2007, when I arrived in Kaluga for the second time, a message was glued at the entrance of the nine-story building in which I was about to live. It read well in the bright north night, despite the late hour: "*The temple will exist! Congratulations to all the residents of Terepec!*" Terepec was the name of the neighborhood. I read further. The message mentioned litigation about the location of the future temple and a court decision dated June 6, 2007, confirming that "the temple will be where it was planned" at the Boulevard of Enthusiasts ['*Bul'var entuziastov*'] that linked the peripheral neighborhood to the city center. As suggested by the leading words that first caught my attention, the large-scale construction and restoration of Orthodox churches cannot go unnoticed in contemporary Russia and still leaves the impression of a triumphant "religious revival" many years after its uneven start in 1988. However, the message also spoke of disputes and struggles in a local context; things which I knew too little about. It was a remarkable reminder of the complexity and contradictions that accompany religious life in Russia after the restoration of religious liberties in the late 1980s.

Kaluga is usually referred to by its inhabitants as a "small city". Indeed, its population numbered 327,500 inhabitants in 2007, during my fieldwork, and had 357,700 inhabitants in 2018.[6] It is a regional center in the Central Region of Russia, about 180 kilometers southwest of Moscow. The city is situated along the Oka River.[7] The first historical record mentioning Kaluga dates back to 1371 (*Pamiatniki*, 1880, p. 136; *Kaluzhskij kraj*, 1976, p. 22). A frontier fortification during the Middle Ages, the city gradually evolved as a trade and industrial center since the early modern period, flourishing with proto-industry and industry (manufactories and factories) in the eighteenth century.

Trade contributed to the formation of the historical architecture of the city as well as to the identity of its population. Many times in conversations with local people I heard the opinion that Kaluga is a city of tradesmen and craftsmen. This judgment, apparently, is part of the local longue durée. Socialist industrialization – testified for everywhere in the urban space – should have made this expression anachronistic. A nostalgic reminder of the pre-revolutionary appearance of the city is the historic architecture in the central city area: Not only the beautiful residences of wealthy merchants from the late 19th and early 20th centuries, but also the smaller wooden houses in "traditional" Russian style.

Nevertheless, during the eighteenth century, Kaluga flourished economically, hardly crippled by the numerous fires and outbreaks of disease. Churches, continuously built and rebuilt, give a symbolic expression of the economic success and of the strong Orthodox affiliation. In 1910, there were at least 40 churches in Kaluga (Malinin, 1992 [1912], pp. 30–67), though the number may have been higher.[8]

In 1910, the city's population amounted to 55,000. The Kaluga province [*gubernija*], of which the city was the capital, was then inhabited by 1,419,949 inhabitants. The population of today's Kaluga province (*oblast'*, according to Soviet administrative vocabulary), has been in decline for more than a century. In 2007, it numbered only 1,009,000 inhabitants. The increased population in Kaluga city, as well as the reduced number of inhabitants of the region, testify to the scale of rural-urban migration processes during and after socialism.

In the last years before the 1917 Revolution, 99.5% of the population in the province consisted of ethnic Russians. Ethnic minorities (although few and mostly Jews, Poles, and Germans) could be found in the cities (Chernyshev and Personal'nyj, 1992 [1912], p. 21). The majority of the population of today's city of Kaluga identify as ethnic Russians, regardless of the influence of migration and ethnic mixing that developed during the Soviet era (Dubas, 2004, p. 216).

In the early Soviet era, Kaluga experienced a period of intense industrialization, and the city was among those selected to support the Soviet military industry. In the 1990s, a significant number of enterprises were closed. During my stay, there were many abandoned industrial buildings. However, the economic development of the city and the region since 2006 can be considered a success story. The city is experiencing a new industrial boom, mainly thanks to large-scale foreign investments. In 2006, Kaluga started construction of a large Volkswagen plant. During my pilot field research in September 2006, the construction of the plant – close to the outskirts of the city – was at its very beginning; only the prepared construction site and construction facilities were visible. By my return in 2007, the plant was already producing cars, and in 2014, it expanded. To date, the plant remains one of the largest foreign investments in the Russian car industry, although Volvo and Mitsubishi plants were also set up in Kaluga after 2009.[9] Global pharmaceutical and food giants are also opening their branches in Kaluga: Since 2011, L'Oreal, Astra-Zeneka and Nestlé have all arrived.[10]

Between 2006 and 2017, 99 new large enterprises (small businesses do not enter the number) were established in Kaluga region. Some 27,000 new jobs were created, and unemployment in the city was less than 1%. The local airport, which was closed in 2001, was restored with international status in 2015, when its first regular flights took place.[11] The successful development of the investment program in Kaluga and the region is largely explained by the flexible local policy for the creation of preferential conditions for investors, conducted by the longtime governor of the Kaluga *oblast'*, Anatolii Artamonov.[12] In the ranking for the development of Russian regions organized by the Civil Society Forum, the Kaluga region was ranked third in 2016 and fifth in 2017.[13]

Without neglecting the investment program and lowering unemployment rates in Kaluga and its region, the success story is "re-read" and relativized through the perspective "from below" of the ordinary people. The anthropologist Jeremy Maurice shows (based on long-term work in the Kaluga region), that the overall economic stability during the first mandates of President Putin (after 1999) was subsequently followed by relatively low incomes and a lowered purchasing power because prices have been similar to those in Western Europe. The high inflation rate and international political crises in which Russia has been involved, especially after 2014, are primarily at fault. Working-class men, in particular, report serious levels of economic uncertainty, low incomes, and demographic collapse (high mortality rates among men) (Morris, 2017, pp. 46–49). These different economic trends – alternately rosy and bleak – are part of the context in which religious life in the city evolves.

I chose Kaluga for fieldwork because of its importance in the history of Russian Orthodoxy, not because it might serve as a "typical case" (the latter was recognized by anthropologists as an irrelevant strategy). Additionally, some pragmatic considerations were important. The proximity of Kaluga to Moscow and the convenient fast rail were important advantages; given the limited time that I had, the prospect of spending some of it on long, fruitless journeys across the vast country was undesirable. On the other hand, my acquaintance with local colleagues was also a weighty argument in favor of the city. I valued their perspective. I also needed an official invitation to obtain a visa and a recommendation from a Russian institution to obtain a registered address (*propiska*) from the Russian Ministry of Interior.

As for the city's place in Russian Orthodoxy, it is worth noting that on the territory of theKaluga diocese are located "some of the most prestigious monasteries in Russia". "The roots of the Orthodox tradition in folk culture and the way of life of the population" in the historical Kaluga province are manifested through the presence of many monasteries, the numerous clergy, and the significant number of works of religious art (Filatov and Lunkin, 2006b, pp. 320–321). First of all, it is worth mentioning the stauropegic monastery, Optina Hermitage [Optina Pustyn'], which is one of the most revered and most visited monasteries in the whole of Russia (Paert, 2010, p. 76, 130; Kuchumov, 2002, pp. 232–238; Zyrianov, 1999, p. 314). It is located 60 kilometers from Kaluga and two kilometers from the small town of Kozel'sk. The monastery was founded in the fifteenth century, and after the beginning of the nineteenth century, it became one of the most important centers of Orthodox monasticism and a symbol of Russian religiosity. It is considered that the important institution of the *starčestvo* originated here (Solov'ëv [1899] 2005, pp. 3–7; Gorbacheva, 2006, pp. 5–23; Kuchumov, 2002, pp. 223–244).[14]

Optina Pustyn' was honored as the "heart" of Russian spirituality. Some of the most significant Russian writers of the nineteenth century, such as Nikolai Gogol, Leo Tolstoy, and Fyodor Dostoevsky, as well as the Slavophile writers Konstantin Leontiev and the Kireevski brothers, repeatedly visited it (Evgin, 2003, pp. 209–220; Paert, 2010, pp. 111, 130–134; Berestov, 2003, pp. 290–325; Duncan, 2000, pp. 23–24; Solov'ëv, 2005 [1899], pp. 3–5). Leontiev even settled in the hermitage in 1886. Dostoevsky's impressions of his meeting (1878) with the *starec* [saint] Ambrose of Optina [Amvrosii Optinskii] in the monastery influenced his novel *The Brothers Karamazov*, while the *starec* became one of the prototypes of the famous hero of the writer, Father Zosima (Solov'ëv, 2005 [1899], pp. 3–7; Dostoevskaja, 1981, p. 329; Pavlovich, 1980, p. 88; Paert, 2010, p. 126). These circumstances are often mentioned in the conversations of local people.

But, indeed, in the works of Mikhail Saltykov-Shchedrin, Leo Tolstoy, and Fyodor Dostoevsky, the *starcy* became literary heroes in the 1870s and 1880s. "Writers were essential in the production of the image of the elder as a typical symbol of Russian spirituality and culture" (Paert, 2010, p. 130). The geographical proximity of the Optina Hermitage to Kaluga has strengthened the local identity among the city's inhabitants and their perception of significance in the symbolic geography of Russia (Avramenko, 2001, p. 95). From the perspective of today, the most important thing is the immediate strong influence that monks from the Optina Hermitage have on the life of the Orthodox dioceses in Kaluga.

To varying degrees, the proximity of the Tikhonova Hermitage [Tikhonova Pustyn'] to Kaluga and the Kazansky Convent in Šamordino (near Kozel'sk) also influenced the local context. The latter is located 12 kilometers away from Optina Pustyn' and was founded in 1884 under the spiritual guidance of the most famous monk from Optina mentioned earlier, (future saint) Amvrosii (Paert, 2010, pp. 93, 153).

At the beginning of the fieldwork, it became clear that there was another factor in Kaluga whose impact determined this city as a suitable place for monitoring the processes of Orthodox resurgence in Russia. The head of the Kaluga diocese (since 1990), Metropolitan Kliment (Kapalin) is among the most influential and ambitious hierarchs of the Russian Orthodox Church (hereafter ROC). In the period 2003–2009, he was one of the eight permanent members of the Holy Synod of the Russian Orthodox Church and was holding the post of Manager of the Affairs of the Moscow Patriarchate. Long before the death of Patriarch Alexii II, the Kaluga Metropolitan was regarded by local citizens as one of the contenders for a future head of the ROC (Mitrokhin, 2004, pp. 193, 202). From the very first days of my stay in Kaluga in 2006, I learned about people's expectations that the local metropolitan would probably be the heir to the patriarchal throne. Shortly after the death of Patriarch Alexii II (December 5, 2008), in January 2009, Metropolitan Kliment was identified as one of three candidates in the election of a new Russian patriarch: Eventually he remained the second choice to the now-Patriarch Kirill (see Papkova, 2013, pp. 250–251; Bodin, 2014, pp. 56–57).

The Kaluga Metropolitan's membership in the highest levels of the Russian Orthodox hierarchy, alongside its proximity to Moscow, defines Kaluga as a place where the ROC's official policies could be closely observed. Relations between the church and the state authorities should have been particularly visible. And they were.[15] Metropolitan Kliment is considered "a highly authoritarian leader." His conservative views, his attempts at interfering with the mass media, and some of his xenophobic manifestations directly reflected on the atmosphere in the Orthodox parishes in Kaluga (Filatov and Lunkin, 2006b, pp. 322, 323, 326). During fieldwork, I repeatedly encountered the consequences of Metropolitan's influence. This was, however, unanticipated on my part. I learned of Metropolitan's reputation and importance only after arriving in the city. Inevitably, his politics left a significant imprint (although indirect) on the course of my fieldwork.

Beyond the "rose garden": The field study of a postsocialist scholar in a post-Soviet environment

Fieldwork in 2006 was organized as a pilot study. Besides general familiarization with the field and specification of the appropriate methods, it aimed at determining the parish or parishes in which the ethnographic work would take place the next year. In 2006–2007 there were 33 operating Orthodox churches in Kaluga, including monastic churches and the so-called home temples. By the end of September 2006, my research assistant, Natalija Makarova, and I had visited about half of the operating churches and, after careful consideration, we identified two of them as suitable places for extended fieldwork. The aim was to apply an approach based on the in-depth study of a parish (or congregational study, as per Warner, 1991, pp. 174–193). The research strategy to divide the fieldwork into two parishes aimed at exploring similar religious practices in different social environments. The chosen approach has proven important because it demonstrated the more sustainable nature of activities in the one parish located in the city center.

The original idea, however, was that one of the two studied religious communities should be a parish that was operating throughout the Soviet period. That left a choice of only two Orthodox churches in Kaluga. Both had been functioning uninterrupted throughout the twentieth century. Of these two, I was drawn to the one that included mainly elderly and conservative believers – a nearly closed social circle that hardly admitted "outsiders". I was interested in it because the people themselves had been practicing since Soviet times. However, their clear distrust of outsiders meant I had to give up. My luck was not much better at the other parish, and it was clear that the consent of the church's clergy to allow a researcher access to the life of the parish was a decisive factor in the selection of a field site.

In 2006, I finally gained the help of two priests. Both were young, educated men in their thirties who had received a secular university education before they entered seminary and became ordained. Consequently, the two Orthodox parishes in which the fieldwork was carried out are similar in the fact that they were both new. Both formed as religious communities after the end of the Soviet era in 1991, although one of the parishes is housed in a church building that was the oldest one in Kaluga. Church St. Martyr John the Warrior is new, not only in the sense of a newly formed parish, but also literally: It was built at the very end of the built-up urban space during the period 1994–1999 in the peripheral working-class district of Silikatnyi.[16] The other parish is housed in a church that dates back to the seventeenth or eighteenth century, the Shroud of the Holy Mother on the Moat [*Pokrova presviatoj Bogorodicy, čto na rvu*].[17] This historical parish ceased to exist during the Soviet period. The temple was revoked by the Russian Orthodox Church in 1930 and used as an incubation station for broiler hen breeding until 1994. At that time, the building was returned to the Church, and the temple was reconsecrated in 1998.[18]

The Shroud of the Holy Mother on the Moat, or Pokrova na rvu [The Shroud on the Moat], as it is most often called, has been recognized as an architectural monument of culture since the early 1990s (Morozova, 1993, p. 157). It is located in the historical center of the city. As a wooden building, it was built before 1626, and after a fire in the eighteenth century, it was rebuilt in its present form as a stone building; it is the oldest of church buildings in the city (Malinin, 1992 [1912], p. 100).

Not only is it historically important, but the Shroud on the Moat is central to the life of Orthodox believers in the city of Kaluga because of its numerous activities. These expand beyond the membership of the parish [*prikhod*]. The newspaper *Vera Molodykh* (*The Faith of the Young*), with uninterrupted publication since 2002, is published with the efforts of parish activists. The Sunday School [*Voskresnaja škola*] at the parish had the reputation of being the best in the city; but since 2009, it has been transformed into a sort of Orthodox Scout formation, involving at present about 300 children of different ages.[19]

In addition to daily observations, I conducted autobiographical interviews (or life stories) with 32 people; some of them I interviewed two or even three times. All interviews (both formal and informal) were conducted in Russian, without the help of a translator. I also documented a lot of informal interviews in my field notes. The autobiographical method of interviewing, despite its weaknesses, provides an insight into how social and personal elements intersect (Bertaux, 1991 [1986], p. 137). It allows us to reveal the social phenomena in the process of their formation (Rosenthal, 2004, p. 50), and this possibility is given precisely by the biographical approach. This is also the reason this approach was preferred here to other interviewing techniques. Moreover, in view of the central importance that the conversion has in a post-Soviet context (from unbelief to faith – see Pelkmans, 2009), personal stories are an especially valuable empirical source for understanding religion. As a natural cognitive and linguistic form, narratives are a means by which the narrators organize and give meaning to their life experiences (Kvale, 2007, p. 38).

The interviewing was balanced in terms of age and social status, but not so in terms of gender. Women predominate among the interviewees (19), and this fact reflects the practices of participation in church life. One of the features of this small sample was not planned: Most of the interlocutors have university or college educations (21, plus two students). This is the result of organizing half of the interviews among and through the personal social network of my research assistant – herself a member of the city's intelligentsia. For reasons already discussed by Köllner (2012, pp. 30–32), this was a prudent strategy to gain traction within the parish communities.

The main strategy of interviewing was to provide information both on ROC institutional strategies "from the top-down perspective" and on the ideals and practices of common people "below". Accordingly, I conducted interviews with: (a) priests (five); (b) parishioners from both parishes (eight); (c) people outside the two parishes who were nevertheless enchurched [*vocerkovlënnye*] in other parishes and involved in ROC strategy and policy in Kaluga (seven); (d) librarians (nine); and (e) people who identify themselves as *pravoslavnye kraevedy* [a kind of semi-amateur expert in local history and culture, discussed more in chapter 4] (three). Talking with librarians aimed at providing information outside the circle of the most dedicated believers. The requirement for the biographical method, i.e. for the stories to be collected in a homogeneous social environment (Bertaux, 1980, pp. 198–199), is satisfied by the fact that this heterogeneous group of people is united by the feature "Orthodox believer".

In conducting the interviews, I kept as much as possible the consistency of the procedures established and widely accepted by the supporters of the biographical method.[20] All interviews followed the outlines of a life story (most often longer, though shorter in a few cases). Their structures also reflected the interviewing techniques of conditional division of the narrative into two parts: (1) period of the spontaneous narrative structured by the narrator and (2) period of questioning, initially "internal" (i.e. clarifying aspects of the narrative), and then "external": Questions beyond the narrative (Rosenthal, 2004, p. 50). Interlocutors were acquainted not only with the topic and objectives of the fieldwork, but also with the way the interview was going to take place.

The place where an interview is conducted also brings information, so it should be noted. In all cases without exception, the place of the meeting was chosen by the interlocutors and, in a large number of cases, this meant we talked in public places. Initially, I found this principled extension of control to my interview partners to be a constraint and a hindrance: I was afraid that communication could hardly achieve depth and sincerity. In most cases, my fears were unmerited.

Twelve of the interviews – with librarians and bibliographers but also with some key interlocutors outside the library staff – took place in the Belinski Science Library building. All these conversations took place in a separate room kindly provided to me by the library's management. Meetings with parishioners and priests were held in both churches, but there we also managed to hold the conversations in private. The church of St. Martyr John the Warrior is open all week, but as the church services took place only on Saturdays, Sundays, and feast days, conversations held on weekdays could be held privately. The *trapeznaja* [dining room] and the priest's office were the meeting place in the Shroud on the Moat.

Only two of the interviews were held at the interlocutors' homes. Two other extensive and emotional autobiographical narratives were shared and recorded at my lodgings; two of the meetings were held in a holiday village (*dacha*) near Kaluga on the same day; three – in the Convent of Kazans' Icon of the Holy Mother (Kazansky Convent hereafter), with sisters from the St. Elisaveta Fëdorovna Orthodox Sisterhood [*Pravoslavnoe sestričestvo imeni sviatoj velikomučenicy Elisavety Fëdorovny*]; and two of the stories were recorded in the workplaces of the interlocutors. After a long hesitation, cancellations and arrangements, one of the conversations took place in a noisy and lively public location: On the Theater Square in the heart of the city, next to a large fountain, whose babble was registered by the tape recorder.

The most extensive formal interview lasted about eight hours. The total length of formal and informal conversations with another key interlocutor exceeded two days. The briefest narrative lasted just 15 minutes. This last was conducted with the only one of my acquaintances in Kaluga who said she was an atheist; she herself wished her opinion of religion and the church to be recorded.[21] No other interviews were quite so brief. Despite the tension with which the choice of the place for conversation was sometimes linked, the different spaces were also a good opportunity to get to know and explore the intimate and not always visible aspects of Russian people's everyday life. The journey to small remote stations on suburban trains overcrowded with colorful human characters; feeling lost in Kaluga forests when in search of sacred little springs; visiting the countryside and touching there the nostalgic tranquility of Russian nature. . . . Going to these places was not just an attempt to systematically study the environment. All this is part of the immersion of the researcher in the distinct stages of social action and conscious effort to achieve a cognitive and moral equilibrium when the "physical, emotional and mental exhaustion" (Delamont, 2004, p. 223) accompanying each ethnographic work was about to get worse.

Field notes (not a diary in the true sense of the word – see Bernard, 2006, pp. 387–398), in which I reflected on what I was seeing and through which I reconstructed informal conversations, I made in Russian, trying to preserve as much as possible of the original meanings. This activity was time-consuming because I had to not only reconstruct the events of yesterday's memory, but also take care with the grammar and expressions of the Russian language.

The information obtained orally through observation and interviewing could be compared with one of the written sources, which is not only historical but modern as well. What I mean here is that some of my interlocutors also contributed to the development of the local church press as authors; I refer here to their publications in support of the veracity of the oral information. I use fictional names when I mention my informants, except for people who have public fame; the latter are presented here with their real names. This is the case of Vitalii Legostaev, an Orthodox *kraeved* and author of about 180 publications, including 15 books.

The time, free of interviews or visits to the temples, I spent in the Kaluga's Belinski Science Library, mainly studying a valuable source from the second half of the nineteenth century to the beginning of the Soviet era: *Kaluzhskie eparkhial'nye vedomosti* [*The Kaluga Diocese Journal*]. The written sources I consulted (periodicals, numerous church papers, books, and the Internet) provided important additional information and shed light on the complex and controversial trajectories of modern Orthodoxy. Following historical background of the religious life is important in the context of the orientation towards the pre-socialist past as a model of piety, which is discussed in chapter 4. What I saw and heard during fieldwork is complemented by and resonated with publications in contemporary local Orthodox periodicals, especially the diocesan magazine *Pravoslavnyj khristianin*[22] [*An Orthodox Christian*] and the newspaper *Vera molodykh [Faith of the Young].*[23]

Switching between different research practices is in fact related to a constant evaluation of previous steps and rethinking of field strategies (Delamont, 2004, p. 223). This also affects autobiographical interviewing in particular, and the need to combine the research and analytical function of this type of study. A longer quote by Daniel Bertaux (1980, pp. 200–201) gives a clear idea of the consistency and practical implementation of this process:

> Collecting several life stories without having to be complete is a good means of penetrating a new terrain to explore the basic processes, the most characteristic traits, the main challenges. In this case, we have extensive use of these stories, with the aim of covering as many aspects of social life as possible, as it is not yet known which ones will be decisive. When they begin to emerge, we will move on to their intensive use, that is, focusing on that aspect which, in our view, deserves in-depth research. Similarly, while in the first conversations the researcher is often forced to interrupt the narrative to ask for an explanation of the meaning of one or another term related to a profession or a local jargon (meaning always some practice, an attitude, a process of local importance), then in the next conversations, the researcher, who has gained a clearer idea of the basic features of the terrain, can specify the initial task (orienting the conversation to professional, family, public or religious life) and then leave an interlocutor to express freely their thoughts. The research approach is self-sustaining, constantly redirecting, following the line of first discoveries.

Accordingly, two moments in the research process often overlap. The first is "the moment of comparison of the phenomena, the typology outline, the transition from 'ideas' to 'hypotheses', in a word – the construction of 'theory', i.e. an idea of what is happening in the 'social reality'". The second is "the moment of verification, or rather of empirical validation of the descriptive proposals and of the interpretations formulated" (Bertaux, 1980, pp. 200–201).

In other words, in the process of fieldwork, the accumulation of empirical evidence stimulated constant testing and reformulation of the initial hypotheses: The theoretical findings were reached in the process of empirical work. Changes in the interviewing and observation strategy were an integral part of the study itself. The reconstruction and reformulation of the hypotheses and, respectively, of the specific tasks to accomplish were made even in the beginning of the fieldwork. My project was initially conceived as a study of the strategies of the Russian Orthodox Church in terms of religious pluralism. The very first interview, however, showed in a categorical way that a change of the pre-designed fieldwork plans and, hence of the project theme, was necessary.

This first conversation[24] was with the then priest of the Orthodox Gymnasium [*Pravoslavnaia gimnazia*] in Kaluga, a teacher who had turned to religious training and a priest's career relatively late, in mid-life. Initially I had to answer his questions (as I did during the other formal interviews, too), mainly concerning the purpose and nature of my research. When I mentioned "religious pluralism", his expression changed markedly, and the smile disappeared. I immediately realized that I had made a serious mistake. As I later understood, my research assistant (who was present for the first and last time in a formal interview) thought that the conversation would not take place at all. She, like me, had noticed that the priest had gone pale and begun to wring his hands. Somehow, I managed to smooth out the unfavorable impression my words produced. Then the conversation went into a relaxed, friendly atmosphere and ended with a welcoming lunch invitation to the dining room of the Kazansky Convent, which houses the Orthodox Gymnasium.

The following meetings and conversations confirmed the conclusions of this episode: Communication with Orthodox believers in Kaluga and a demonstrated interest in other confessions are mutually exclusive. "Religious pluralism" is an antithesis to the energetic struggle of the ROC – largely successful (see Papkova, 2013, pp. 244–253) – to secure hegemony over the Russian religious field.[25] Gaining access to study the ROC required me to relinquish the study of "religious pluralism". The decision to take this direction was made quickly, all the more because repeated attempts to establish contact with the "other" religious communities in Kaluga (Lutherans, Baptists, Catholics, Pentecostals, Mormons, Krishna consciousness, Neo-pagans, etc.) ended in failure. I could never connect, despite my repeated phone calls.

In Kaluga, there is a different attitude toward one special group of "other" religious communities: Old Believers. Historically, Kaluga (the city and the district) has been an important center for Old Believers since their emergence in the middle of the seventeenth century; about 50,000 Old Believers inhabited the territory of the area at the beginning of the twentieth century (Malinin, 1992 [1912], pp. 21, 44).

Thousands of them were killed during Stalin's repressions in the 1930s. As early as 1989, at the beginning of the restoration of religious life in Russia, this community was officially restored in Kaluga and, by the orders of the local Party authorities, it received at its disposal one of the most ancient and precious architectural church buildings in Kaluga: Znamenskaja.[26] In short, there is an attitude of tolerance towards the contemporary Old Believers, and their religious life is undisturbed. Interviews with two Old Believers and a visit to Znamenskaja Church revealed that Old Believers are perceived as "authentically" Russian and part of the country's "antiquity". One of my two interlocutors had even converted from contemporary Orthodoxy to the Old Faith, led by the perception that it is the true, "authentic Russian faith".[27] Despite their historical reputation as schismatics, the Old Believers are still perceived through the filter of national ideas as an indispensable part of Russian cultural history. It was the only religious community outside the Russian Orthodox Church thatI could contact easily.

Particularly discouraging were attempts to determine whether the local people knew about neo-pagans and their activities. The events of the latter were (and are currently) documented on the Internet,[28] and Kaluga is reputed to be one of their most significant centers of activity (see Filatov and Lunkin, 2006b, p. 347). However, the only person who had ever heard of them was a reader in the Kaluga Science Library whom I chatted with incidentally. He had a vague idea of the existence of neo-pagans in the city and surroundings, but that was all. All other interlocutors in my numerous conversations (formal and informal) in Kaluga responded with astonishment to my questions, reporting that they did not know anything about neo-pagans. Most likely, the activity of neo-pagans on the Internet and their actual significance and presence in the life of the city and region do not coincide.

Thus, because of the impossibility to establish contact with "other" religious communities, changing the research strategy became not only desirable but necessary. Meanwhile, in the course of work among Orthodox believers, I was in a unique world that quickly absorbed me. To continue in this direction was the only possible solution.

Participant observation: Theoretical considerations and ethnographic practices

Theoretical discussions on the epistemological validity of participant observation have long been in their most acute phase. Although the infamous "crisis of representations" (which occurred after the books of Clifford and Marcus (1986) and Marcus and Fischer (1986)) can be considered overcome, the sensitivity to the relevance of this method remains. Pierre Bourdieu, ironizing the extremes of "textualism", proposes the concept of "participant objectivation" instead of "participant observation" (Bourdieu, 2003, pp. 281–283). The polemical criticism of other authors in relation to the semantic "fogs" of postmodern writing and "textualism" in anthropology is in turn combined with reflexive and responsible reconfirmation of the epistemological value of the field study based on the live presence of the researcher "being there". We must maintain that ethnographic practice and reflective writing can together "produce knowledge that can acknowledge its relationality and still aim for truth" (Borneman and Hammoudi, 2009, p. 8).

In this context, there is no way to circumvent the question of the nature of the observation during fieldwork in Kaluga. The short duration of the empirical study, with all its intensity, raises the question: Can the observation be participant when two or three months of stay are insufficient to get the local people accustomed to the researcher's presence? If Bourdieu is skeptical of the researcher's opportunity to "immerse" himself/herself in the worlds of "others", a more pragmatic approach to the participant observation claims that "researchers are totally immersed in the culture under study, twenty-four hours a day. This is usually about a long stay (a year or more) in a foreign country" (Bourdieu, 2003, p. 281; Delamont, 2004, p. 218).

My immersion in Kaluga was "total" but for a shorter time. It coincided with the recommendations of H. Russell Bernard that participant observation in a foreign culture occur over no less than three or four months (Bernard, 2006, p. 349). In view of the fact that there was no need for language learning, I estimated that the three months I had at my disposal would be adequate but set myself the task, too, of using fieldwork to test the limits of the method. The forms of active social control over newcomers – such as myself – in an Orthodox parish make it impossible to remain unnoticed, even on Sunday and festive liturgies, when 100 people or more come into the temple.

Field observation also includes a phase of feverish and chaotic gathering of a large amount of information: All sorts of data related to the study. The researcher is overwhelmed by the voluminous amount of information. Bernard recommends a brief interruption of the fieldwork after the end of this phase so that the scholar can reconsider the results so far (Bernard, 2006, p. 382). The research in Kaluga proceeded in this way. I returned home to Bulgaria in a state of confusion and unable to rediscover the focus of the study under the weight of the abundant information I had gathered.

The Russian anthropologist Sergei Abashin describes and analyzes in a remarkably open and frank manner the state of uncertainty that often accompanies an ethnographer's effort to master the voluminous and heterogeneous material collected during fieldwork. This, he writes, can force the long-term "freezing" of an ethnographic study. So it was with the long pause between his first fieldwork in Tajikistan (1995), the return to its theme in 2009, and the publication of a related book in 2015. Of course, as he points out, in addition to the cognitive and intellectual problems presented by fieldwork, academic precarity (in postsocialist conditions, but not only) tends also to contribute to a long pause between fieldwork and publication of a monograph (Abashin, 2015, pp. 5–9).

To the problems mentioned by Abashin, we have to add the weight of the – at times – very emotional nature of the fieldwork in Kaluga. The perception (explicitly stated) of autobiographical interviews as a type of confession by some interlocutors was related to the sharing of sensitive intimate information as well as the super-emotional flow of the narrative itself. After such meetings, it was difficult to continue working the next day. Clearly, the emotional burden blocked, at least temporarily, the possibility of research distance and impartial analysis.

What I described must not be understood as a complaint or posture. Fieldwork is not a "rose garden" if we paraphrase a popular song of the early 1970s. It is accompanied by "physical, emotional and mental exhaustion" as already mentioned previously. It is not accidental that Hammoudi and Borneman use the dramatic metaphor of the "agony" of fieldwork (2009, p. 260). As much as it contains experimental moments, field research is not only an "encounter", but also a participation in the existing human drama. Mentioning here the emotional nature of these "participations" is intended to provide a credible testimony of what is seen and experienced in fieldwork.

However, there is also another specific type of participation to mention. Fieldworkers face various dilemmas in how to balance participation and observation. My dilemma was both research related and moral: Was I to participate or not in the religious practices of the studied communities? In view of my Orthodox and Bulgarian identity, it was both an issue of professional relevance and of practical relevance. What is more important: Keeping the necessary distance and impartiality over the observed groups and personalities (and, respectively, not participating in prayer practices) or participating in prayer life for the sake of convergence and integration?

This awkward dilemma, a choice between two ethnographic commitments – distance or engagement, urgently required a solution at the very beginning of the empirical study. As far as the fieldwork was carried out as an equal dialogue, my belonging to Orthodoxy was constantly discussed, tested, and contested. The Orthodox identity, albeit Bulgarian, rather than Russian, mitigated the personal dimension of the moral dilemma of whether or not to participate in liturgical life. I would not, after all, perform against my own beliefs. Still, there remained other layers. While the researcher of a fishing village is not obliged to fish (see Delamont, 2004, p. 218), the passive observation (as in a theater) of such a sensitive social sphere as the religious may place the researcher in the position of "voyeur" (Borneman and Hammoudi, 2009, p. 14).

When questioned by the *Anthropological Forum Journal* (2017) about the desirability of the personal involvement of a scientist in the religious traditions he studies, 33 anthropologists proposed an equal number of answers. Two answers, opposite in a sense, illustrate the overall agreement about the pros and cons of participation versus distancing. Simon Coleman is skeptical of the idea that those participating in a religious group have privileged access to it (2017, p. 92). Sonja Luehrmann, in turn, perceives the opposite, moreover, in groups with different affiliations (Baptists and Orthodox). She opines that participating offers the possibility to learn from the bodily experience of religious practices. In addition, participation mitigates somewhat the mistrust of foreigners, which is commonplace in terms of modern political moods in Russian society. Luhrmann cites a religious activist: "*Sonja is here, she prays with us. So we know that she is not a foreign spy who has come to watch us*" (Luehrmann, 2017, p. 29).

My decision was to favor participation in prayer practices without being definitely certain that this was the relevant choice.[29] The fieldwork process further revealed that the position of a secular observer would have made access to some communities and places difficult or virtually impossible. Participation in religious practices unlocked the possibility not only of learning through bodily experience (in Luehrmann's understanding) but also of spontaneous and long-lasting debate with the interlocutors about their normative notions of the "real" (or not) Orthodox practices. By participating, believers perceived me and responded to me as a neophyte who was, indeed, seeking to join the community – a position related to a number of challenges. Certainly "participating while observing" led to unplanned and unexpected situations. Before interviews, for example (often involving having a meal together – an act of hospitality) or in different ritual contexts, believers sang prayers or contemporary authors' religious songs. This required learning "on the go" the Russian melodies of the most popular prayers, *The Lord's Prayer* [*Otče naš*] and the *Akathistos of the Holy Virgin*: "Rejoice, Unwedded Bride!" [*Bogorodice, Devo, radujsia!*], as well as the songs.

The present field study is characterized therefore, among other things, by my specific position with respect to the studied culture. Contrary to the neverending discussions in the scientific literature of the power relationship between the researcher (often a representative of the hegemonic "North") and the people he/she studied (often inhabiting peripheral and exotic regions of the world), my position among the people of Kaluga was radically different. In their eyes, a Bulgarian scholar is a representative of a former socialist country, and indeed of the former and most servile ally of the Soviet Union. At the same time, the radical redrawing of geopolitical boundaries after the end of socialism was a fact whose meaning was clear to everyone. The fieldwork in 2007 took place in the year when Bulgaria joined the European Union, and this brought the ambiguity, ambivalence, and tension between "before" and "now" into the picture.

In fact, Bulgaria's changed relationship with Russia had less importance in my dealings with women than in those with men. Nationalism and xenophobia were present in Russia even in 2006–2007, but they had not yet conquered the Russian public space as they have since the Crimean annexation of 2014. I did not hear aggressive or openly unfriendly comments about myself or about my home country (see Morris, 2016, pp. 110–126). A Bulgarian anthropologist is still not a British or American anthropologist; geopolitics has not yet brought about a perception of stark distinctions in the cultures of Bulgaria and Russia.

Unlike the "West", a concept with vague misty shapes in Russian media, Bulgaria is a country that is a very specific place. Especially among the older generations in Russia, many have visited Bulgaria and have personal impressions of places and people. Once during my fieldwork, at the gathering held the day after a wedding for the newlyweds' closest relatives – an event that unfolded in an intimate and warm atmosphere – Bulgarian-Russian relations were unexpectedly put into discussion. The groom's father raised to me the question of how to understand the political situation in Bulgaria. Had Bulgaria indeed become hostile towards Russia? He sounded worried, not aggressive. He continued to recall how, during socialism, he had many professional and close friendly relationships with Bulgarian engineers. "*If the Bulgarians have also turned against us now* . . ." he said. There was no verbal finish to the sentence. He only struck his fist against his chest expressing frustration and sorrow. The unequivocal gesture speaks more than words: It is not only about dissatisfaction with Russia's lost political hegemony, but also about purely personal disappointment with the ruined human ties. I had to answer something. I replied (quite impromptu) that in Bulgaria, the monuments of the Soviet Army were not destroyed. This was accepted well, and the subject of conversation was changed. This was the most memorable episode of "testing" during fieldwork, but it was not the only one.

Unexpectedly, the *Bulgarian* aspect of my Orthodox identity outlined a border of "close otherness", which, without being overwhelming, proved to be sometimes difficult to cross.[30] The notions of Russian religious exclusiveness, which will be discussed later, make everyone of non-Russian origin, albeit with Orthodox identity, subject to doubts expressed by the notions of "purity" and "danger". The intermediate position of the researcher, both internal (as an Orthodox) and external (as a person of foreign nationality, albeit of Slavic origin), means she is confronted with a series of dialogues that constantly challenge and renegotiate the boundaries of "one's own" and "alien".

It will be misleading, however, to argue that mistrust and "testing" apply only to foreigners. An examination of the affiliation and involvement in Orthodox practices also applies to Russians who apply for jobs in Orthodox institutions (Medvedeva, 2016b, pp. 94–95). In this thread of thought, it seems reasonable to conclude that the internal/external distinction is "frequently situational, depending on prevailing social, political and cultural values in a given social context" (Morris, 2016, p. 114). Intimate knowledge of foreign culture (starting with language and competence in the field of Russian literature and art) is able to soften these borders over time.

* * *

Since the field study in 2007, there was no opportunity for a further trip to Kaluga. Despite the large amount of written information cited – primary and secondary sources – and the meticulous tracking of "field changes", this study was built on the basis of the "ethnographic snapshot" from 2006 to 2007. Its conclusions should be considered above all in the context of this particular period of development of Orthodoxy in Russia.

The structure of the book. Chapter 1 addresses the paradox of a high level of Orthodox identification among the Russian population with the low level of church attendance. The community of the most devoted believers ("little flock") makes Orthodox revivalism possible, despite the low overall level of actual participation in liturgical life. Both this chapter and the whole book explore this community, its ideas, and social practices. Chapter 1 also discusses theoretical problems: Relevance of the concepts of vicarious religion (Davie, 2007), public religion, desecularization, post-secularism, and religious revivalism as social movement. **Chapter 2** focuses on a particular aspect of the socio-cultural portrait of the "little flock": On the ethical search among its representatives. Value preferences and "ethical reasoning" (Keane, 2014, 2016) among believers bring about the strong will to achieve moral perfection in religious terms. On the other side, "negative moralizing" (Luckmann, 2002) is related to the discourses and practices of obedience and humility. The problem of religious morality finds continuation in **chapter 3** as it focuses on the way believers forge their new moral selves, through narratives of conversion from atheism to Orthodox faith. This chapter turns to considering similarity – though not identity – between conversion models within Christianity. It picks up Robbins' (2004, 2014) concept of "moral torment" to prove that a model of "break" and "rupture" is neither exclusively Protestant nor Pentecostal. It also explores how narratives of miracles strengthen the positive identity of Orthodox communities and contributes to their sacralization.

While the narratives of conversion reveal personal moral trajectories, **chapter 4** addresses collective ideas marked by religious exclusivism and nationalism as it explores various manifestations of the politics of memory. In particular, it considers the veneration of "special dead" promoted by both church and state: (a) canonization of "new martyrs" (victims of atheist repressions during Soviet times); and (b) dead heroes of WWII who are commemorated. This chapter also gives attention to *kraevedy* as being among the main social actors engaged in the politics of memory. Their politics of memory diligently reshapes traumatic Russian memory into a non-conflictual vision of the past. The **Conclusions** synthesize the main empirical findings and theoretical inferences of the book. As it considers the community of zealous believers ("little flock"), the book suggests an integral view on the phenomenon of post-atheist religious revivalism. Essentially, the book addresses a global problem of religion going public from the specific Russian perspective. This grassroots perspective brings to the conclusion a consideration of the essence of religious social movements. In particular, it sheds light on the capacity of a minor group to implement major social change.

Notes

1 My translation [Milena Benovska] from Russian (Coleman, 2017, pp. 89–90).

2 Old Believers are heirs of centuries-old conservative tradition, and a group that suffered repressions after they split (seventeenth century) from the official Russian church. Old Believers are also Orthodox, but because of their particular history of divergence from the official Russian Orthodox Church, I do not address them here. The interested reader will find a large body of literature dedicated to them by Russian and international scholars alike.

3 *Trudniki* normally refers to laypeople who work in a monastery for shelter and food or for modest wages. See Mitrokhin (2004, pp. 56, 116).

4 See the Internet page of the Center for Anthropology of Religion: https://eu.spb.ru/car/about. Last accessed: 5.08.2018.

5 Projects in "Religion and Morality" were integrated into the research program of Max Planck Institute for Social Anthropology in Halle/Saale (2006–2008); they were carried out in three regions: East Germany, European Russia, and Taiwan (Hann, 2010).

6 Krogius (2009, pp. 133–134); Seliverstova and Zaharova (2019, p. 49).

7 Historically, Kaluga was built on the left bank of Oka River. Yet since the city started enlarging after 2007, the right bank of the river has also been built up. This extension was preceded by the construction of a bridge linking both banks of the river (it was completed during my fieldwork). A second bridge has been built and a third one is

planned (see: Kaluga-poisk.ru/новости-калуга/новости-калуга-благоустройство/в-Калуге-построят-третий-мост-через-Оку-и-новую-окружную-дорогу).

8 Another source indicates that already at the beginning of the nineteenth century, there were 47 churches (Kliment, Mitropolit, 2005). Different figures partly reflect the existence of so-called home churches [*domovye hramy*], smaller churches that are sometimes located inside of another larger building. The total number of churches differs depending on whether these churches were counted.

9 See Ivkin and Gusev (2007, p. 2); www.volkswagengrouprus.ru; http://volvotrucks.com/trucks/russia-market/ru-ru/kaluga_factory/Pages/firstpage.aspx.

10 According to the site specialized in foreign investments: www.investkaluga.com. Last accessed: 1.08.2018.

11 https://airkaluga.ru. Last accessed: 1.08.2018.

12 On February 13, 2020, governor Artamonov resigned and Vladislav V. Shapsha was appointed by President Putin as a temporary executive governor of the Kaluga region. – Znamia, 2020, n.p.

13 Gubernatory (2015).

14 Derived from the Church Slavonic *starec* (spiritual elder), this is a specific type of monk ascetic largely popular and venerated by the laity. See Paert (2010, pp. 130–131), Solov'ëv (2005 [1899], pp. 3–7).

15 According to Nikolai Mitrokhin (2004, p. 209), three types of ideological orientations exist among high Russian clergy: fundamentalists, conservatives, and liberals.

16 '*Hram sviatogo velikomučenika Ioanna Voina*'. Completion works continued until 2005 when the first church service took place. See more about it: http://drevo-info.ru/articles/11683.html. Last accessed: 2.08.2018.

17 The name '*Pokrova Presviatoj Bogorodicy čto na rvu*' has its explanation in the historic urban topography of Kaluga in the sixteenth–seventeenth centuries when the city was surrounded by a wooden fortification. The place where the church had been built was part of the castle moat on which the temple was named. See Malinin (1992 [1912]).

18 See http://drevo-info.ru/articles/4966.html. The site was visited on July 23, 2015. A source of more detailed information about the history of the temple building and the parish was given during my "temple excursion" held on July 8, 2007. This is an event that is held periodically for visitors to learn about the history of the temple. It was led by the conductor of the church choir, who was then also the director of the Sunday School.

19 See site of the parish: http://kaluga-pokrov.cerkov.ru/voskresnaya-shkola/. Last accessed: 23.07.2018.

20 Concerning this technique see Rosenthal (2004, p. 50).

21 Interview with Ekaterina Vasilievna, university education, bibliographer, 60, 17.07.2007, Kaluga.

22 Published since 1991, six issues per year. See: http://eparhia- kaluga.ru/periodika/gazeta-nasha-vera.html. Last accessed: 14.08.2018

23 *Vera molodykh* has been published since 2002 under the editor Marina Bogomolova. From 2002 to 2018, 88 issues were published. Since 2008, the edition has had an online version: http://eparhia- kaluga.ru/periodika.html. Last accessed: 15.08.2018. There are two more religious editions in the Kaluga Diocese, but they do not have the same popularity among the believers as the two cited above. See them on the site of the diocese: http://eparhia- kaluga.ru/periodika.html. Last accessed: 18.08.2018

24 Interview with Father E. č., 55, university education, a teacher/ priest. 22.09.2006, Kaluga.

25 See also Knox (2005, pp. 175–247).

26 For this church, see Malinin (1992 [1912], pp. 141–143).

27 An interview with Ilya Karpovich, 30, university education, a lawyer/priest. 12.08.2007, Kaluga.

28 See for example *Soiuz slavianskikh obščin slavianskoj rodnoj very'*. – www.rodnovery.ru; www.rodnoverie.org. Last accessed: 17.08.2018

29 In a similar situation, also carrying Bulgarian and therefore presumed Orthodox identity, Tocheva (2017, p. 22) took the opposite stance. She did not engage in Orthodox liturgical practices during fieldwork, though she did follow the "minimum dress-code for women" appropriate in Orthodox settings.

30 Similar problems are described by Tocheva (2017, pp. 23–24).

1 The vicarious religion

The strength of the "little flock" of believers

Introduction

The restoration of religious life in Russia began about a year before the fall of the Berlin Wall, in 1988, during *perestroika* and during the anniversary of the millennium since the baptism of Kievan Rus' in 988. Although the chronology and meaning of these events are presented in the literature (Powell, 1991, pp. 328–329; Tsypin, 2012, pp. 547–563; Bourdeaux, 2000, pp. 9–10; Ellis, 1996, pp. 27–42; Davis, 1995, pp. 59–69), it makes sense to recall them here, since every beginning is important for the understanding of socio-historical processes. This reminder will also show the limited extent to which the return to religious life in the last years of the Soviet era was "top-down" (driven by central state policy). Beyond the surface of events, the picture is more complex.

Without neglecting the political strategies from the "top-down", this study privileges the perspective of ordinary people, from the "bottom-up", in the local context. This chapter therefore aims to show the role of the core of the most devoted Orthodox believers, the "little flock", as a "motor" of Orthodox religious life. Such an analysis requires addressing theoretical problems of a more general nature: The trends (or not) towards desecularization and the essence of "vicarious religion" (Davie, 2000, 2007).

"*Orthodoxy is in the soul of every Russian person!*": The establishment of religious liberties during *perestroika*

During the first years of Mikhail Gorbachev's rule (1985–1991), the atheistic politics of his predecessors continued to exist, and another hundred churches were closed. Then came 1988 – a turning point for religion in the USSR. On April 29, 1988, Mikhail Gorbachev met in the Kremlin with Patriarch Pimen I of Moscow and all Rus' and representatives of the Holy Synod of the Russian Orthodox Church. This was only the second such meeting of a secretary general of the Central Committee of the Communist Party of the Soviet Union (CC of the CPSU) with the Supreme Orthodox clergy following Stalin's meeting with Metropolitan Sergius during World War II in September 1943. In his statements at that meeting, Gorbachev said that he regretted the "tragic events" that occurred to the Church during the Stalinist repression. He promised, firstly, official commemoration of the anniversary of the millennium since the baptism of Kievan Rus', and secondly, the introduction of a new law on religion to replace that from 1929 (Tsypin, 2012, pp. 547–550; Bourdeaux, 2000, pp. 9–10; Ivanov, 1994, pp. 30–31; Pospielovsky, 1995, p. 97; Chaplin, 1995, pp. 41–47; Knox, 2004, pp. 58–60).[1]

The anniversary celebrations began only a few weeks later, on June 4, 1988, and surpassed all expectations in scale, international participation, and attention to what was happening in Russia. Tens of thousands of citizens participated in the festivities, and there was unprecedented media coverage of the Church ceremonies (Bourdeaux, 2000, p. 10).

That same week, June 4–12, 1988, the Local Council, the supreme authority of the ROC, was convened as the Anniversary Local Council. It adopted the first Statute for the Administration of the Russian Orthodox Church [*Ustav ob upravlenii Russkoj Pravoslavnoj Cerkvi*] (Tsypin, ibid.; Pospielovsky, 1995, pp. 42–43) and canonized nine saints (Ellis, 1996, p. 206).[2] Metropolitan Alexii of Leningrad and Novgorod was elected, along with five other senior clerics, as a representative in the State Duma in the April 1989 elections (Powell, 1991, pp. 9–10; Knox, 2004, pp. 11–12).

After the death of Patriarch Pimen, on May 3, 1990, the Bishop Council was convened, and on the next day, the Local Council, and a new Patriarch was elected: Alexii II. On October 1, 1990, a new Soviet law was adopted: On the Freedom of Conscience and Religious Organizations [*O svobode sovesti I religioznyh organizatsiyah*] (Tsypin, 2012, pp. 547–563; Powell, 1991, p. 329; Pospielovsky, 1995, pp. 42–43; Bourdeau, 2000, p. 10; Knox, 2004, p. 7). It radically changed the conditions in favor not only of the ROC but also of other religious organizations. The law not only restored religious freedom, but also made a step forward: It introduced religious pluralism for the first time in Russian history (Agadjanian, 2001, p. 481).

These events triggered a swift avalanche of changes. "The church bells could toll again in the Soviet Union, and the religious organizations were again empowered to do charity work. Many churches, mosques, prayer homes, as well as cathedrals, monasteries and other religious buildings were reopened and new ones were built or are currently being constructed" (Powell, 1991, p. 328). Tens of thousands of copies of the Bible and the Qur'an were imported from abroad or printed in the country; Muslims could perform pilgrimage to Mecca; charity activities of religious organizations were restored; Sunday schools were opened (ibid., pp. 328–329; Walters, 1994, pp. 98–99; Tsypin, 2012, pp. 547–563). The most visible part of these processes was the massive opening, repair, and restoration of the once-demolished temples, the return of the property rights to the religious organizations, and the construction of new temples.

In an interview with *Foma* magazine in 2005, Patriarch Alexii II described the events since 1988 as a "miracle" and as "a revival from the ashes of Christianity in Russia" (Alexii, Patriarch, 2005).[3] Of course, the "miracle" was prepared and carried out by real social actors in a particular socio-historical context. Various explanations for how the context for a sharp turn in the relationship between the state and the religious organizations in the Soviet Union in the late 1980s became possible include: The discrediting of the Soviet regime through the policy of *glasnost'* during *perestroika* combined with nostalgia for the pre-revolutionary epoch (Tsypin, 2012, pp. 547–563) and the desire of Mikhail Gorbachev to legitimize his policy and his search for allies (Powell, 1991, p. 329; Davis, 1995, p. 59; Ellis, 1996, p. 20). Perhaps certain international factors also had an impact, such as UNESCO's call for "celebrating the anniversary as the most important event in world history and culture" (Tsypin, 2012, p. 548).

It is harder to identify how various social actors brought about the societal turn. Twenty years after the remarkable events of 1988, some "little-known facts" were made public by Konstantin Kharchev. In an anniversary interview with *Novaya Gazeta* on September 17, 2008, Kharchev, who had been chairman of the Government Council of Religious Affairs [*Soviet po delam religii*] from 1984 to 1989, revealed some important circumstances surrounding the millennial celebrations of 1988. The import of 60,000 copies of the Bible, printed by the Bible Translation Institute in Stockholm through donations from Christians in Northern Europe, he said, had taken place with the knowledge and cooperation of the KGB. [The Fifth Chief Directorate of the KGB on Religious Affairs was certainly involved in the complex puzzle (Smirnov, 2008, p. 1)]. Decisions such as the return of Optina Hermitage to the Church in 1988 and the opening of church schools were carried out following decisions made by the Central Committee of the Communist Party (CCCP) of the Soviet Union and with the permission of the Council of Religious Affairs. In other words, it could be concluded that by 1988 there was clearly support for the return of religion among top leadership in key state institutions.

However, it was already known that with the restoration of religious freedoms came tensions and struggles between the reformist and hardliner wings (Alexii, Patriarch, 2005) of the CCCP. Party leaders at the local level created obstacles and conflicts over the manifestations of believers (Powell, 1991, pp. 331–332). Thus, the question of human agency is at least double: It is not only "how did support for religion develop", but also "how did it win out over support for atheism"? The personal role of Konstantin Kharchev matters. Between May 1988 and October 1989, Kharchev gave three unprecedented interviews to the journalist Alexander Nezhny, which were then published in *Ogonëk* Magazine (Ellis, 1996, pp. 43–54). In the first one, Kharchev numbered the believers in the USSR at 70 million and argued that this quarter of the Soviet population could not be ignored. Some researchers believe that this first-ever public recognition of the significant number of believers in the USSR put pressure on opponents, no to get on the way of the anniversary celebration and of the new CPSU policy.

The other two interviews discussed the difficulties that believers encounter when restoring new churches and parishes, despite the new policy towards religion, and mentioned ideological opponents of the new policy. The latter became Kharchev's personal opponents. Kharchev lost his post in mid-1989, before the interviews were completed. The lines of alliance were hardly clear-cut: Some of the higher Orthodox hierarchs supported Kharchev's dismissal (Davis, 1995, p. 70; Ellis, 1996, p. 47). Still, as Kharchev maintained 20 years later, during the years of Soviet rule, a whole layer of atheistic activists who literally lived with atheism was grew up. Huge state money was spent for atheistic propaganda, and if these religions and atheism were to equalize, the active atheists would lose not only their ideological positions but also their material well-being (Smirnov, 2008, p. 1).

These developments show that the "old guard" did not lose its power at the time of *perestroika*. But religious liberalization was certainly helped along by efforts, like those of Kharchev, to make information about internal party struggles publicly available (Ellis, 1996, pp. 43–54).

From what has been said, the process of religious renewal at the end of the 1980s is marked by a high degree of complexity and contradiction. It was not a sudden triumph, nor was it a "miracle". This latter definition of Patriarch Alexii II must be understood rather metaphorically. The liberalization of religious life was not the result only of Mikhail Gorbachev's work (Bourdeaux, 2000, p. 13), nor was it only a "top-down" process.

The responsiveness of the population to the "top-down" opening of religion was prepared through various "bottom-up" processes, such as "readiness for religion", since at least the 1960s. These processes included dissidents' activities in defense of the religious rights of Soviet citizens; an interest in Orthodoxy among the intelligentsia; and the gradual rethinking and re-conceptualization of Orthodox Christianity in terms of (national) cultural heritage (Agadjanian, 2001, p. 473; Kormina and Shtyrkov, 2015, p. 11). "The religious enthusiasm of the early 1990s was conditioned by a prolonged legalization of religion in Soviet times through its localization in the sphere of 'culture'" (Kormina and Shtyrkov, 2015, p. 9). During *perestroika*, these processes became more publicly visible thanks to *glasnost'*. Various groups and individual activists called for the mitigation of the restrictions on religion; they published letters and initiated petitions in the 1980s. In the 1980s, remarkable works of film, fine art, and literature with religious themes appeared in Soviet artistic culture (Ellis, 1996, pp. 11–26; Kormina and Shtyrkov, 2015, pp. 34–35).

Researchers also note the survival of rural religion "in the remote province" [*v gluši*] as one of the ways of preserving the memory of Orthodoxy. Orthodox Christian communities, which survived and existed underground, should also be noted. During the Soviet period, a secret religious life existed in the face of severe repression: There were traveling priests, secret theological courses, and secret stores of icons and liturgical books (Orlovskii, 2014). Formed at the beginning of the twentieth century, the religious stratum or subculture, which will be referred to as *pricerkovnyi krug* [around church circle] – survived in isolation during the Soviet period. It seems this fact was not reflected by researchers (Tarabukina, 2000, p. 4)[4]; I claim, though, that it is precisely this circle of people, as small and isolated as it was, that had a crucial role in the postsocialist resurgence of Orthodox Christianity in Russia. Although members of this small circle could not change the atheist character of Soviet society, in the isolated and hidden forms of Orthodox life, they preserved (and later transferred) the memory and cultural knowledge of religion.

None of these factors – religious dissidence, transformation of religion into a national cultural heritage, or the isolated informal religious communities – can alone explain the "religious boom" in Russia since the late 1980s and 1990s. All of them put together, however, create the readiness of the population for the return of religion during this period. While finishing her biographical narrative, one of my interlocutors gave strong metaphorical expression of the same conclusion, phrased in everyday language: "When it became possible to go to church freely in *perestroika* times, it turned out that all this was buried. And it was reopened, because Orthodoxy is in the soul of every Russian person".[5]

Since 1988, statistics have testified to the rise of religion in the country. According to official ROC sources, during the meeting of the Local Council in June 1988, the Church had 6,893 parishes and 22 monasteries (inhabited by 1,190 monks and nuns). By the end of 1988, some 1,000 temples had been returned to the ROC, most of them in the territory of Ukraine; 176 were returned within the territory of the Russian Federation. The next year, 1989, marked the beginning of an acceleration: On January 1, 1990 only 3,120 parishes were operating in the territory of the Russian Federation, while the total number of parishes in the ROC exceeded 11,000. Ten years later, at the end of 1999, the ROC had more than 19,000 parishes (of which 8,168 were in Ukraine and 1,080 were in Belarus). The actively preaching priests in 1988 numbered 7,397; at the end of 1998, there were 12,378 (Tsypin, 2012, pp. 547–563). But not everything was going smoothly. Shifting the ownership of the temples from state to the Church was a process accompanied by struggles and obstacles, mainly at the local level by the "old guard". However, "in the religious sphere, between 1991 and 2001, there was more change than in any other decade in Russian history" (Knox, 2004, p. 11). Thirty years after the restoration of religious freedoms in the Soviet Union, the Russian Orthodox Church claimed 39,414 priests, 36,378 temples, and 1,000 monasteries.[6]

How to explain the inconsistency between the number of actively practicing believers and the mass identification with Orthodoxy among the Russians?

The engagement of large masses of people in religious practices in post-Soviet Russia invites analysis. It is reflected in an avalanche of sociological research that either disputes or supports the thesis of the genuine nature of the resumption of religious life, especially among Orthodox Christians. There have been numerous analyses based on quantitative data, in addition to that on Orthodoxy and on the study of other religions and professions in Russia.[7]

The process of the resumption of religious life after 1988 is often called "religious revival" in Russia, especially at the *emic* but also at an *etic* level (Greeley, 1994, pp. 253–272; Agadjanian, 2001, pp. 473–488; Dubas, 2004, p. 216; Garadzha, 2005, p. 287; Dubin, 2006, p. 68). This term requires clarification, especially in view of a peculiarity that is consistently confirmed by periodic sociological research: The discrepancy between the declared religiosity, on the one hand, and the frequency of temple visits and religious rituals and sacraments, on the other hand. This is the reason for the skepticism of part of the Russian scholars (and some foreign ones – see Kääriäinen, 1998, pp. 155–162; Kääriäinen, 1999, pp. 35–46; Borowik, 2001, pp. 47–49) regarding the level of religiosity in post-Soviet Russia and of the supposed "religious revival".

Finnish researcher Harri Heino considers this discrepancy a "unique" feature of post-Soviet Russian religious life (2000, pp. 289–304). Filatov and Lunkin, in turn, define this discrepancy through the term "cultural religiosity" (2006a, p. 36). This, they say, should be distinguished from "religious observance" (ibid., p. 40), which is active participation in religious life. Regardless of the growing number of people identified as "believers" (75% of the total population of Russia according to 2010 data,[8] or 82% of ethnic Russians), "it can be said that between 2 and 10 percent of the population, between 3 and 15 million people are Orthodox practitioners" (Filatov and Lunkin, 2006a, p. 43). Different researchers refer to different numbers of "traditional" or "practicing" Orthodox believers, but their numbers never exceed 10% (Kääriäinen and Furman, 2000, pp. 16–24). The difference between identification with Orthodoxy and practiced religiosity, registered in the 1990s, has been invariably noted by researchers, including in recent publications (see Köllner, 2012, p. 18; Tocheva, 2017) as a specific feature of Russian Orthodox life in the post-Soviet era.

Doubts about the genuine rise of Orthodoxy are further reinforced by the strong government support for the Russian Orthodox Church during the Putin era since 2000. The "symphony" between the Church and the state has been repeatedly commented on by researchers. They have concluded that (whether or not belief is genuine) there is an "Orthodox consensus" in Russian society, according to which Orthodoxy is an important component and a symbol of national identity.[9]

In the context of this study, it is legitimate to raise the questions again: Are religious practices and values increasingly central to the everyday life of millions of Russian citizens who identify themselves as Orthodox Christians? To what extent is this religious renewal genuine? Or how spurious is it?

Religious revival or religious revivalism?

The question of the genuineness of the religious rise in modern Russia also puts into question the validity of the expression "religious revival". Skeptics on this issue pay attention to a few more peculiarities of contemporary Russian religious life. The media coverage of Orthodox problems has gradually become a powerful factor in the influence of the ROC on Russian society. The presence of ROC is unprecedented in the Internet through the thousands of "Orthodox sites" that continue to grow monthly and even weekly.[10] Moreover, some authors even suggest that the rise of Orthodox religion is a media phenomenon created and reinforced by the practices of multi-hour TV viewing. There is no doubt about the strengthening of the public aspects of Orthodox Christianity, illustrated, for example, by the successful introduction of the school subject *Fundamentals of Orthodox Culture* [*Osnovy pravoslavnoi kul'tury*], a problem to be discussed later in this chapter.

The terminological application of the phrase "religious revival" is problematic in some respects. Apart from its use by the clergy and religious activists for the purposes of political mobilization, its figurativeness also brings inconveniences. This is the primary metaphorical, non-terminological meaning of the word "revival" that generates an "organismic analogy" for a "new life" (Wallace, 1956, p. 256). The same applies to the term "revitalization": "Human society is considered here as a certain type of organism" (ibid.). In turn, a "religious renaissance" – which might be synonymous with a "religious revival" – is a concept already applied to another past: It is used in connection with the flourishing of religious philosophy and art from the early twentieth century until the outbreak of the Russian Revolution of 1917 (Zernov, 1963).[11]

For analytical purposes, the term "religious revivalism" has been suggested. It is largely discharged from the metaphorical character of the phrase "religious revival" although the two are partially synonymous. According to Lindekinde and Kühle, religious revivalism is an academic label, close to terms such as deprivatization, public religion, and desecularization in the sense of José Casanova and Peter Berger's ideas as described in the Introduction of this book. For their part, Lindekinde and Kühle link religious revivalism with theories of social movements and a consideration of political activism.

This religious revivalism equates to greater visibility of religion in many parts of the world, especially in its fundamentalist forms. Revivalism does not mean increased respect for religion or that religion before revivalism has not played a significant role as a source of cultural and ideological innovation. Historically, there are no examples of links between religious practices and political mobilization. However, since the 1980s, religious revivalism has emerged as concept of growing importance to social movements advocating political change (Lindekinde and Kühle, 2015, p. 173).

At first sight, this understanding of religious revivalism as grassroots movement appears to be inadequate, considering the evidence of state support that the ROC has enjoyed since 2000. However, this concept can also include the adaptation of religious mobilization to the existing state-church relationship (Ibid., p. 174). It is present in the maneuvering of religious activists and clergy in accordance with the turns of government policy towards religion in Russia/the Soviet Union from the late 1980s onward. In addition, the term revivalism refers to two semantic meanings: Revivalism as a "voice" (i.e. as a struggle for recognition in society), and revivalism as an "exit" (i.e. a passive closure of religious communities in their own spaces) that is marked by a strong emphasis on the personal transformation of believers through purification and improvement (Lindekinde and Kühle, 2015, pp. 174, 178–180). At the various stages of the restoration and stabilization of religion (in particular Orthodox Christianity) in Russia, both strategies are found – together or separately.

In the outlined sense, I will later use the term "religious revivalism", especially in the context of the 1990s, when religious life in Russia is particularly marked by a confrontation between believers and the adherents of atheistic politics and/or heritage. The phrase "religious revival" is retained in the text in the citation of authors who use it.

The minority of the most devoted Orthodox believers: How little is the "little flock"?

From this position, I turn back to the apparent paradox of the difference between the high level of identification with religion and the relatively low levels of participation in Orthodox practices. A closer look at the research methods shows that the criteria for measuring religiosity in Russia are formulated in a maximalist way. In other words, the questions asked in sociological studies outline a pattern of total immersion in religious practices – as they are normatively outlined by early Christian patristics (I-VI centuries). In practice, these questions ought to best describe – not the ordinary Christian – but the most devoted core of believers. From the outset, it should not be surprising that the number of people who meet these criteria is relatively small. "To require every Orthodox Christian to perform all canons prescribed in the ecclesiastical way of life – this is an unrealistic approach because Orthodoxy is not a military statute" (Chesnokova, 2005, pp. 19, 28). The discussion of revival, or revivalism, thus need not stumble repeatedly over the question of number of the regular churchgoers.

Certain researchers who do not insist on skepticism do find a rise of Orthodoxy in Russia (Greeley, 1994, pp. 253–257; Bourdeaux, 2000, pp. 9–21; Tomka, 2001, pp. 13–25). Among them are scholars who write from the position of believers (Sinelina, 2001, pp. 89–96; Sinelina, 2006, pp. 88–97; Chesnokova, 2005; Sinelina, 2006, pp. 89–97; Klimova, 2005, pp. 3–4). However, there is also a third, more flexible approach to the issue which differentiates aspects of religious revival. For example, the former professor of scientific atheism, Viktor Garadzha, found that there was a "revival" of the religious institutions in post-Soviet Russia, but still holds the position that it is premature to talk about religious revival in relation to "mass consciousness" (Garadzha, 2005, pp. 328–329). The reconstruction of religious institutions has been described by another author as follows:

> The main indicator of the obvious revival of ecclesiastical and religious life in recent years is the creation of new parishes of the Russian Orthodox Church, the opening of monasteries, the creation of brotherhoods, the publication of numerous canonical literature and religious periodicals.
>
> (Tsekhanskaia, 2015, p. 5)

Like Garadzha, Tsekhanskaia concedes revival exists as the restoration of church institutions. Alexander Agadjanian, in turn, tries to get beyond the skepticism aroused by figures that point to a low level of participation in church life (2–6%) by looking at "not just the number of deep conversions but the whole spectrum of religious presence". The boom in baptisms and marriages in the 1990s, for example, speaks of "responsiveness to the religious symbols that operate in society" (Agadjanian, 2001, p. 476). Therefore, Agadjanian does not deny the rise of religiosity, although he remains cautious

> about the very notion of "religious revival" because of manipulative use by the clergy for social mobilization.
>
> (ibid., p. 484)

We can also apply what Mikloš Tomka said about Eastern and Central Europe in general as valid for Russia:

> There is a clear "religious revival" in three respects. Majorities in individual societies state that they are religious. . . . Religion becomes a topic in public discourse and in the media. Finally, churches gain or maintain an influential social status and a decisive, albeit often contradictory, role. This overall picture differs from the situation and trends in Western societies.
>
> (Tomka, 2001, p. 25)

What does my fieldwork show? One particular episode eloquently illustrates the complexity of the questions that the anthropologist faces beyond quantitative methods and the language of figures. After the end of the church service on a Saturday night in August 2007, on the way home, I tried to sort out my impressions. I could not get rid of the extremely emotional images of a group of devoted parishioners who were in no hurry to leave the temple after the end of the long and exhausting ritual: They worshipped, kissed, and embraced each of the numerous icons. My route passed by a nearby grocery store, to which many late customers had rushed. The contrast of this hustle and bustle with the drawn-out manifestations of devotion in the little prayer community was striking. The parish looked like another universe, an island in this sea of people engaged in the cares of "profane" everyday life.

According to my approximate estimation, the attendance of Orthodox temples in Kaluga is not different from the average figures for Russia. Depending on various external factors (the absence of some parishioners during summer vacations or because of very low temperatures and frosts in the winter), participation in Saturday, Sunday, and holiday services varied (in 2007) between 100 and 150 people.[12] But as suggested earlier, these figures hardly give an adequate idea of the level of religiosity, nor of the repercussion and influence of Orthodoxy on Russian society in Kaluga – let alone in Russia.

In search of an answer to the research questions, I will formulate two theses. The first one states that the specificity of post-Soviet religious revivalism is determined by the combination of several characteristics that seem to be mutually contradictory: A high level of identification with Orthodoxy and the transformation of the latter into a symbol of national identity (Filatov, 2007, p. 16); large-scale reproduction of Orthodox institutions (Tsekhanskaia, 2015, pp. 5, 12); and the formation of a specific "minority" of most consistent believers, often called *vocerkovlënnye* (enchurched) (Tarabukina, 2000, p. 1). According to Sergei Filatov, "It is precisely this identity that is a political factor, not the real religious practice which from 2% to 10% of Russian citizens are attached to, according to various surveys" (Filatov, 2007, p. 16). On the other hand, the *vocerkovlënnye* have a key role in the current and future development of Orthodoxy in Russia. The question is: How do they play this role?

In fact, it would be hardly possible for regular worshippers to be much more numerous. Reflecting on the revival of Orthodoxy in Russia, the consequences of the extremes of atheistic politics during socialism should not be forgotten. Although "a strong sense of continuity pierces the post-Soviet feeling of the Orthodox person" (Benovska-Sabkova et al., 2010, p. 16), whole generations have lost (partly or completely) cultural knowledge related to religion. As Alexander Agadjanian and Kathy Rousselet note, this loss means that religious practices in modern Russia

> [are] carried out in a situation of a sharp rift in the religious traditions, as a result of the radical anti-religiousness of Soviet culture. Post-Soviet societies, as before, feel the consequences of this deep rift; it is evident in the intergenerational transmission of religious knowledge, religious practices and their meanings.
>
> (Agadjanian and Rousselet, 2006, p. 18)

The sense of loss is confirmed by field observations in Kaluga. Phrases such as "We do not know" and "We do not know anything" were so insistently repeated in one of my interviews that they became its refrain. It is no exaggeration to conclude that for many Russians, Orthodoxy is a new religion (Burdo and Filatov, 1999, p. 140). Not only the believers but also the clergymen in Kaluga admit that they continue to study the norms and cultural expressions of Orthodoxy (e.g. the techniques of Orthodox choral singing) through their stays in nearby monasteries.

There are also other factors influencing the level of participation in religious practices. Weekly visits to church services, regular communion, and observance of long and exhausting Orthodox fasts require a serious effort and a radical reorganization of the everyday life of a believer. Another episode of the fieldwork in 2007 shows this well. During the interview with a popular church *kraeved*, I asked: "How often do you go to church?" Surprisingly for me, my interlocutor said that he is not a very regular worshipper:

> *It takes too much time. I do not have the time. I work on the computer until midnight, I get up in the morning and work on the computer, then [go] to the archive, then – journeys to the villa. Now it's a summer season. And in the winter, I constantly work on the computer. There is no time. And the temple. . . . You understand – one has to renounce all these thoughts.*[13]

Indicative in this regard is a remark of a Kaluga woman believer, who I will not name because of the deeply intimate nature of what she said. When asked why her husband had accepted communion alone without her during the Sunday liturgy, she replied that she did not support frequent communion because it "interferes with normal marital life" [*mešajut normal'noi supruzheskoj zhizni*]. The practices of communion are the subject of discussions, including historical and theological ones:[14] how often to receive it, how long and how strict the fasting that precedes it should be. Strict fasting demands sexual abstinence too – as implied by my interlocutor.[15] Moreover, it is not difficult to imagine how frequent communion (i.e. once a week or more) – which some of the believers are willing to receive – combined with weekly fasting on Wednesdays and Fridays, would greatly weaken the body's health with such regular and severe food deprivation. After the Sunday sermon at the end of the Mass, the parish priest repeatedly used to invite sick or elderly believers, especially before the beginning of one of the four annual fasts, to discuss with him exactly how to keep fast and which of the nutritional prohibitions can be mitigated.

The mentioned episodes of the fieldwork highlight the problematic compatibility of traditional Orthodox practices with the rhythm of modern life. *Vocerkovlenie* requires full time attention, participation, and energy; the organization of everyday life must be made according to the rhythm of the church bell – an effort that not everyone can make.

According to Kormina and Shtyrkov (2011, p. 173), "Church has good reason to represent irregular religiosity as legitimate and Orthodox". Unlike them, I argue that today's Russian Orthodox clerics are reluctant to compromise in the name of attracting more believers to the temple; strict observance of the rules and canons is required by the churchgoers. In other words, the strategy of the Russian Orthodox Church is not inclusive – rather the opposite is true. Indicative of these moods is an article published in the official magazine of the Diocese of Kaluga, under the eloquent title of "Dead Souls" ['*Mërtvye duši*'].[16] The author is one of the most conservative priests in Kaluga. Openly controversial, the article insists that (newly) baptized people who do not regularly visit the temple should not be considered Christians and should be excommunicated from the church: "Three Sunday liturgies, omitted without a good reason, are grounds for excommunication from the church" (Kazancev, 2006, p. 11). Tsekhanskaia reports on a softer form of the same "policy of exclusion", which is already implemented in practice and not only as an intention: "In some Moscow parishes today there is repentance for the failure of several consecutive Sunday liturgies" (Tsekhanskaia, 2015, p. 4).

Intolerance rejects those believers who have religious feelings "but refuse to be pressed by the institutions" (Wanner, 2018, p. 90; see also Kormina and Shtyrkov, 2011, p. 172). In these cases, religious experience remains atomized and deinstitutionalized. For instance, Tamara, a librarian from Kaluga, was baptized as a child in Soviet times and said she was a believer, but explained her rare visits to the temple was due to her difficulty in communicating with the priests: "I do not know how to deal with them! I'm afraid of them!"[17]

Vicarious religion: A portrait of the "little flock"

I mentioned above the problem of compatibility of traditional Orthodox practices with the rhythm of modern life. The next thesis states that the "little flock" of the most devoted believers is an important driving force (in cooperation with the clergy) of the religious life in modern Russia. This particular "minority" of actively practicing Christians makes the discussed paradox possible. Following are the arguments in favor of this statement.

The "politics of exclusion", defined by Vasilios Makrides as rigorism (Makrides, 2004, pp. 511–521), is shared, discussed, and negotiated between the priest and the narrow circle of the most devoted parishioners. Priests are often put under tension: Between their own desire to engage a wider circle of believers and the views of the most conservative part of the parishioners. The latter seek the religious salvation in asceticism and support even the introduction of monastic practices in urban parishes (e.g. monastic service worship with a duration of three and one-half hours). The expropriation of some believers is undoubtedly a cause for concern and is discussed both in conversations among the worshippers and in the pages of the Orthodox periodicals. However, legitimacy for this exclusion strategy is sought and found in a quote from the Gospel by Luke: "*Fear not, little flock*" ['*Ne bojsia, maloe stado*'].[18] The most devoted believers of the "little flock" perceive themselves as the bearers of "true Orthodoxy", and this is an argument by which the policy of exclusion is implicitly accepted: The adherence of more people to the circle of Christian practitioners has been limited.

The concept of vicarious religion, introduced by Grace Davie, is the appropriate analytical tool that brings clarity to the outlined context. It is the understanding that "a relatively small number of people could 'take care of' the memory (and especially the Christian memory) on behalf of others" (Davie, 2000, p. 177). When she introduced the concept, Davie meant it to apply first and foremost to the clergy who take care of religion "on behalf of others", while the phrase "believing without belonging" applied to those who rarely participated in parish life. Davie has since adjusted her view on the varied relations between belief and practice, proposing an expanded concept of vicarious religion that allows the "retirement" of "believing without belonging" from the conceptual repertoire. According to this updated understanding, vicarious religion is "the notion of religion performed by an active minority but on behalf of a much larger number, who (implicitly at least) not only understand, but, quite clearly, approve of what the minority is doing" (Davie, 2007, p. 22).

How can the notion of vicarious religion be applied to observations formed in the midst of contemporary Russian Orthodoxy? The Russian Orthodox environment shows that the community of the most devoted believers, interacting with clergy, is the main social actor who takes care of religion on behalf of others. From the point of view of religion, the state of contemporary Russian society can also be defined as a post-atheistic one. In this context, it must be understood that the clergy provides the institutional stability of religious life. Without the active support of the most dedicated believers, however, the Church, understood as a single body of believing laymen and clergy, could not carry out its day-to-day activities, much less its ambitious program of transformation and influence on Russian society. Moreover, the emphasis here on the importance of the minority of the most active believers makes it possible to regard religion not solely in the instrumental sense, but to pay due respect to value rationality (Weber, 2002).[19]

In order to gain greater clarity in these theoretical considerations, it is necessary to present the social actors and analyze the practices in which they are involved. The *vocerkovlënnye*, mentioned several times so far, form the "little flock" of consistently practicing worshippers. Taking into consideration all the cultural specificity of this layer of contemporary Russian society, it would be relevant to give it a more general definition – of people who "have absorbed an all-encompassing religious way of life" (Ammerman, 2007, p. 219). The word *vocerkovlënnye* derives from the ecclesiastical term *vocerkovlenie* [enchurchment], which I will tackle first.

Vocerkovlenie is a term whose original meaning refers to a church ritual known in Russia since the fourteenth century: The first introduction of the child into the temple (Petrovskii, 1902, p. 1020). This term (still known in its original meaning in other Orthodox Slavic countries) has a multi-layered character in the Russian environment. Characteristic of Russian Orthodoxy is a second, broader understanding: A continuous process of bringing man to the church at different ages, and full harmonization of the life of the worshipper with the canons of faith (Grozovskii, 2006, p. 46; Torik, 2007, p. 2; see also Agadjanian, 2011a, p. 22). A clearer idea of this understanding can be found in quotations from popular readings. One such example, written by a respected priest, explains to believing parents how to "enchurch their children" ['*kak vocerkovit'detei*']:

> We can think of a child as enchurched when he is happy to go to church for the early service or the late one; when he prepares for confession and receives the Holy Communion; shows obedience to parents, honors them; without urge participates in domestic prayers; reads the Gospel; takes the blessing of the parents, and most importantly – there is love for God and for the people.
> (Grozovskii, 2006, p. 46)

It is clear from the last citation that the notion of *vocerkovlenie* is not limited to the ritual introduction into the temple or religious socialization. It covers the basic aspects of life under the sign of faith: Participation in church life, fulfillment of basic sacraments, contact with the sacred books, and mastering the most important postulates of Christian ethics. Such an understanding has a certain third, post-Soviet specificity when *vocerkovlenie* also means the catechization of people socialized in the Soviet era and unfamiliar with the basic postulates of Orthodox Christianity. This third use of the concept brings it somewhat closer to the concept of conversion, in the specific postsocialist sense of the transition from unbelief to faith. From the aforementioned, it is also implicit that *vocerkovlenie* affects not only the beliefs, but also the overall adjustment of individual behavior.

An attempt to perceive sociologically the notion of *vocerkovlenie* is worthwhile. Valentina Chesnokova, who is an often-quoted author, objects to those attempts of her colleagues to relativize Orthodox affiliation by emphasizing the inconsistency between Orthodox self-determination and the degree of participation in religious practices. Chesnokova insists to the contrary that nobody has the right to question the self-determination of respondents in sociological research: "Believers are the ones who call themselves Orthodox". Chesnokova rejects the often-used argument that "superstition", belief in astrology, magic, etc. testify to the absence of religiosity (Chesnokova, 2005, p. 7). Instead, she turns to break down into several layers the notion of *vocerkovlenie*, introducing a five-step scale of assessment on each of five criteria: Visiting the temples, receiving Communion, reading the Bible, praying, and fasting. She aims at determining the degree of *vocerkovlenie*, but points out: "The attainment of a high indicator of at least one characteristic of the Orthodox way of life – that is already a great victory for man" (Ibid., pp. 19, 28). The introduction of five criteria brings clarity about the scope of the concept of *vocerkovlenie* and increases the possibility of its application for analytical purposes instead of operating with the ambiguous, as we have seen, rather intuitive understanding related to the church circles.

In turn, the derivative term *vocerkovlënnye* [the enchurched] is used at both *etic* and *emic* levels. In its broad *emic* meaning, popular in Russian society, this concept encompasses the entire class of regularly practicing and church-attending worshippers. Here I propose a different, narrower (*etic*) use of *vocerkovlënnye*, which allows a clearer outline of the typology of believers. For analytical purposes, I will distinguish between the two similar but not fully matched categories of active believers: *Vocerkovlënnye* and *pricerkovnyi krug* [literally, "around-the-church circle"]. Regardless of the "permeability" of the boundaries between these two layers, the distinction between them is beneficial in that it allows us to avoid the essentialization of a whole stratum of Russian society as homogeneous or static.

The people in the *pricerkovnyi krug* form the layer of the most devoted believers. *Pricerkovnyi krug* is an *etic* concept introduced by the Russian folklorist Arina Tarabukina (Tarabukina, 2000, p. 1). Following this author, other Russian scholars define the *pricerkovnyi krug* as a religious subculture or environment formed at the beginning of the twentieth century under the influence of popular Orthodox preachers that existed underground in the Soviet era. The *emic* name, with which they more often identify themselves, is *cerkovnye liudi* [church people]. The majority of them do not engage in jobs (or do not identify themselves with their professional status); they have no permanent dwelling or have given it up for "spiritual reasons". Their ideal is ascetic monasticism; they exclude secular influences from their lives and limit their social contacts (possibly their activities as well) to the boundaries defined by the "church fence". In their search for holiness, they often settle in a monastery or convent for long periods of time, even for months or years.[20] *Cerkovnye lyudi* have a distinctive appearance: Clothing, body control, manners of behavior; they are easily recognizable, first and foremost by their characteristic clothing (long, free skirts and headscarves for women; beards and ponytails, a specific type of shirt – for men) (Tarabukina, 2000, p. 1; Akhmetova, 2004, pp. 240–241; Kormina, 2011, p. 192, 2013b, p. 202).

An excerpt from the autobiographical narrative of a zealous believer from Kaluga, who corresponds to the previous description, gives an idea of the mentality and feelings of the people of this stratum:

> *Working at the temple, naturally, gives more opportunities to participate in the service. The circle of worship with all the saints, with all the holidays. When you experience this ecclesiastical year every day, being in the choir, singing poetry of the lives of the saint: this is certainly a completely different feeling,*

> *than when a person, to the extent of his employment, the need for social service, has to dedicate only days of the holidays to the church. And here [it is granted] by the grace of God. . . . That is, you cannot imagine: here a person lives in the church practically church life every day, speaks about internal . . . about sorrows, does his favorite thing, that is, I don't know, what else you can dream about.*[21]

Some of the most devoted believers sometimes change their behavior: "They completely change their lives and return to the secular world" (Tarabukina, 2000, p. 1). The number of people joining the core of the most devoted believers, however, is more than the number who leave it.

Some researchers claim that *pricerkovnyi krug* also includes part of the clergy – monks and priests (Tarabukina, 2000, p. 1; Akhmetova, 2004, p. 240). Jeanne Kormina defines people in this circle as "religious professionals" (Kormina, 2013b, p. 202). With regard to *pricerkovnyi krug*, I take a different approach and exclude the clerics.

The reason that Russian researchers assign clerics to the *pricerkovnyi krug* is that they share common beliefs and ideas, worldview, and a narrative repertoire with the lay members. My reasons to exclude them are of a theoretical nature: For the purposes of my analysis, the boundaries between laymen and the clergy must be clear and not blurred. Clergy are the backbone of church institutions. They possess "office charisma" (in the terms of Max Weber), and their religious ministry is a profession from which they earn their income. The people of the *pricerkovnyi krug* can develop in the direction of religious professionalization by performing the functions of church singers, readers, managing the church stores (*lavki*), which offer candles and various church supplies for sale. However, these and some other functions are often performed on a voluntary basis: The laypeople in the *pricerkovnyi krug* support priests and their parishes.

Thus, a core of eight women from the parish to the temple of the Shroud of the Holy Mother [*Pokrova na rvu*] dealt voluntarily with the cleaning and maintenance of the church building (where building and repair activities took place during the fieldwork in 2007). The transformation of the church yard into a flower garden with facilities for young children was also the voluntary work (called "obedience" [*poslušanie*]) of certain parishioners.

The people of the *pricerkovnyi krug* are also a "resource" for Orthodox life in another, different way. Because of their search for closeness to the monasteries as a model of holiness, they can also be defined as a "reserve" from which the ranks of monks and nuns are completed (see Medvedeva, 2016b, p. 93). This trend is clearly evidenced in Kaluga: The activity of the St. Elisaveta Fëdorovna Orthodox Charitable Sisterhood, founded in 1992,[22] is a good example. It is associated with the Kazansky Convent and performs charitable activities with the material support of the convent and of the diocese of Kaluga, and with the personal support of Metropolitan Kliment (Kapalin).[23]

The first cohort of the sisterhood has been working voluntarily since 1995 for the physical restoration of the Kazansky Convent. Periodically, some of the "sisters" integrate into the same convent as neophytes or nuns. At least once, the spillover of "sisters" from the charitable organization into the convent largely exhausted the human resources of the sisterhood itself. In 2003, the sisterhood had to re-form itself with a second cohort of volunteers. But the process continued: In 2007, two sisters from the second cohort also went to the convent.

> *On the basis of this sisterhood, in 1995 we started restoring our Kazansky Gurski Convent. All the forces and knowledge have been given to recover the convent. And from their circles the sisters in the convent were appointed. Well, they went to the convent, became neophytes, nuns. Our matuška [Mother Superior] was also in the first sisterhood. . . .*
>
> *In 2003, then, Mother Superior blessed the creation of the new [second] sisterhood. . . . Because that [first] sisterhood seemed to be . . . not working. It seemed to have transformed itself into the convent. . . . Here, two of our sisters also went to a convent from the second sisterhood. We have sisters who can be so high on a spiritual vocation: I think we will have more sisters who can go to a convent.*[24]

However, not all members of the sisterhood could be referred to as belonging to the *pricerkovnyj krug*. Some of them have families and an autonomous professional and private life. Interviews show the different attitude of the "sisters" towards the prospect of monastic life, even though they spend most of their time on the territory of the cloister. The sisterhood develops there some of its activities (it maintains a year-round soup kitchen for homeless people; the other charity activity – care for the seniors and the sick in the nursing home[25] – is developed on the territory of the latter). Some of them do not associate their future with the adoption of monastic rank, inasmuch as they have not mastered obedience as a manifestation of humility: A moral quality, considered to be the main Orthodox virtue in a monastic environment (Dubovka, 2015a, pp. 327–333): "*I am not fit for the convent, I am self-opinionated*", says one of them.[26]

Others are prepared to accept monasticism, such as Sister G., who is involved daily in preparing food and feeding the homeless in the soup kitchen. The head of the sisterhood in 2007, the "senior sister" (*staršaia sestra*), lives in the convent, although she is not a nun. This allows her to help in the work of the abbess in everyday activities. Regardless of individual life strategies or future decisions, the prospect of entering the religious world ever more deeply is a topic that is the subject of much discussion. The intermediate status of the sisters, with the status of the laity but actually immersed in the monastic environment, is symbolized by the wearing of formal clothing (discussed in direct dialogue with the bishop),[27] which externally resembles monastic rigor but avoids the color black.

In her typology of Orthodox regimes of sociality, Jeanne Kormina distinguishes three "regimes": Parishioners, pilgrims, and networkers. The third of these is related to the specific culture and behavior of the *pricerkovnyi krug*, as outlined by Tarabukina (Kormina, 2011a, pp. 189–211, 202–205). Although part of Kormina's argument needs further elaboration, she does draw attention to an important feature of the community: "[E]x-territoriality and a claim to empathy for the narrow circle of the chosen" (ibid., 205). Importantly, this "regime" of contemporary Orthodox religiosity also exists outside territorially established religious communities with a (relatively) stable composition and structure, such as parishes. The radical anti-modern values and ideologies typical of the *pricerkovnyi krug* are not in conflict with the speed with which modern technologies become the usual companions of everyday life for the benefit of mobility and human connectivity. Mobility as a regular feature of life in later modernity, as well as modern communications, also greatly facilitates the plurality of connections between territory and holiness.

The socio-cultural profile of the networkers, outlined by Jeanne Kormina, corresponds to another attempt for typology, this time of religiosity proposed by Tünde Komáromi: Distanced, passionate, and balanced religiosity (Komáromi, 2011, p. 96). The definition of "passionate religiosity" may serve as another approach to the collective portrait of the *pricerkovnyi krug*. Their specific ideology and worldview, shown in the first study devoted to them (Tarabukina, 2000), are characterized by a demonology that includes images, narratives, and language clichés. The observations from Kaluga allow their portrait to be compacted: Not so much by unfamiliar traits, but rather by linking it to specific contexts and circumstances.

As Tarabukina (2000, p. 4) proves, from the beginning of the twentieth century, when this stratum (or subculture) formed, the "church people" have been marked by a "feeling of tension". Moreover, their behavior testifies to the state of alarming eschatological expectation, which is expressed both at the narrative level and in everyday communicative situations. The strategy of self-isolation characteristic of this socio-cultural environment in order to avoid "satanic influences" (ibid.) is a cause of suspicion among representatives of secular culture. In the process of fieldwork, I became familiar with two of the main narrative genres spread among the *pricerkovnyj krug*: "[J]oint prayer" and "situational communication"; I have not witnessed a "spiritual talk".

The behavior and discourses characteristic of "church people" can be considered a semiotic system. Their world is "ethically saturated" in the terms of Webb Keane (2014, pp. 318–320). Their shared picture of the world is based on the fundamental binary opposition between two poles: The powers of light and of darkness, respectively the divine and satanic forces. However, the poles have an asymmetrical "weight": The light in the world is getting less, and the powers of darkness overwhelm it (ibid.); so between the two poles, there is no balance: Darkness and evil gain more power.

When communicating with people who share this culture, one falls into a world of anticipated encounters with evil, where it is neither an abstraction nor a metaphor, but a part of the close profane environment of mundane everyday life. "Satanic forces" are all pervasive and are at hand. Furthermore, insofar as evil is in battle with the powers of light and holiness (embodied by the monasteries and the monastic way of life), it attacks the holy places and the people who are committed to virtuous life.

The latter idea is also known and accepted and outside the *pritserkovnyi krug*. In response to my apologies that I found it hard to stand and suffered during three-and-one-half-hour liturgies, I heard from various believers – and one priest – the explanation that I was being attacked by the devil because I was trying to do a good deed.[28] The explanation of evilness came easily to people: "*If laymen are followed by a horned one, then there will be ten horned ones after the monks: When a person strives for spiritual perfection, the enemy attacks him more*"[29] – said a devoted believer with a smile, as if talking about the weather outside.

Meanwhile, this statement also points to reasoning in a different direction. It multiplies demonic power into ten "horned ones" and thus reminds of popular demonology featuring multiple images, partially depersonalized precisely because of its multiplicity. The omission of the name of the evil power – Satan – and its substitution with a synonymous epithet also belies faith in the magical power of speech (i.e. Satan's name is not said because to pronounce it is to call the devil to the present place). This particular statement is a remarkable reminder of the discussions on the division of Christianity into "high" and "low", "official" and "popular". It shows how ideas and images popular in a monastic environment (i.e. in "high" Christianity) touch and mingle with mythologies typical of "popular" peasant culture.

At one of the meetings of the Orthodox Sisterhood, I could hardly overcome the suspicion of one of the interlocutors that I was "infected" by the "unclean power" of darkness. During the conversation, which tested my belonging for Orthodoxy, I crossed some significant spatial boundaries and before each of them I was thoroughly watered with holy water until I was completely wet. I was initially admitted into the courtyard of the convent where a woman sprinkled me with holy water. The next stage of socialization was at the door of the Rotunda (a cylindrical building where the sisterhood develops its activities). After we crossed its threshold, the woman sprinkled the room, then she sprinkled another sister who was cleaning, and then me again; the procedure was repeated once more after we climbed to the second floor. Since no explanation was given as to the meaning of this unusual "ritual", I came to the conclusion that the opposition between "purity and danger" (Douglas, 1966) was being materialized: Treated as unclean, I was dangerous until the perceived impurity was neutralized.

The notions and discourses among the "church people" are a clear example of what Keane calls "semiotic ideology": "[P]eople's assumptions, either tacit or explicit, that guide how they do or do not perceive or seek out signs in the world and respond to them" (Kean, 2014, p. 314). In a wider interpretation, the signs are a set of symbols, images and language clichés that are shared intersubjective knowledge. People use this knowledge as they interpret their everyday experiences and adjust their behavior accordingly.

By way of illustration, I will present some of my field notes describing the most significant episodes of an unplanned encounter on July 23, 2007, with a typical representative of the *pricerkovnyj krug*. I will keep her anonymity by calling her X.[30]

> Zinaida Anatolievna and I were in a place where there had been a fire. The home of X was burned on June 29, 2007 because of the negligence of an

alcoholic neighbor. . . . When we entered, the first words of X were: "*The Lord sends me trials. And I have to accept them*." This was about the fire. I immediately understood that I had come across a representative of the *pricerkovnyi krug*. X pulled off her hat and put on a headscarf. . . . Zinaida Anatolievna brought food, X boiled eggs. She boiled tea. And she invited us to pray towards the east, against the icon. We performed the ritual, we sang [prayers]. Then I managed to hear almost the entire repertoire of the *pricerkovnyi krug*. The conversation mentioned the *babuška* (old lady), cared for by X. She was now in hospital, about to be discharged, and X did not know where to accommodate her because there was no place in the burned house. It turned out that this was a completely strange woman to X – not a relative. Zinaida Anatolievna emphasized that fact, as if speaking of the virtues of X, and she honestly replied: "*Well, Zinaida Anatolievna, what you say is so embarrassing*" – she did not want to be praised. Christian ethics.

At teatime, X could not get away from the topic of moral decay, the manifestation of which was the fire. A hint of apocalyptic expectation: "*Indeed, as if these are the last times. The Lord loves us, he still tolerates us. And how to find salvation?*" Unbelief is the reason for this. It divides parents from children ("*The children complain about parents, parents about children*", i.e. because of unbelief). . . . X also believed that another neighbor was responsible for all this because she dealt with spells. . . . "*She* [the perceived sorcerer] *cannot look in my eyes. So, she passes by without looking me in the eyes*." X spoke without anger about what had happened. Her actions to overcome the fire were completely rational [she filed an application in court]. . . .

[X was born in Siberia, in the Far East, where her family settled. During World War II, her grandfather died in 1943, though they had not known where.] "*And can you imagine, in 2003, my mother received a statement that my grandfather was killed near Kaluga!*" [In 2005, X and her mother attended the Kaluga celebrations on the 60th anniversary of the Soviet victory in World War II; then X moved to Kaluga]. In a very categorical tone, X notes: "*All this is the Divine Providence! Coincidence does not exist. . . . They* [the Jews] *waited for Messiah, but when the Lord came, they did not recognize Him and sent him to the Cross. They are sending to Russia moral crisis, because one can't easily conquer Russia*." When we talked about her arrival in Kaluga, she noted that it was very difficult to leave the city where she used to live. There was a "*lot of darkness*" (i.e. actions of satanic forces).[31]

This portrait of X should add two peculiar features to the people of the *pricerkovnyi krug*: The spiritual connection with an informal charismatic leader, a "spiritual elder" (Paert, 2010), and settling if not in a monastery, then near it, in search of holiness. After her resettlement from the far northeast of Russia, X settled not in Kaluga, but in a village in the immediate vicinity of a large ancient monastery. Her "spiritual mother" was a known hermit [*skimonakhinia*]. Though she died in 2006, she still served as a resource for a higher spiritual authority and status for X among other believers: X held a strong respect for Zinaida Anatolievna as her elder; but the latter spoke with sincere admiration and respect for X.

The conversation with X, presented here in summary, relates to the genre of "situational communication" described by Tarabukina (2000, p. 3). It shows how a real-life situation of a burned-down-house (indeed not a rare incident in Russia due to the easy flammability of traditional wooden buildings) is integrated into interpretive models of a significant character. The interlocutor's speech is "ethically saturated": "[T]here are no accidents, and no neutral causality, and any event or thing might turn out to be a sign of an agent (and most significantly when they are divine or satanic), something subject to ethical evaluation" (Keane, 2014, p. 319). The anti-Semitic motive in X's speech seems out of context, but only at first glance: It is a must-have part of the narrative repertoire and explanatory clichés within the *pritserkovnyi krug* and related to the anti-Semitism of some iconic monks – "spiritual elders" – at the end of the nineteenth century, such as the Reverent St. Ambrose of Optina (Amvrosii Optinsky) [Grenkov].

The specific ideology and narrative repertoire of *cerkovnye lyudi* [church people] are also known among other believers, but they are not shared by the reflexive part of the educated *vocerkovlënnye* [enchurched people] who are looking for moral improvement.[32] In contrast, anti-modern and xenophobic attitudes resonate in the ideologies of political Orthodoxy – far-right Russian nationalist parties and movements (see Verkhovsky, 2003, pp. 34–95; Knorre, 2014, p. 70).

If we go back to the main features of the *pricekovnyj krug* in contemporary Russia, we will find a basis for comparison between this class and examples from other religions and denominations following the model of religious exclusivity and revivalism. On the demographic characteristics and propensity for self-isolation, Eric Kaufmann bases the parallels between ultra-religious communities such as those of Mormons, fundamentalist ultra-Orthodox Jews (or Haredi), and the followers of Salafi Islam. All of them are characterized by segregation and pronatalism (Kaufmann, 2010, pp. 252–253). Alexander Agadjanian uses almost the same examples when he finds such a link existing, or parallelism, between Russian and international examples. The analogy is based on the model of the split religious authority: The traditional power of the priest against the charismatic power (in Weber's terms) of the spiritual elders (Agadjanian, 2011a, p. 20). High birth rates are, however, not so easy to find among Russian ultra-religious believers (rather, people without families are not rare within the *pricekovnyj krug*). In this sense, such a comparison should rather be deduced within individual signs and not as a general typology of ultra-religious communities. Despite the indispensable caution, it is important to note that Russian examples are not isolated from internationally presented trends.

In turn, *vocerkovlënnye*, understood in the narrow *etic* sense that I put here, have another sociological profile. This is the part of regular churchgoers who have an autonomous professional and family life. In this respect, they are distinguished from *cerkovnye lyudi*. They do not wish to be recognized on the street in their appearance, and they do not avoid communicating with people who are not believers. As one explained, "*Believers are not obliged to distinguish themselves externally. They must be distinguished internally. . . . No one forbids communication with unbelievers.*"[33] Their everyday life is not limited to the church or monastic space. Field observations in Kaluga show that often *vocerkovlënnye* are people with respected professions and influence in society (engineers, doctors, teachers, computer experts, journalists, heads of state-owned enterprises, or private entrepreneurs).[34] They are also actively involved in the life of their parish and diocese (serving as tour guides for pilgrimage groups, Sunday school teachers, Orthodox journalists who write on religious matters in secular and religious media, singers in the church choirs, or members of various parish and diocesan committees). Often (albeit not always), they develop these activities on a voluntary basis.

Among the representatives of this environment are people with high social standing. Thanks to their access to resources, their prestige, and their participation in secular social networks (economic and political), they have the opportunity to contribute to important church projects concerning church property, the construction and development of temples, and charity funding. It is worth noting the role of two of the interviewees who occupy significant economic positions in Kaluga.[35] This allows them to carry out important links between the Diocese of Kaluga, the city administration, and the economic elite in the city: To help restitution of the ecclesiastical properties or to provide donations – cash or in kind – in the form of building materials, food, or other material benefits. For example, the dining room [*trapeznaia*] at Pokrova na rvu was entirely built (in 2005) with building materials afforded by donations;[36] indeed, the golden crosses that crown the domes of the same temple were donated by a citizen.[37]

Because of their full social life, *vocerkovlënnye* (in the narrow sense of the word) are able to convey religious messages to society and to mediate between society and the church institutions. Their role as mediators is important for both the functioning of everyday religious practices and their role as one of the bridges through which the church influences society at the local and national levels.

Thus, as we can see, there is an overlap between the two conditionally distinct layers of the "little flock". In real life circumstances, a believer can change his or her behavior. A *vocerkovlënnyj* can become a representative of the *pricekovnyj krug* or vice versa. Although the boundaries between the two categories are shifting, the cases of such a transition from one state to the other demonstrate that such boundaries exist. The main criterion for distinguishing between the two affiliations (or states) is the level of participation, at a particular time, in the parish or monastic life. As noted, those belonging to the *pricekovnyj krug* socialize almost entirely in ecclesiastical or monastic environments, but they did not always do so, and some return to more secular life patterns.

The transition from one state to the other is also evidenced by the interviews held in Kaluga. Thus, Vadim Nikityč, a young man with a medical profession, became deeply engaged in religion during his student years. After completing his medical education, he began a theological training, (temporarily) abandoning the medical profession and serving on a voluntary basis as a deacon in one of the Kaluga monasteries for two years. A sudden escalation of an internal conflict in the convent caused him to radically change his life again: Vadim excluded himself from church circles, terminated his ministry in the cloister, and returned successfully to his medical profession. Religion continued to be an important factor in his life, but something that he pursued alongside his professional career. In short, when I met him, Vadim remained among the *vocerkovlënnye* but no longer belonged to the *pricekovnyj krug*. According to the wise comment of another interlocutor – a patient of Vadim's – "*the Church lost; medicine won.*"

The daily life of the two ecclesiastical parishes [*prikhody*] could hardly be organized to function normally without the participation of the "little flock". Its members are the source for much of the church *pričt*[38] – altar assistants, readers, singers [*altarniki, ponomari, pevčie*]. Here, too, we have to add the *svečnicy* – women who are responsible for selling in the church *lavka*.

In certain cases, such as the one at St. Martyr John the Warrior in Kaluga, the role of these women is essential and is not limited to the sale of religious goods. In this church (as in a number of others), worship is performed only on Saturdays and Sundays, but the temple is also open during the week. Believers and visitors who stop by on weekdays are welcomed only by the shopkeeper. She is the person they consult to receive information on spiritual and other questions, order church rituals, or reach the priest. The two women who work in shifts at the *lavka* of St. Martyr John the Warrior are important gatekeepers of the temple life. How they welcome the visitor – patiently and courteously or unresponsively and rudely – may determine whether this man or woman will open the church gate again.

For example, I witnessed a dialogue in which a young woman who came to the church to negotiate a day and hour for the baptism of her newly born child came with an attitude similar to that of a customer in a shop. She was impatient and asked "when" and at what time the church ritual could be performed. She was right to expect that the shopkeeper could do the scheduling, but – following the priest's instructions (which are also written in a special notice), the shopkeeper explained that the mother should talk to the priest first. Only after such a conversation could the shopkeeper negotiate the day and the hour for baptism. The priest insisted that the ritual should be preceded by preliminary explanations of the meaning of baptism, and about the spiritual blessings and responsibilities that it brings.[39] He was not in a hurry to attract new members or customers, even though the execution of *treby* (i.e. basic church sacraments) forms an important part of a parish's income. Indeed, insisting on such a preliminary conversation is part of the catechism work of the ROC in Kaluga that Metropolitan Kliment requires of the priests. In the repeated exchange of the same words – "when" and "you must first make an appointment with *batiuška* [Father]" – the shopkeeper invariably showed respect and patience. But it is fair to note that such a visitor would not meet such a respectful approach in all of Kaluga's churches.

It is not possible to determine with precision whether and in what cases the work related to everyday church activities is paid or voluntary. Interviews and observations show that each individual case is negotiated and decided with the priest. Nor is it possible to predict which work can be voluntary and which not. "I do not work for them, I only help them [*Ja u nikh ne rabotaju, ja im tol'ko pomagaju*]", came the answer to my question in a random street meeting with Nina, the smiling middle-aged woman who cooks in the kitchen at Pokrova na rvu.[40] Some of the Sunday school teachers at the same church teach children on a voluntary basis; others do the same for a fee.[41] The church choir [*pevčie*] does not sing every day, but participation requires some training, specific skills, and talents, and a small amount of pay might help secure some good singers. Normally, the *matuška* (the priest's wife) is a member of the choir or conducts it (as is the case in both studied parishes) without payment; but one singer does not make a choir. Due to a shortage of candidates, one person is likely to do several different activities: He or she might work in the *lavka*, teach at the Sunday school, work as an "Orthodox journalist", or guide pilgrimage trips [*palomničeskie putešestvija*]. The reasons for such "collaboration" are not only the modest pay rates (if any) of each activity, but also the requirements of church institutions; an important filter is the demand for candidates to be *vocerkovlënnye* (see Medvedeva, 2016b, pp. 94–95).

This aspect of the mechanisms of everyday life also testifies to something else. The impression of a virtually unproblematic and triumphant resurgence of Orthodox Christianity during the post-Soviet decades in Russia, which is conveyed by the restoration of temples and other persistent signs of religion in Russian public spaces, outlines only the visible side of Orthodox life. However, there is a real shortage of people who are prepared and sufficiently motivated to implement the full range of religious practices and services at the churches. Therefore, believers face a fundamental contradiction between the ROC's ambitious program to have a comprehensive influence on all spheres of social life and the constraints imposed by social life. This contradiction shows the essential role that regular churchgoers – the "little flock" – really play in the life of Orthodox communities. Both the *vocerkovlënnye* and the *pricekovnyi krug* contribute to the translation of religious culture within the Orthodox parishes: They support neophytes and less experienced believers in the attainment of religious norms and especially in the rules of conduct during church services.[42]

Let us return to the role of the St. Elisaveta Fëdorovna Orthodox Sisterhood. The story of their donation campaign for the Home for Seniors testifies to the importance of the "little flock". The most dedicated believers are important not only within the temples but also in serving as intermediaries in the communication between the Russian Orthodox Church and the secularized part of the Russian society in Kaluga:[43]

> *When we finished this job, well, we had to go to the temples, to all the acquaintances. Well, thank God, I have many such acquaintances who are wealthy – for example, a lawyer, a prosecutor – such people whom I know do not live poorly. There is a director among them, and a shop owner, and so on.*
>
> *I began to select such people and go to them. And thank God, no one refused me. They even gave large sums of money – well, three, five thousand* [rubles]. *Then, they gave some material – for the ceiling, and tiles, and ground coat, and all the cement mixes. They gave a lot. Even, well, I went to a shop, looking for timber. And I also went there – I think they were from the "new Russians" – young. I turned to them, I said, "Guys, we need this for the temple". They*

> *immediately cut down the prices. And they gave me cheaper. And they offered me their car, they brought the things . . .*
>
> *That's how people helped. So, they helped. And thank God.*[44]

The "little flock" can be effectively mobilized for political action and provide the legitimacy of clergy ambitions for influence and power in Russian society. Among the most visible examples in this respect are rallies in Moscow in 2006 and 2008 to support the introduction of religious education in schools[45] or the more controversial *molitvennye stoyanija* [prayer standings]. For the latter, 60,000 people gathered in Moscow on April 22, 2012 to protest "in defense of the church" and to condemn the performance of the anticlerical female punk group *Pussy Riot* (Schroeder and Karpov, 2013, p. 295; Uzlaner, 2014, pp. 23–58; Wanner, 2018, pp. 91–94). As it happened, this was also a pro-government position.

It has to be concluded that representatives of the "little flock" have an essential role in the day-to-day functioning of the Orthodox parishes, fulfilling part of their daily and liturgical activities; they do social and charity work; serve as a reserve from which the roles of the clergy are often filled; participate in the post-Soviet context of the process of restoration of temples and monasteries; have an important role in the transmission of Orthodox culture; reinforce the sources of Orthodox identity among the majority (which is not in a hurry to enter the temples on Sundays); and legitimate the political ambitions of the clergy.

Grace Davie suggests that in different societies, vicarious religion can function differently (Davie, 2007, p. 32). The Russian examples show, firstly, that the concept of vicarious religion can also concern a particular social class of laymen associated with clergy but not coincident with it; and secondly, that vicarious religion can have a much more central role than that of reminding the population of religious traditions in times of crisis. The "little flock" of the most devoted believers in modern Russia reaffirms observations about the potential of radical minorities to be a catalyst for social movements and social changes.

A "symphony" between the Russian Orthodox Church and the state

That the support of the state institutions for the ROC, which emerged with Mikhail Gorbachev, was contradictory but tangible with Boris Yeltsin and became firmly established during the Putin and Medvedev era (see Knox, 2005, pp. 105–132; Knorre, 2014, pp. 42–103), is also among the important factors for the character of post-Soviet religious life. At the beginning of the second decade of the twenty-first century, state legislative initiatives in favor of the ROC reinforce the positions of the church in a way that surprised even the most confident researchers of the Russian religious field. The establishment of the military priests in the Russian army in 2010, the restitution of church property in the same year (see Köllner, 2018),[46] and the introduction of religious education in secondary schools in 2012 throughout the country[47] show that forecasting in this area is a risky business.

While in Russian society and media since the end of the 1990s there has been a long and heated debate for and against the introduction of the subject *Fundamentals of Orthodox Culture* [*Osnovy pravoslavnoi kul'tury*] and its compatibility with the secular nature of the Russian state, its introduction with a governmental decision makes this discussion immaterial. By 2008, the ROC projects mentioned (military priests, religious education, property restitution) had failed "spectacularly", which is why Irina Papkova made a conclusion in her book (Papkova, 2011) about the political weakness of the ROC; but she was disproved by subsequent developments only two or three years later. The same author devoted a separate article to this turn (Papkova, 2013, pp. 244–253).

The list of phenomena, processes, and events that show the increasingly influential role of the ROC in the public world is much longer – even in its very non-exhaustive version. Apart from the tangible presence of Orthodoxy in Russian public and political life, this list cannot miss the cases of sharp confrontation with groups or individuals not in line with the policies of the ROC. Such an event is the fierce public debate on the protest letter of ten academicians from the Russian Academy of Sciences from July 23, 2007 addressed to President Putin (Anderson, 2007, p. 197) and the subsequent political scandal widely disseminated by the

Figure 1.1 Entanglement of the secular and religious: Newlyweds' pilgrimage at the shrine of St. Tikhon near Kaluga. July 7, 2007.

Source: Photo: Milena Benovska

media. Of the cases of religious-based confrontation in the field of art or with representatives of the artistic world, the scandalous lawsuit against the performers of the female punk group *Pussy Riot* in 2012 has achieved the greatest popularity (see Schroeder and Karpov, 2013, p. 295; Uzlaner, 2014, pp. 23–58; Wanner, 2018). In response to the case against *Pussy Riot*, the "Law for the Protection of Religious Feelings" was adopted in 2013.[48] But of course there have been other conflicts between "religion" and the arts. Cases such as the exhibition in the Sakharov Musical Center "Beware, Religion" [*Ostorozhno, religiia*] in 2003, which was vandalized by religious activists (Agadjanian, 2006, pp. 169–184; Schroeder and Karpov, 2013, pp. 37–41), as well as a number of related events that have not received the same national or international publicity.[49]

The influence of Orthodoxy on public life in Russia and the successes achieved by the ROC and Patriarch Kirill during the presidency of Dmitry Medvedev (2008–2012) are an incentive for a theoretical quest. In attempts to theoretically master empirical reality, a number of researchers have tried to find the right conceptual models. Among the most popular are efforts to apply theories of desecularization (Karpov, 2013, pp. 255, 258; Schroeder and Karpov, 2013, pp. 303–307); post-secularism (Kyrlezhev, 2008, pp. 21–31, 2014, pp. 7–22; Knorre, 2014, pp. 42–103; Uzlaner, 2014, pp. 23–58); and "desecularization from above" (Karpov, 2013, pp. 254–283). Some authors use synonymously the terms "post-secularism" and "desecularization" (Knorre, 2014, pp. 42–43; Uzlaner, 2014, pp. 23–58). Indeed post-secularism (intensely debated globally as well) is almost always used somewhat vaguely, giving grounds for doubting its analytical value (Molendijk, 2015, pp. 100–105). Certainly, the applicability of the ad-hoc definition of "desecularization" in the Russian contexts is controversial, especially considering the subordinate role of the ROC in the state-church relationship. It is about "asymmetric" symphony (Anderson, 2007, pp. 197–201; Köllner, 2020, p. 19).

What is important to address at this point of this chapter is the moral panic of scholars that is detectible in the whole discussion. Indeed, behind the theoretical quests mentioned here, scholars have to reckon with the face of considerable clerical authority in Russia, and the perceived possibility that modern Russian society will secede from the orbit of contemporary rationality. If we take the discussion from here – perhaps asking: How real is this danger? And: Does this give us reason to talk about desecularization? – then we get to the more flexible approaches of several scholars concerned to understand the balance of the secular and desecularized aspects of Russian society.

The starting point of the analysis proposed by Catherine Wanner is the concept of public religion in the sense of José Casanova. According to her, "religion is going public" in Eastern Europe, and she considers that "public religion includes all forms of expression of religion that have direct bearing on the public order" (Wanner, 2018, pp. 88, 89). Along with this, public religion, according to Wanner, is not secularization in reverse: Rather, religious resources are mobilized for a variety of purposes. This leads the writer to the conclusion of "syncretic secularism", meaning a blending of belief, doubt, and non-belief with the desire to belong and the refusal to be coerced by institutions (ibid., 90). According to Irina Papkova,

Russian examples conform to Peter Berger's model of desecularization. Along with this, the (political) forces of secularism in the face of anti-Putin opposition have not surrendered and have a fierce anti-clerical resistance (Papkova, 2013, p. 249).

Boris Knorre's analyses present examples that can serve as empirical support for Papkova's thesis. Knorre shows that the widely demonstrated Orthodox religion among the high echelons of the Russian political elite in the middle of the first decade of the twenty-first century played the role of a kind of political correctness. Orthodoxy, taken on by the ruling elite, serves as a resource for various political discourses. Some of them portray Orthodox Christianity as the backbone of the Russian modernization project and even national security. In fact, the rulers are seeking political support, relying on high levels of identification with Orthodoxy among the Russian population – something that Mikhail Gorbachev also relied on at the beginning of the "religious revival" in the late 1980s (see earlier). On the eve of the 2012 elections, Dmitry Medvedev articulated this position when he called on the elite of the ruling party, *Edinaia Rossia*, "to associate themselves with the set of values that [people] will always vote for". In turn, the many concessions to the demands of the Russian clergy are interpreted as "benevolence to the ROC as an institution that strengthens power" (Knorre, 2014, pp. 52–54, 90). However, "desecularization from above cannot make people go to church regularly" (Karpov, 2013, p. 259): The low level of participation in church services remains unchanged in Orthodox Russian religiosity.

In a local perspective, a different, more complex and controversial picture emerges. Based on field observations in two Russian regions (Vladimir and St. Petersburg), Tobias Köllner shows that local restitution of church property is a disputed and controversial process. Aligning the law of restitution of church property into action not only encounters difficulties and obstacles, but often has an unpredictable outcome or simply does not take place (Köllner, 2018, pp. 1–20).

In turn, through analyses of religious education in the southern Russian city of Rostov on Don, Agata Ładykowska shows the interweaving of religion with worldly authority through the participation of female teachers in the teaching of religion in various formats. This gives her reason to see this area of religious life as "internal secularization", referring to Mark Chaves for the latter (Ładykowska, 2018, pp. 104–105).

By presenting observations from Kaluga, I will use examples of a different nature that, however, support similar conclusions. These examples show how the secular and the religious share and challenge common public spaces. The latter concerns, first, the specific semiotics of clothing in a public environment. Along with the silhouettes of ecclesiastical architecture, public apparel reinforces the Orthodox identity of Kaluga. Some people of the *pricekovnyi krug* almost always follow their specific "dress-code". The Bishop of Kaluga even requires the sisters of St. Elisaveta Fëdorovna Orthodox Sisterhood to wear their formal clothing when they move about in the city, as well as when they are at the convent. Other believers, crossing the boundaries between private church spaces and public urban geography, make changes in their appearance. For example, when going out in the street, women may replace their headscarf with a more neutral cover like a hat. At the end of one interview, I watched a typical representative of the *pricerkovnyi krug* change the headscarf she wore at home for a specific hat when she left home on her way to work. Changing to a hat allows the believer to dress in a fashion that is congruent with both church and secular conventions: The head is covered, but in a more secularly acceptable way.

On an August day in 2007, in Kaluga, I stood on the street just outside a church, waiting for the arrival of one of my Russian friends, who would introduce me to the priest. My acquaintance did not come, but during that time I saw how, when *matuška*, the priest's wife, a young woman in her twenties, went out of the church, she quickly took off her headscarf.

These are not the only cases, though they are the most prominent, of change in clothing when entering public space. The manner in which women belonging to the *pricerkovnyi krug* are dressed is the subject of discussion, careful negotiation, and sometimes of *economy* (Old Greek *οικονομία*).[50] From conversations with interlocutors on this topic,[51] I understood that recommendations for appropriate female clothing are not always imperative but rather provide guidelines and choices. The minimally required "long" skirt or dress need only be knee length. Even some of the priests' wives wore knee-length skirts.

If a hat is worn instead of a headscarf, it can follow an indefinite number of variations, which suggests that no norm has been defined in this respect and that the rule is still being invented. This uncertainty is probably due to the difficulty of finding historical patterns: The many preserved photographs of the early twentieth century (until 1917, a time marked by liberalism of church life) show priests' wives with uncovered heads. Moreover, clothes-related practices are changing in time: Many women's faces which were covered by headscarves in 2006 and 2007 when I met them, watch us today from photographs on the Internet uncovered. We do not know what the explanation is, but more important is the fact that norms (formal or otherwise) are in the process of being invented and negotiated.

Clothing choices are important because they make visible, or indistinguishable, religious signs in public space. The flexibility in the Orthodox "dress code" saves believers from active confrontation with the possible disapproval, perplexity, or curiosity of the social majority (which does not follow the code). Expectations of unfriendly reactions from those who share public space motivate believers to switch from one type of symbolism to another, a clear sign that secular norms and expectations continue to dominate public space, even as religious symbols re-appear.

Besides clothing, the compatibility and possible tensions between secular and religious norms and habituses was a topic discussed in formal interviews. A mother of two children and a regular churchgoer shared her concerns about the future socialization of her children, and especially of her five-year-old daughter. The child was socializing in a religious spirit, attending Sunday school at the parish church, and willingly demonstrating her knowledge, especially about the icons. The mother worried that at school, the girl might be bullied because religiosity makes her different:

> *I have always been afraid: They [kids] will go to school. They will see that we are different. We are fasting, and in school there is obscene music, obscene pictures. . . . S. [the daughter] listens to Orthodox disks and cassette tapes: Our grandmother is a believer . . . she will go to school and will be laughed at.*[52]

This quote from an interview shows the feeling of tension of the *vocerkovlënnye* that they are a minority among the majority who is less (or not at all) committed to church life. In fact, the problems of sharing come not so much from the "hostility" of the secular environment as from the forms of social control among the local communities of colleagues, peers, neighbors, etc.

Believers are often the subject of suspicions and direct, face-to-face criticism of opportunism: They face accusations that their religiosity is not sincere but demonstrative. I heard such comments about some believers repeatedly in Kaluga. People who had a Communist career in the Soviet era were especially perceived as opportunistic "believers". This is consistent with Catherine Wanner's observation (in Russian and Ukrainian contexts) of sensitivity to religiosity, coupled with "cynical suspicion" towards clergy or religious activists (Wanner, 2018, p. 90). In response, believers are uncertain about spaces filled with secular forms of culture. The latter are perceived as a possible antithesis of religious life ("obscene music and pictures").

Whether or not Russian society is "de-secularizing" in any theoretical sense hardly matters from the perspective of believers. For them, the predominantly secular nature of public space is a banal fact that does not need to be proven. It is they who are perceived as different, and it is they who experience themselves as different.

As secularism cannot be ruled out of the contemporary Russian religious landscape, let us leave the related discussions to the side. The concept of "public religion" provides a more flexible analytical tool – at least in the Russian context. Further, let me recall that when Casanova defines a "public religion", he makes the provision that this notion does not deny the validity of the theory of secularization – as a concept at three levels in its main assertions. (It is only Berger who dismisses secularization as a fundamentally erroneous theory.) These and other arguments set forth so far show that the "desecularization" theories of Russian society are premature despite the growing public presence of religious power, symbols, and discourses.

What has been said so far outlines the complex contradiction of the religious landscape in contemporary Russia and requires us to return to the initial basic question: Is Russian religious revivalism genuine or spurious?

The upheaval of religion in Russia began in 1988 in the context of *perestroika* as a "top-down" process that was enthusiastically accepted from the "bottom-up". The resurgence of Orthodoxy, "unlocked" after the abolition of atheistic bans, was the result not only of the political will of Mikhail Gorbachev, but the process was also possible due to the persistence of responsiveness to religion in the depths of Soviet society. This responsiveness was due to several factors, including the continued practice of Orthodox religiosity in remote rural areas [*v gluši*]; survival and underground ministry of a small part of the clergy and the most loyal laity, including small subculture groups such as the *pricerkovnyi krug*; the legitimacy of religion as a national cultural heritage of the 1960s onwards (Kormina and Shtyrkov, 2015); and the activity and protest actions of a few religious dissidents.

Post-Soviet Russian Orthodox religiosity has several peculiarities: Massive restoration of religious institutions; state support in favor of the Russian Orthodox Church; mass identification with Orthodoxy among Russians; *and* a relatively low level of actual participation in religious practices. However, a key role for the renewal of Orthodoxy in Russia over the past 30 years has been the formation of a group of devoted believers – the "little flock" that, along with the clergy, forms the core of religious life and practices religion on behalf of others.

The concept of vicarious religion, formulated by Grace Davie, meets these peculiarities of today's Russian religious landscape. Russian examples allow the concept to be understood in a different "key". Without diminishing the role of the clergy, it is necessary to conclude that it is the milieu of the most devoted believers that is at the root of the vicarious religion, enabling the everyday life of the church and legitimizing clerical power in Russian public life. This stratum is called metaphorically the "little flock" – borrowed from the Bible and also from its own vocabulary. The interaction between the clergy and the comparatively limited circle of the "little flock" is a significant (and also political) factor to influence the "agenda of society".

The distinction, albeit conditionally, of two types of engagement in religious practices and, respectively, of two social profiles within this community allows one to avoid the essentialist presentation of it. Self-isolation, the denial of secular professions, and specific ideology and values dominated by millenarian expectations, characterize in general the specific counterculture of the *pricerkovnyi krug*. In contrast, *vocerkovlënnye*, in the narrow sense of the word, are people who have an autonomous professional and family life, as well as successful socialization in society as a whole. This also allows them to play a mediating role and to convey important messages between clergy and society.

The upsurge of Orthodox Christianity is a process that runs at different speeds in different social segments and cannot be said to be a homogeneous social phenomenon. However, heterogeneity cannot play down the genuine nature of religious upheaval in an Orthodox setting, including because the phenomenon of vicarious religion makes it possible. Despite the success so far in the re-instatement of religious institutions, the relatedness between the latter and the political power in Russia implies a dependence of religion on the political processes in the country. In this sense, the future will show to what extent Orthodoxy will continue to be an influential factor in Russian society.

Notes

1 On December 17, 1985, Metropolitan Alexii (later Patriarch Alexii II) turned to Mikhail Gorbachev with a letter in which he set the question of revision of religious law. The initial letter did not produce any results – see Tsypin (2002–2005).

2 Andrey Rublëv, Maxim the Greek, Dmitry Donskoy, Makarii Moskovsky, Paisii Velichkovski, Blessed Xenia of St. Petersburg, Ignatii Bryanchaninov, the spiritual elder Amvrosii, and Theophan the Recluse.
3 Alexii II, Patriarch (2005).
4 Tarabukina's work is available only as an Internet publication without pagination of the pages. In the citation here I do not mark a page but the numbering of a dissertation chapter; 04 means here chapter 4. Further quotations follow the same principle.
5 In Russian:

> *Kogda v perestroečnye vremena stalo vozmozhno svobodno khodit' v cerkov', okazalos', chto vsë eto bylo zasypano. I otkrylos', potomu čto pravoslavie – v duše kazhdogo russkogo čeloveka.*
>
> – Interview with Victorija Leontievna, 51, university education, a bibliographer. 30.07.2007, Kaluga.

6 According to the official site of the ROC from 29.11.2017: "The Holy Patriarch has published statistical data on the ROCs life" – www.patriarchia.ru/db/text/5072750.html.
7 Greeley (1994, pp. 253–272), Vorontsova, Filatov and Furman (1995, pp. 81–91), Kääriäinen (1998, pp. 155–162), Kääriäinen (1999, pp. 35–46), Karriainen and Furman (2000, pp. 21–59, 79–104), Borowik (2001, pp. 43–56), Tomka (2001, pp. 11–29), Dubin (2004, pp. 35–44), Mitrokhin (2004, pp. 35–34), Dubin (2006, pp. 69–88), Filatov and Lunkin (2006a, pp. 33–49).
8 Data from the Russian Center for the Study of Public Opinion, published by the Interfax news agency on 30.03.2010. See Rossijane (2010).
9 See Knox (2004, pp. 105–131), Filatov (2007, p. 16), Kääriäinen and Furman (2007, p. 20), Agadjanian (2011, pp. 17–18), Papkova (2013, pp. 244–253), Karpov (2013, pp. 254–283), Tsekhanskaia (2015, p. 11).
10 The image of the latter, for example, is given by the Orthodox portal www.hristianstvo.ru, which comprised over 42,000 sites in 2018.
11 Some sociological theories do not use the term "religious revival", but this understanding is implicit in their analysis. These are the theories of: (a) "pendulous movement" of "mass consciousness" between opposing states of religiosity and atheism, and vice versa (Vorontsova, Filatov and Furman, 1995, pp. 81–91); and (b) alternation of secularization cycles and return to religion (cyclical hesitation between secularization and the "return of religiosity" between the eighteenth century and the Russian Revolution of 1917 – see Sinelina [2003, pp. 88–96]). The "pendulum model" in fact encodes another variant of "sociological skepticism". In comparison with the "pendulum model", "religious revival" deprives of sense and that is probably one of the author's goals. Compared to the "cyclical model", it acquires the meaning of another phase in the *longue duree* of the civilization development of Russia from early Russian modernity to the present.
12 See a similar assessment expressed by Father E. K. From Kaluga in 2010 (Slabova, 2010, p. 4).
13 In Russian:

> *Očen' mnogo vremeni otnimaet. U menia net takogo vremeni. Ja sizhu do polnochi za komp'iuterom, utrom vstaju – komp'iuter, potom v arkhiv, potom poezdki, dača, sejčas letnij sezon. A zimoj voobšče iz-za komp'iutera ne vykhozhu. Nekogda. A khram – eto vy ponimaete, nado otreč'sia ot vsekh etikh dum.*
>
> – Interview with V. L., 59, secondary education, writer and photographer. 9.07.2007, Kaluga.

14 See a special document of the Russian Orthodox Church on the issue of communion, adopted on 2–3.2.2015: "For the Participation of the Faithful in the Eucharist" ['*Ob'učastii vernyh v Evharistii*']. – www.patriarchia.ru/db/text/3981166.html. – Last accessed: 3.08.2018.

15 Communion is typically preceded by a three-day fast which, under certain conditions, may be relieved by the priest, but fasting almost always remains obligatory for at least one day or one night; in all cases it includes complete deprivation of food and water for six hours before the communion. – See the cited document above, note 12.

16 The title is ambiguous because it also refers to the title of the novel *Dead Souls* (*Mërtvye duši*, 1842) by the Russian classicist Nikolai V. Gogol.

17 Interview with Tamara Kirillovna, 46, secondary education, administrative position. 17.07.2007, Kaluga.

18 In this case, my interlocutor uses the Gospel quote "*Fear not, little flock, for your Father has been pleased to give you the kingdom*" (Luke 12: 32) to support the view that compromises with Orthodox canons in the name of attracting more worshippers to the temples are not desirable. Here she refers to the authority of the Kaluga Metropolitan Kliment, who has adopted this argument, along with the quote supporting it. – Interview with NN, 52, university education. 13.07.2007, Kaluga. I omit part of the information concerning this particular interlocutor to keep her anonymity, due to highly sensitive character of the information she shared (see chapter 3).

19 The instrumental rationality has been opposed to the value rationality by Max Weber (2002).

20 In the monasteries, they most often receive the status of *poklonniki* (pilgrims), which gives them the right to earn their bed and food by helping with the work in the monastery.

21 In Russian:

> *Rabotaia v hrame, estestvenno, yest' bol'še vozmozhnostej na sluzhbe byvat'. Krug bogosluzheniia so vsemi sviatymi, so vsemi prazdnikami. Kogda prozhivaesh' tak etot cerkovnyj god uzhe kazhdyj den', nakhodias' na klirose, zhitiia sviatogo propevaiut stikhi, eto konečno sovsem drugie oščuščeniia, nezheli kogda čelovek v meru svoej zaniatosti, neobkhodimosti social'nogo sluzheniia, emu prikhoditsia prazdnikam posviaščat' tol'ko dni v cerkvi. A zdes' vot: milost'iu Bozh'ej. . . . T.e., Vy ne predstavliaete: vot čelovek zhivet v hrame praktičeski cerkovnoj zhizn'iu kazhdyj den', govorit o vnutrennikh . . . o pečaliakh, zanimaetsia liubimym delom, t.e. ia ne znaiu o čem eščë mozhno mečtat'.*
>
> – Interview with Ekaterina Viačeslavovna, 36, university education, teacher/religious activist. 12.07.2007, Kaluga.

22 See the official site of the Kaluga diocese http://eparhia- kaluga.ru/kaluzhskaja-eparhija/monastyri/kazanskij-monastyr.html. Last accessed on 28.08.2015.

23 It has been difficult to determine precisely the number of members of the sisterhood as far as its composition has varied over the various periods of its existence. At certain periods of time, its number has reached about 40 members. – Interviews with Zinaida Anatolievna, 66, university education, an engineer/ pensioner, held in Kaluga and Lev Tolstoy village on 18.07.2007, 23.07.2007, 2.08.2007. Except the formal interviews conducted with two of the "sisters", I also engaged in informal discussions with three more of the "sisters".

24 In Russian:

> *Na baze etogo sestričestva, v devianosto piatom godu nachalos' vosstanovlenie nashego Kazanskogo Gurskogo monastyria. Vse sily i znanija otdali na to, chtoby monastyr' byl vosstanovlen. I iz ikh sredy byli naznačeny, značit, sëstry monastyria. Nu prišli v monastyr', priniali poslušničestvo, inočestvo, monašestvo. Matuška naša, tozhe tak byvaet, ona v pervom byla sestričestve.*
>
> *V 2003-yem godu matuška, znachit, blagoslovila sozdat' novoye sestrichestvo. Potomu-čto to sestričestvo uzhe kak by . . . ne stalo rabotat'. Ono kak by pererodilos' v monastyr'. Vot dve sëstry u nas tozhe ušli v monastyr'. Iz vtorogo sestričestva. . . . U nas est' sëstry, kotorye mogut po dukhovnomu prizvaniju dovol'no takim vysokim: ja dumaju, čto u nas eshchë budut sëstry, kotorye smogut ujti v monastyr'.*
>
> – An interview with Zinaida Anatolievna, 66, university education, an engineer/ pensioner. 2.08.2007, Kaluga.

25 Kaluga Nursing House for the Seniors and Disabled - www.kdi40.ru. Last accessed: 28.08.2013.
26 An interview with Zinaida Anatolievna, 18.07.2007.
27 In the early 1990s, the sisters did not yet wear uniforms.

> *Then we were offered such blue shirts and they became our uniform. And then we also got festive silk headscarves. The bishop said the heads should be covered.*
> – An interview with Tamara Fëdorovna, university education, a pensioner. 18.07.2007, Kaluga.

28 Komáromi reports concerning similar demonic beliefs expressed during her fieldwork in "Mirgorod" (Komáromi, 2017, p. 132).
29 "*Esli za mirianinom khodit odin rogatyj, to za monahami budut desiat'; kogda čelovek stremitsia k dukhovnomu soveršenstvovaniiu, vrag bol'še napadaet*". – An interview with Vadim Nikityč, 41, higher medical education, a doctor. 9.08.2007, Kaluga.
30 X was born in 1955, higher education, a pensioner.
31 Key phrases from this conversation in Russian:

> *Gospod 'prisylaet mne ispytaniia. I nado ikh priniat'. Deistvitel'no, i eto kak-by poslednie vremena. Nas Gospod'miluet, eščë terpit. A kak spastis'? Ona (sosedka koldun'ja) menia v glaza smotret'ne mozhet. Tak prohodit mimo menia" "I predstavliaete, v 2003 godu mama polučila izvestie, čto deduška pogib u Kalugi! Eto vsë Bozh'ia promysel! Nikakoi slučainosti net. Oni [evrei] zhdali Messiiu, a kogda Gospod'prišël, oni ego ne priznali. I otpravili na krest. Oni posyljut Rossii nravstvennyi krizis, potomu-čto Rossiju tak-to ne pobediš".*
> – Informal interview. 23.07.2007, village of Lev Tolstoy.

32 Nevertheless, the field observations of Agata Ładykowska (2018, pp. 101–102) show that such educated and humanistic believers do not fear the occasional taking-up of the opinions of authoritative "elders" whose views directly shape the ideology of "church people".
33 *Veruiuščie ne dolzhny vnešne otličat'sia. Oni dolzny otličat'sia vnutrenne. Nikto ne zapreščaet obščenie s neverujuščimi.* – An interview with Nadezhda Sidorovna, 32, university education, a housewife. 30.06.2007, Kaluga.
34 For the latter and their specific role, see Köllner (2012, pp. 39–42, 94–112).
35 To keep their anonymity, I will not quote the interviews with them.
36 An interview with A. B., 36, priest. 5.07.2007, Kaluga.
37 An informal talk with Ekaterina Viačeslavovna, 36, university education, a teacher/ religious activist. 8.08.2007, Kaluga.
38 *Prič*t: ecclesiastical unit comprising ordained priests and "lower clerics" serving at a church/ parish (Stefanovič, 2002, pp. 10, 47). See, for example, the Optina Hermitage Monastery site: www.optina.ru/rites/about/. Last accessed: 28.08.2018. An informal conversation, 13.08.2007, Kaluga. The Sunday school in the Shroud of the Holy Mother (existing since 1998) was transformed in 2009 due to the expansion of the Youth Club of Explorers and the increase of the number of participants to 300. See the site of the church: http://kaluga-pokrov.cerkov.ru/voskresnaya-shkola/. Last accessed: 21.08.2018.
39 At present (2018), some Russian monasteries accept via the Internet orders to perform memorial services, but only them. Rituals such as baptism or marriage are not included in the list of *treby* which can be ordered remotely, probably for the same reason – the need for catechism. See, for example, the Optina Hermitage Monastery site: www.optina.ru/rites/about/. Last accessed: 28.08.2018.
40 An informal conversation, 13.08.2007, Kaluga.

41 The Sunday school in the Shroud of the Holy Mother (existing since 1998) was transformed in 2009 due to the expansion of the Youth Club of Explorers and the increase of the number of participants to 300. See the site of the church: http://kaluga-pokrov.cerkov.ru/voskresnaya-shkola/. Last accessed: 21.08.2018

42 This issue has another side too. It is known that the intervention of more experienced worshippers, often referred to ironically as *babuški* [grannies] by both believers and researchers, can often be rude and put other believers off church life.

> *These babuški are a scourge of Orthodoxy because they push people away. . . . There used to be such* [in our temple too]. *I see that people do not enter the temple because of this group. The Father reproves them for behaving like that. Now there are none in the temple.*
>
> – An interview with Maksim Andreevič, 22, secondary education, a student, 11.07.2007, Kaluga. See also Mitrokhin (2004).

43 For more information about this temple, see chapter 3.

44 In Russian:

> *Kogda my eto delo sdelali, nu prišlos' idti po khramam, po vsem znakomym. Vot. Nu, slava Bogu, u menya mnogo znakomykh takikh, kotoryye bogaty: dopustim tam, jurist, prokuror, takiye liudi, kotorye ja znaju, čto oni zhivut nebedno. Vot i tam direktor tam, magazin i tak dalee.*
>
> *I ja stala takikh lyudej podbirat' i k nim khodit'. I slava Bogu, mne nikto ne otkazyval. Prichem davali bol'šie summy deneg: tam po tri, po pyat' tysyač. Potom značit, material dali nam: i dlya potolka, i plitočki, i špaklëvki i smesi vse cementnye. Očen' mnogo davali. Dazhe vot ja v magazin ja ezdila, iskala derevo. I tuda tozhe prišla, kazhetsia – novye russkiye – molodye. Ja podošla k nim, govoriu:*
>
> *– Rebiata, vot nam nuzhno na khram.*
>
> *Oni tut zhe skidyvajut ceny. I dajut mne podeševle. I mašinu svoju dajut, privoziat. . . .*
>
> *Vot tak liudi pomogali. Tak pomogali. I slava Bogu.*
>
> – An interview with Zinaida Anatolievna, 66, university education, an engineer/pensioner. 2.08.2007, Kaluga.

45 NEWSru (2006).

46 Law No 327 [2010] "*O peredače religioznym organizacijam imuščestva religioznogo naznačenija, nahodiaščegosia v gosudarstvennoi ili municipal'noi sobstvennosti*" [On the transfer to religious organizations of religious property being in state or municipal ownership.]. – *Rossijskaja gazeta* [Russian Newspaper], 3.12.2010. *Federal'nyi vypusk* [Federal Issue] № 5353 (274), available at: www.rg.ru/2010/12/03/tserkovnoedobrodok.html. Last accessed: 30.08.2018.

47 The first major experiment to introduce *Fundamentals of the Orthodox Culture* in fifteen Russian *oblast'* dates back to 2006. In 2010, with a governmental decision, religious education was introduced at the national level, and in 2012 the subject was introduced throughout Russia (see publication of governmental decisions in: NEWSru (2006), Rossiiskaia gazeta (2009). On the issue of the introduction of religious education, see: Mitrokhin (2004), Glanzer (2005, pp. 208, 215–216), Willems (2006, pp. 288–291), Mulders (2008, pp. 7–9), Ładykowska (2018, pp. 96–107), Karpov (2013, p. 258), Papkova (2013, p. 245), Knorre (2014, pp. 86–87). In 2007, *Fundamentals of Orthodox Culture* were already taught in Kaluga (city and *oblast'*) and several of the priests I knew were engaged in teaching.

48 "*O zaščite religioznyh čuvstv*" [On the protection of religious feelings]. – See Sergazina (2015).

49 A review of a series of church censorship events in the area of culture and art, See Sergazina (2015).
50 This is a specific church term, sometimes with a negative connotation, which denotes adaptation of one or another canonical rules. For the various theological meanings of this concept, see Dimitrov (2016, pp. 59–70).
51 Interview with Larissa Makarovna, 50, secondary medical education, a paramedic. 4.08.2007, Kaluga-2; informal conversation with Zinaida Anatolievna, 20.08.2007, Kaluga; interview with Natalia Emelianovna, 55, secondary education, a pensioner/housewife, 19.08.2007, Kaluga.
52 In Russian:

> *U menia vsegda strakh – oni [deti] pojdut v školu. Oni uvidiat, čto my raznye. U nas – posty, a v škole muzyka nepriličnaja, kartinki nepriličnye. . . . S. [doč'] slušaet diskov pravoslavnyh, i kassetki. U nas babuška veruiuščaja . . . poidët v školu, nad nei stanut smeiats'sia.*
>
> – An interview with Nadezhda Sidorovna, 32, university education, a housewife, 30.06.2007, Kaluga.

2 Multiple moralities and religious power

Humility is born of true obedience and the postponement of self-reflection when we do not trust in ourselves, but cutting off our will and our own reason, we entrust ourselves to others who can guide us.

St. Reverend Makary of Optina[1]

Introduction

The previous chapter addressed the issues of the peculiarities and the driving forces of the contemporary Orthodox upsurge in Russia and, above all, the way in which vicarious religion drives the everyday mechanisms of religious life. The second chapter is dedicated to the same group of people – devoted worshippers – but focuses on the links between their personal ethical pursuits, group moral concepts, and the nature of religious power. These heterogeneous issues are united by the concept of multiple moralities. Contrary to expectations, the moral views of the "little flock" are not homogeneous. It is these multiple moralities that facilitate the efforts of the most committed believers to respond to the challenges of the contemporary world.

In the pages that follow, I will look at the role of the ROC as a mentor and a moral entrepreneur in modern Russia; the moral reasoning of believers; the problem of negative moralizing, discipline and authority in Orthodox communities; the empowerment of women in contemporary Russian Orthodoxy; and the search for the good as a central moral category.

The overarching concept, which unifies the various values, concepts, beliefs, and social practices presented herein, is multiple moralities. I discussed this concept in the Introduction. The present chapter draws too on theoretical incentives from other sources. The term "entrepreneur" (Stockl, 2016, pp. 132–151), derived from political science and applied to the ROC, outlines the perspective of religious "top-down" policies from the position of the top management of the ROC. Another two concepts that I bring to the discussion belong to that field in which the anthropology of Christianity crosses the anthropology of morality. These are "ethical saturation" and "moral imagination". The understanding of the "ethical saturation" of the life-world has been applied to the Russian Orthodox context by analyzing materialities (icons, relics) (Keane, 2014, pp. 318–320), but I find it sufficiently comprehensive to fit beyond the concrete context of the material manifestations of the sacred. In the context of my analysis, the notion of "moral imagination" (originally from cognitive science) has proven its usefulness in the study of narratives. At its base, this concept holds that "human beings are fundamentally imaginative moral animals", and that "the quality of our moral understanding and deliberation depends crucially on the cultivation of our moral imagination". This includes our ability to walk in other people's shoes so as to understand their situation and direct our own actions according to this (Johnson, 1997, pp. 1, 188–200).[2]

The analyses in this chapter are enriched by the overall achievements in the recent anthropology of morality.[3] However, I do not examine definitional questions or distinctions between the partially overlapping concepts of morality and ethics (see Johnson, 1997, pp. 1–12; Robbins, 2009, pp. 277–285; Zigon, 2011a, pp. 6–12; Keane, 2016, pp. 16–21, 134–135). I will adhere to the common understanding that "ethics does include the morality system – morality is just a special kind of ethics"; in simple words, ethics includes "people's ability to evaluate acts as good or evil (Keane, 2016, p. 19, 2014, p. 316)".[4]

And, this chapter includes an analysis of heterogeneous phenomena from different spheres of contemporary Russian social life, united by their belonging to or linking with Orthodox Christianity. The analysis of these heterogeneous practices benefits from the overarching notions of discipline and power, in the understanding that Talal Asad (1993, pp. 125–170) invested in the study of medieval monastic practices.

The dissolution of the Soviet Union was a rapid social change that, like the collapse of socialism in other European socialist societies, involved a total shift of social strata and the degradation of personal and collective statuses. In addition, former Soviet citizens also experienced a loss of collective political identity as their country disappeared from the political map of the world. The economic and political chaos of the 1990s, called *bespredel* by Russians, destroyed collective and individual cognitive stability. It reduced orientation abilities amidst the rapidly changing events. In the same context, the unilateral moral resilience of Soviet society, based on political and (quasi) religious teleology (the notion of a "bright future" as a positive eschatology), drastically lost relevance. Different, competing systems of values and of public and personal morality appeared, contributing to what can be called "multiple moralities" (Zigon, 2011a, pp. 3–15). With the former socialist morality no longer a relevant choice, an intensified search for alternatives was a traumatic personal and collective experience. Under these conditions, Orthodoxy (and the ROC in particular) offered an alternative choice of positive identity, legitimated as a return to "traditional" values for Russian culture and history (Agadjanian, 2017, pp. 39–60).

In this context, Webb Keane's understanding of ethical saturation adequately describes the contemporary world of Russian Orthodox believers, especially when it is used beyond the narrow understanding of the sacred semiotics and expanded in the direction of everyday social relationships and human interactions. The subject of Orthodox Christianity as a corrective of the morally disoriented Russian society after the end of socialism is invariably articulated in a different environment. It was a kind of leitmotif during fieldwork in Kaluga in 2006 and 2007. Predictably, morality and religion "work together" in a general semantic field.

Normative entrepreneurship and public participation policy of the ROC

The topic of moral healing is one of the main arguments of the church and the high clergy during the ongoing (and continuing) public debate on the introduction of religious education in public schools.[5] Moreover, the ROC's top management used to engage actively in norm entrepreneurship ("normative agency of actors in transnational governance regimes") in the field of international relations, especially after the enthronement (2009) of Patriarch Kirill.

As Kristina Stoeckl shows, the ROC's entrepreneurship is expressed in the active promotion of international projects aimed at changing human rights philosophy (after a period of rejection of the concept itself). The aim is to integrate the concept of "traditional values" with the philosophy of human rights (Stoeckl, 2016, p. 132). A basic moral area in which the church fights for supremacy in public debate – not only in Russia but also internationally – are issues related to the human body, family, and "traditional" family values: Homosexuality and same-sex marriages, abortion, surrogate maternity, and juvenile penal codes, and courts (Agadianian, 2017, pp. 39–60). Some of these topics were also discussed in Kaluga. Two specific projects interwoven with secular and religious policies in the field of culture, for example, support marriage and the family. One of them is the widespread popularization of the cult of the Sts Tsar Pëtr and Tsarytsa Fevronia, figures not very well known in the Russian public space until recently, which, through successful political and cultural engineering, have become symbols of marriage, love, and marital fidelity since 2008. The second is a purely secular project: The Parade of the Brides Initiative [*Parad nevest*], which started in 2005. The messages of these newly invented traditions (in the sense of Hobsbawm & Ranger) are aimed at the revalorization of traditional family values such as marriage. The local cultural environment in Kaluga actively participated (and participates) in both projects.

The most visible manifestation of the cult of Sts. Tsar Pëtr and Tsarytsa Fevronia is the festive Day of Family, Love, and Fidelity. Tobias Köllner (2020, p. 134; 108–136) explores it "as an example for interrelation between politics and Orthodox religion" introducing the concept of "entangled authorities". I address it looking for diverse facets of the multiple moralities. The veneration of Sts. Pëtr and Fevronia, which rapidly gained popularity throughout Russia, intends to strengthen the institution of marriage among young people. This intent to encourage the young to marry is connected to the ambition of different institutions, religious and secular, to oppose a Russian "tradition" to the expansion of the imported Valentine's Day (Köllner, 2020, pp. 122–126). The new initiative was undertaken first by the ROC: In 2004, with the blessing of Patriarch Alexii II, the program "In the Circle of the Family" [*V krugu sem'i*] was set up, financially supported by one of the major Russian state-owned corporations – Rostechnology. From 2008 onwards, the ecclesiastical feast of Sts. Pëtr and Fevronia on July 8 was declared by government decision as the Day of Family, Love, and Fidelity [*Den'sem'i, liubvi i vernosti*]. The committee for the creation of this nationwide holiday was headed by Ms. Svetlana Medvedeva, the wife of the third Russian president, Dmitry Medvedev. At the first all-Russian celebration of the holiday, it was accompanied by solemn liturgies and prayers to the saints.[6]

From 2009, the initiative continued with the placing of sculptural compositions of the saints in public urban spaces: Initially in the city of Murom where the cult was born, and then in 60 Russian cities, including Kaluga in 2012. The monument of the saints was erected in the courtyard of one of the Kaluga churches and was consecrated by Metropolitan Kliment.[7] As patrons of marriage and family, Sts. Pëtr and Fevronia were well known among Kaluga believers during the time I performed my fieldwork, that is, before the Day of Family, Love, and Fidelity was introduced nationwide. Their lives were read at the Feast of the Saints, on July 8, 2007, in the parish of the Shroud of the Holy Mother, evidence that the saints were already gaining popularity among the faithful, most probably due to the efforts of clergy.

However, who were Sts. Pëtr and Fevronia of Murom? They were canonized in 1547. It is not known whether they actually lived, and if so when, because documents referring to them as historical persons have not been found. Stories about them, however, have circulated since the beginning of the thirteenth century. *The Tale of Sts. Pëtr and Fevronia*, written by Ermolai-Erasmus presumably after 1547, is far away from the genre of lives of saints. Because of its fairy-tale character, the work is usually considered to be a masterpiece of medieval Russian literature (Skripil', 1949, pp. 131–167; Likhachev, 1987, pp. 237–277).

The aim of building monuments to the saints is "to create a positive image of family values, faithful and chaste relationships, love and devotion in marriage, childbirth, and education of children in the spirit of love for the Motherland", says Alexander Kovtunets, president of the In the Circle of the Family program. Therefore, family values (religious and secular), pro-natalist policies, and "national sentiments" (Bendix, 1992, pp. 768–790) are entangled, as Köllner proves (2020). The sculptural compositions are designed to create space for the development of ritual actions on the Day of Family, Love, and Fidelity. Marriage, releasing pigeons into the sky, and the placing of flowers can all be staged at the monuments. Sculptors Konstantin Chernyavsky and Olga Kravchenko have created seven different projects for the monuments from which copies are produced for different cities.[8]

The In the Circle of the Family program evolved in full cooperation between the ROC and the central state institutions, involving the mutual transfusion of secular and religious practices. In Kaluga, however, this is not the only case of erecting a statue of hagiographic characters: There are three in the urban area. In addition to the one dedicated to Sts. Pëtr and Fevronia, there are also monuments to St. Kukša Pečerskii (twelfth century) and St. Lavrentii of Kaluga (sixteenth century) – both connected to the Kaluga lands. The statue of St. Kukša was consecrated by Patriarch Kirill on September 9, 2014,[9] and that of St. Lavrentii by Metropolitan Kliment on August 22, 2015.[10]

Taken together, these details raise questions for the researcher, first, concerning the semi-legendary character of the saints, and second, concerning the questionable character of erecting monuments (i.e. statues) vis-à-vis Orthodox canonicity. The initiative for the In the Circle of the Family program came from the ROC, and even from its highest representative – the Patriarch – in 2004. Its rapid development, however, came a few years later and was possible thanks to the initiative of the state legislature which made the celebration of Sts. Pëtr and Fevronia a legal national holiday in 2008. Moreover, the holiday seems to be popular because of its syncretic character as both a secular and a religious holiday. The semi-legendary character of the saints is not, in fact, unusual in the context of Christian hagiography (see e.g. Delehaye, 1909). Perhaps ironically, St. Valentine's Day, the Western holiday to which Sts. Pëtr and Fevronia's celebration is explicitly opposed, follows a similar pattern. The Valentine prototype is also semi-legendary, transformed from popular imagination into a symbol and later into a powerful stimulus of the consumer industry. The list of similar examples may be extended.

Neither the secular possibilities of the celebration nor the uncertain historical origin of the saints, however, pose an obstacle to the development of a full-fledged contemporary respect for them. One of the publications on the Internet dedicated

Figure 2.1 Parade of the brides: A secular initiative supported by the church. Kaluga: Theatre Square. July 8, 2007.

Source: Photo: Milena Benovska

to their lives is followed by several hundred prayers submitted by the faithful. Clearly many believers call on these saints for their mediation and divine help.[11]

Once ROC and the state turn Sts. Pëtr and Fevronia into national symbols, the saints become a point of reference for family values. They are central to religious ethics and laden with potentially political content. So the problem is settled on another level. The semi-legendary hagiographic characters, whose trajectories in the late medieval past are vague, have become the subject of a syncretic cult, both secular and religious. Since 2003, certain events, such as the Orange Revolution in Ukraine, have signaled a lack of social cohesion in post-Soviet space and have emphasized to Russia's ruling elite the need to invest effort in nation building. The introduction of the Day of National Unity (November 4) as a national holiday is a move in this direction, according to Tobias Köllner (2012, pp. 169, 177–182). Similarly, the Day of Family, Love and Fidelity contributes to this project, despite its more specific connotations with pro-natalist politics, aiming to strengthen the institution of the family and public morality.

At the same time, the placement of three-dimensional religious images raises other questions concerning the ROC's strategies of public presence. Since the medieval iconoclastic controversy (727–787, 814–843, see Mango, 1977, pp. I–XII), three-dimensional images have not been allowed in Eastern Orthodox churches or their grounds. In Kaluga, the Orthodox elite is apparently aware of this policy and applies a careful policy to the placement of commemorative statues. Statues of saints are located outside church grounds, but the three monuments in Kaluga – Sts. Pëtr and Fevronia, St. Kukša, and St. Lavrentii' – have been placed in close proximity to churches. This may make them less secular and less political than they might otherwise be; moreover, they have been sanctified with the blessing ritual (see Köllner, 2012, p. 184). Close placement to churches and sanctification, however, enhances the ambivalence of these three-dimensional images, continuing to prompt believers to decide how to place them in the balance of the religious and secular worlds.

The policy of enhanced public presence obviously has priority over strictly following the inherited aesthetic canons of Eastern Orthodoxy. Herewith two conclusions can be made. First, the placement of monuments with religious content in the public space is also a means of transforming the public environment through the visible presence of religious symbolism. That means the elegant term "ambient faith" (Engelke, 2012, pp. 155–170), which may well describe a contemporary British context, does not correspond to the results of the ROC's vigorous actions to symbolically transform Russia's public urban environment, though both national spaces may be saturated with religious symbolism. This shows once again that Russian Orthodoxy turns into a public religion (without yet meaning automatic desecularization). Second, the practices in question demonstrate that Orthodoxy is being rediscovered and reinvented. As Miklos Tomka notes (2001, p. 8), "religion has been resurrected in Central and Eastern Europe. The resurrected body is, though, not identical with the old one". The same proves valid concerning Russian Orthodoxy: It is not being "dug out of the ashes" intact, nor is it a faithful copy of past patterns.

Before leaving the topic of how political and religious projects combine in support of family values, we have to briefly reflect on the Parade of the Brides [*Parad nevest*]. Kaluga was one of the first cities to engage in a local version of the parade in 2007, following its first edition in Moscow on September 27, 2005. From the *Parad nevest* website it becomes clear that the original parade was an advertising and marketing initiative by the Studio for Wedding Photography, owned by the Moscow photographer Ekaterina Aleshinskaja, who owns the copyright. The short information on the site announces that the goal is to encourage young people to engage in a wedding celebration as a glamorous event – at the center of which will be the newlyweds – and thereafter to love each other and be happy. After the first parade in Moscow in 2005, the initiative expands to 26 cities in Russia and even to some post-Soviet countries. In 2017, there were such parades in about 50 cities.[12]

The first edition of the parade in Kaluga took place on July 8, 2007, on a gloomy rainy Sunday. That same morning, after the Sunday liturgy at the Church of the Shroud of the Holy Mother, I discussed the upcoming event with some of the church activists. The subject of love and family is a central concern for this parish, especially because it has specialized in "*working with young people*", as confirmed by the title of the parish newspaper *Vera molodyh* [The Faith of the Young]. The parade was viewed positively: "*Somehow we have to act towards the restoration of family values in Russia*", I was told. They were so interested in the topic, I even promised to write a notice for the parish newspaper.

On the previous day – July 7, 2007 – there were an unusually high number of weddings in the city. Still, the parade was not enjoyed very much, perhaps because of the rain or perhaps because of the lack of spectacle. Brides arrived by white Cadillacs. A dozen brides were arranged on a special stage in front of the city theater façade and served more as a decoration or background to onstage formalities than as a "parade" of themselves. Onstage, didactic messages about the significance of marriage and family in Russian traditions came booming from the microphone, and an award was given to an elderly couple who were celebrating their 50th wedding anniversary. It went on and on. During the third hour of the event, I felt under the weather and left, so I could not write the short article describing the whole event.

This secular initiative is important. While it is a small event in Kaluga, it is nevertheless spreading and finding supporters and participants across Russia (and Orthodox space). Importantly, church circles are not indifferent to it, and actually support it, despite its secular and consumerist nature. The Parade of the Brides fits well with state and church policies of popularizing marriage and affirming traditional values as a "soft" expression of pro-natalist politics. (The latter is also an aspect, albeit specific, of nation-building – Köllner, 2020, pp. 109–136.)

The various actors, driving initiatives in favor of family values, have different motivations. In this case, the ROC has more than one purpose. On the one hand, it plays the role of a moral entrepreneur (in the field of domestic politics, central and local). On the other hand, it pursues its long-term goal of establishing hegemony in the religious sphere of the multinational Russian state.

Ethical reasoning

The Kaluga believers are deeply involved with the problems of Christian ethics, seen through the prism of personal biographical experience and expressed in autobiographical narratives during interviewing. The replacement of the unitary official Soviet morality with the post-Soviet multiplicity of competing value systems is only one possible source of tension. Various authors call this tension one of ethical reasoning (Robbins, 2004, p. 314), morality of freedom (Robbins, 2009, pp. 283–284), moral problematization (after Foucault), or moral breakdown (Zigon, 2006, p. 133).[13]

Conversion from unbelief to belief (as a result of post-Soviet social change) is another, second source of moral tension. Among other things, this change also means changing ethical systems. Nadezhda Sidorovna went through a conversion from unbelief to belief six years before our meeting in 2007. Her narrative (written in two interviews) is filled with her inner dialogue, in which various moral alternatives are confronted. It begins: "*I came to Orthodoxy through my husband. I liked that he did not push me to do it. And I started little by little – alone, he helped*".[14]

The hesitation, the moral judgment, and the tense moral demand are expressed by multiple statements of "ignorance". The latter is to be understood as a dual expression of the lost cultural knowledge of Orthodoxy (see chapter 1) but also as an expression of uncertainty as to which is the "right" moral choice. Ethical self-control, the effort directed at personal improvement in Nadezhda's narrative, is called a "struggle" – with herself, with her own moral instability. These concepts are translated into the language of Christian ethics and Christian anthropology:

> *How difficult it is – to walk down the street and not to judge* [the others]. *This is the most difficult. How to get rid of this? It's hard. When a person begins to fight – it's hard. Christians are the ones who need Christ – to save us from ourselves. If we check this in practice: "I will not think bad things today!" – when one sees that he cannot do it alone, it does not happen, then you begin to pray to the Lord as the Savior and not as the sender of earthly goods.*[15]

Nadezhda's narrative switches between different moral codes in search of continuity with the Soviet past and as an attempt to seek stability in the uncomfortable world of moral hesitation. This is also the state of transition, crossing from one moral domain to another: "*The Pioneer's obligations – they are from the Gospel, however, [they] are called otherwise. Then* [in Soviet times] *there were very good people, too, but they were unaware* [concerning Christianity]".[16]

The messages that Nadezhda makes are not monolithic; the narrative is polyphonic and contradictory. The search for its place in the ethically saturated space of contemporary Russian culture passes as a consistent repulsion between at least three alternative ethical systems: Between the individualism of the secular environment, Orthodox ethics, and the moral utopian project outlined by Leo Tolstoy with its theory of the non-resistance to evil. These are consistently opposing one another. The hidden, implicit center of this opposition is the search for an active position in the world, the search for human dignity that is compatible with Christian ethics and excludes humiliation.

> *Humility – this is not about being a downtrodden but seeing your sins. This is not non-resistance to evil. Humility is to see that you are sinful. The non-resistance to evil is when you do not respond* [to insults]: *"If he has spoken* [badly] *of me, then I really am bad". – To humble yourself.*
>
> *And if someone treads on an icon, you have to protect it. The boy will go to school, he will see another one being beaten: You have to protect him; or if he himself is being beaten, he has to protect himself. This is entirely the opinion of my own.*
>
> *Seraphim of Sarov – he was a saint: The robbers attacked him. He was cutting wood. When they attacked him, he threw the ax away. He was strong, but they beat him, hit him.*
>
> *The Christian must be a warrior, to fight – above all within himself.*
>
> *Everyone should be taken as the image of God. This is very difficult, but you have to strive for it. The chief commands are: "Love the Lord" and "Love the neighbor as yourself".*[17]

I quoted this story here with some shortening but kept the sequence of key statements. This consistency shows that the meaningful center of the narrative and its purpose is the search for legitimation. Nadezhda is in favor of an active position of the believer in the world, and in defense of human dignity. She seeks legitimation of this position. The themes of humility and non-resistance to evil are introduced to support the narrator's position by reconciling it with normative supports borrowed by Orthodox ethics and from the competing utopian position of Tolstoy's "non-resistance to evil". By distinguishing the Christian humility from the non-resistance of evil, Nadezhda expresses her belief in the necessity of actively protecting the Christian values ("*if anyone treads on an icon, you have to protect it*") but also personal dignity. She seeks support for the latter, referring to one of the undisputed authorities of contemporary Russian Orthodoxy: St. Seraphim of Sarov.[18]

The story she refers to is an episode of the saint's life when he humbly lets robbers hurt him badly. They cripple him for life, but he did not even try to defend himself. With an ax in his hands and his extraordinary physical strength, Seraphim almost certainly would have beaten his attackers if he had tried. It is not difficult to notice that the expected moral message of this story is the opposite to which the interlocutor binds him. Normally, this episode in the saint's life is used to show how one might follow the sacrificial example of Christ as a model of humility. On the contrary, Nadezhda puts it to service in her narrative about the need to actively oppose evil.

The reference to St. Seraphim of Sarov is followed by another reference – to Jesus as a supreme sacral example ("*the Christian must be a warrior, to fight – above all within himself*"). A hidden source of controversy is the evangelical texts themselves that combine the image of the Savior as a sacrificial lamb with his image as a warrior. This, however, does not abate the contradiction in the narrative:

Nadezhda chooses to refer precisely to the image of Christ as a warrior, not the alternative. The controversy of the narrative is significant not as a manifestation of logical inconsistency but as evidence of moral reasoning, of the state of intense moral demand. This story is also a manifestation of ethical saturation (Keane, 2014, pp. 318–320) at the level of personal narrative. Nadezhda strings together familiar episodes of "fighting" against evil, aligning her own moral reasoning, as much as she can, with Christian narratives.

One not obvious reason for the contradictory character of the narrative, following the ethical axis "humility-evil-resistance", lies in the tacit influence of the moral trajectories of the Soviet ideological heritage. A person born and living her formative years in Soviet times inevitably experienced the influence of the socialist humanist project. Born in 1975, Nadezhda was indoctrinated in various information paths during socialism and her formative education. The ideology of "harmoniously developed (socialist) personality" is influenced by the legacy of the Enlightenment and the Renaissance. The Sixth Principle of the Moral Code of the Builder of Communism (1961)[19] requires: "Humane relations and mutual respect among the people: A man for a man is a friend, companion and brother"; the Ninth Principle – "irreconcilability to injustice, parasitism, dishonesty, careerism, self-interest". In the 1986 version, the moral principles are not referred to as a "code", but in return, it mentions that the Communist morality is a "humanistic morality" and has absorbed in itself both "universal moral values" and those held by the masses of the "centuries-old struggle against exploitation" (27th Congress, 1986).[20] This conceptual context, whether or not realized by the interlocutor, is also an unnamed source of ideas in her moral repertoire.

At the end of the narrative, the interlocutor introduces a theme of Christian anthropology: Of the man as the image and likeness of God. Thus, she returns to her original narrative position by repeating the postulates of Christian ethics – respect for others, as well as the theme of moral difficulty ("*it is very hard*"). In this way, the narrator brings out the second moral accent in the narrative (Christian love and humility), reasserting a value that is close to her own spiritual quests. This is understandable in the context of her preference for an intellectual theological reading of Orthodox ethics. This preference is detectible in her explicit references (at other points in the interview) to the authority of the theologian Prof. Alexei I. Osipov, whose lectures she and her family listen to on electronic media.[21] In particular, she followed Osipov in discussing the internal moral inconsistency of practices and currents in contemporary Russian Orthodoxy. The subject came up in the interview on June 30, 2007, but almost filled the second interview with Nadezhda on July 4, 2007, which I will discuss later.

Nadezhda's narrative illustrates well the role of moral imagination in situations of moral reasoning. The narrator uses imaginary situations – metaphors (in the sense of Johnson, 1997, pp. 37–49) – which challenge and collide with basic moral concepts. By changing the point of view of the narrative, the interlocutor consistently replaces her voice with an imaginary scenario. This in itself "is an act of imaginary experience and a dramatic rehearsal" (Ibid., p. 200). The narrative patterns that she uses are tools of moral reasoning. The multiple instances of "ethical affordance"[22] also produce the sense of internal contradictions in Nadezhda's narrative on June 30, 2007.

Nadezhda's ethical reasoning concerns, as mentioned previously, the "inside" assessment of the meaning of different religious practices, or the types of religiosity, among contemporary Russian Orthodox believers. This topic was briefly discussed in some parts of the first interview with her and was developed in the second. As the first interview was lengthy, the interlocutor agreed to a second meeting to finish the conversation. In this sense, the second interview is a direct sequel to the first, and they present a semantic entity which I divide conditionally according to the dominant topic (ethical or internal-Orthodox).

In summary, Nadezhda's second narrative is organized around an axis that opposes the manifestations of external ritual piety against the search for internal personal self-improvement in the spirit of Orthodox ethics. Even the brief overview of the keywords in it shows that these are topics that are widely discussed in Russian society and especially in the Orthodox periodicals and the media. Like most interlocutors, Nadezhda notes a decline in church attendance since the initial "boom" of the 1990s. Her story includes her personal assessment of religious practices and ideas that have gained wide popularity in Russia, often with no commitment to the ethical self-transformation required by the spirit of Orthodox ethics. Here again, the polemic nature of her reasoning is markedly pronounced. She criticizes the model of religiosity where believers expect to solve their earthly problems through transcendental intervention without trying to change themselves or the model of godliness, which is mainly based on the fulfillment of ritual prescriptions in Orthodoxy (fasting, communion, etc.):

> *Everyone goes to* [the temple] *to get something: work, bride, groom – on life issues. And they go to the "spiritual elders" to ask: "Do I marry or not?" It seems that people do not try to improve their lives . . . and nobody wants to change themselves. . . . When they turned to Orthodoxy* [in the 1990s], *it was its ritual aspect. And the worst thing is that we are Orthodox, believers, and we do not know that the ritual side leads to* [a feeling like this]: "*I have fulfilled* [the ritual prescriptions]", *that is*, "*well done! I am righteous*". . . . *We are Christians only in words. The most important thing is to purify man from passions – the external performances* [rituals] *can bring pride, and nothing separates man from God more than pride.*[23]

It can be seen that for Nadezhda, religion should be much more than a routine or cultural habit: The reflexivity of her narrative testifies to intense spiritual search for the path to God through moral improvement. Still, there are apparent contradictions in her second narrative. These center on the roles of the *starčestvo* and on the interest in miracles among modern Orthodox believers. In the passage cited earlier, she is critical of the specific magical thinking attached to both. Yet she too believes in miracles: Commenting on the phenomenon of the myrrh-streaming icon of St. Seraphim of Sarov at St. Nicholas Church in Kaluga in 2002,[24] which she personally witnessed; she spoke with admiration for the "non-earthly smell" and concluded "well, obviously it is a miracle" [*nu, čudo iavnoe*].

Figure 2.2 Charitable activities: St. Elisaveta Fëdorovna Orthodox Sisterhood used to run a soup kitchen for homeless people. Catechism before lunch. Kaluga, July 18, 2007.

Source: Photo: Milena Benovska

However, her critical reflections on the nature of Orthodox practices in contemporary Russia are followed by a balancing summary: "*The Russian people feel that they need to turn to God. It's hard if you do not believe! You live – and what do you live for?*"[25] For Nadezhda, the "for" of living should be personal moral improvement, conceptualized as "purifying from passions" (i.e. sins).

Obedience, discipline, and power: Negative moralizing in Orthodox communities

Over the past decade, research attention has been drawn to the attachment to conservative values in contemporary Russian Orthodox communities, along with other trends and processes. Scholars note the importance of moral notions such as discipline, obedience, humility, and related or synonymous notions. My attention was drawn to these moral issues during the fieldwork in 2007, when on a hot August day, I received a phone call. It was Larissa Makarovna, one of my interlocutors. Visibly excited, she invited me to visit her at home to take part in an important event.

> *Do you remember I was telling you about a young matuška, how great an impression she made on me? Now she is travelling with the priest and the*

> *children; they are coming to visit me. Come and meet them, it will be very interesting for you.*[26]

The priest's wife that she wanted me to meet was, for Larissa Makarovna, a model for a woman's behavior. Twenty-six years old at that time, the *matuška* was a student of philology and a mother of four. She chaired the church choir and took care of a great home farm. Larissa Makarovna had mentioned this young woman in our previous conversation:

> *And just how she behaves! He* [the priest] *calls her, "Matuška" – and she replies: "Yes, Father! As you say, Father!" Such obedience! She never contradicts him! I want my daughter to see her and learn from her.*[27]

A few years later, publications appeared that confirmed my observations but also presented far more extreme examples and conclusions (see Zabaev, 2007a, 2007b; Knorre, 2011, pp. 317–340; Rousselet, 2011b, pp. 298–316, 322–344; Medvedeva, 2016b, pp. 92–108; Dubovka, 2018, pp. 192–211). Thus confirmed, the value of obedience remains to be analyzed in this chapter.

Next, I will elaborate on the following specific questions: The influence of the monastic tradition (historical and contemporary) on the formation of conservative values such as humility, obedience, and submission; humility and obedience as negative moralizing; the relationship between obedience, discipline, and power; humility as an aspect of the pursuit of moral improvement; the question of the empowerment of women in contemporary Russian Orthodoxy; and "good" as the main moral category. This chapter, not by chance, has as its motto a reflection by St. Reverend Makary of Optina (1788–1860) on obedience and self-denial – the path to humility as a prime virtue. This reference is intended to highlight the impact of ethical codes followed by Orthodox monasticism on the moral values of today's Russian Orthodoxy.

The influence of the monasteries as a model of holiness in Russian Orthodoxy on the parish life of the laity (both past and present) has been noted repeatedly by researchers.[28] Moral values such as obedience, submission, and humility have been studied through the use of these concepts as a reference to labor activities in a monastic environment and in the context of economic ethics (Zabaev, 2007a, pp. 5–26, 2007b, pp. 36–62). Apart from presenting the ethics of monastic life in remote and hard-to-reach religious centers, Ivan Zabaev also analyzes historical written sources that directly shape monastic piety, as well as the ethics of the parish in modern times. Through these writings, monastic ethics are transferred directly to laymen, but this fact raises a question of whether such ethics are compatible with the radically different, technologically and economically modern world (Zabaev, 2007b, pp. 42–43, 60). Authors focused on the sphere of parish life raise similar questions (Knorre, 2011, pp. 317–340; Rousselet, 2011b, pp. 301–302).

In the monastic environment, obedience is declared normatively as a path to the salvation of the soul. In practical terms, the word *poslušanie* means monastic or church-related labor tasks of a different nature.

In the Russian language, the word "obedience" [*poslušanie*] simultaneously directs both the attitude towards the will of God and the type and mode of action. . . . In the course of participant observation, it seemed to us at some point that the terms "humility" [*smirenie*] and "obedience" [*poslušanie*] refer simply to the specific monastic rhetoric concealing army methods of attitude towards the inhabitants of the monastery (Zabaev, 2007a, p. 20).

However, the analysis of historical Orthodox literature dedicated to the monastic structure shows that the methods in question are described there too, and that the contemporary picture is consistent with the theological sources (ibid., pp. 20–21). In fact, both of Zabaev's observations hold: "[H]umility" may be the replication of historical and theological arrangements, but it can also "motivate the despotism and the managerial arbitrariness of the rector of the parish or simply of the priest in regard to the layman" (Knorre, 2011, p. 324). Published excerpts from interviews show this unambiguously: "*We, the workers of the temple, were told, 'You have only duties, but you have no rights'. . . . So I left the temple*". A former pupil of spiritual school says, "*I was woken at night in the spiritual school and was sent to wash all the toilets . . . Or on a weekly watch – to the kitchen because my appearance was 'not humble'*" (Knorre, 2011, p. 324).[29] An uncompromising discipline, requiring blind and mechanical obedience (and not only voluntary obedience) in nunneries and Orthodox sisterhoods, was observed by multiple researchers. The unreasonable physical effort (leading to inability to perform prayer practices) and exhaustion is also in certain cases the cause for leaving the monastic community (Dubovka, 2018).

By using the Orthodox vocabulary (obedience, humility, blessing), some priests and spiritual fathers unceremoniously control the lives of not only monks, but also laypeople. Important decisions in the lives of the latter are made under the influence of a cleric or a priest. Priests may order believers to take up or abandon their careers (see Zabaev, 2007b, p. 45), as well as who and when to marry, as Nadezhda noted. However, the overall picture is far from homogenous. Often, it is believers who seek "blessings" (i.e. permissions) on all occasions and activities. Not a few parish priests express reservations about this practice. They underline the responsibility of clergy to respect the autonomy of the believer's personality (Rousselet, 2011b, pp. 211–215).

My observations in Kaluga are in line with the comments and conclusions made by the other researchers previously quoted. But interlocutors brought out additional perspectives. One man, who had spent two years as a deacon at a convent in Kaluga, explained that Russian convents lack the continuity of spiritual experience that the important male monasteries have. He confirmed that physical exhaustion is a rule and often leads to severe bodily injuries. For example, one of the lay sisters at her convent had overstrained herself by lifting heavy weights at the order of the abbess. But, said my interlocutor, the abbess was not prepared to guide a monastic community: The two-week missions on which abbesses are sent to gain spiritual experience are insufficient for training them to lead. "*There is no experience in the monastic spiritual life. Optina* [Hermitage] *has continuity, there were* starčestvo. [The nuns] *had no such experience. The churchwarden* [of the monastery] *must be spiritually rich: Not to be an administrator, but to be a person who will not destroy people*".[30] Still, he continued: "*A normal priest will never go to a monastery.*[31] *There is collision of strong characters*".[32] My interlocutor explained that there is an emerging rivalry between abbesses and priests. An abbess may allow herself to enter the altar and even to make a remark to the priest that he does not serve properly. Such an occurrence would seem unthinkable in Orthodoxy, because women are not allowed into the altar space, but my interlocutor assured me that it happens.

Historically, in Russian Orthodoxy, female monasticism has evolved with attention to the need for spiritual training. Important and respected nunneries from the eighteenth and nineteenth centuries were founded under the supervision and direct guidance of experienced and highly respected monks. It is sufficient to mention exemplary cases such as the Kazansky Convent of Ambrose Hermitage in Shamordino (near the town of Kozel'sk) or the Convent of St. Trinity in Diveevo, established and guided by emblematic monks like Ambrose [Amvrosii] of Optina and Seraphim of Sarov, who were later canonized as saints (Tarabukina, 2000, p. 1; Filippova, 2001, pp. 135–137; Shamordino, 2006 [1908] pp. 13–45). Conflict situations such as those mentioned earlier are apparently something new, the result of the modern dynamic social environment and, in particular, of changes in the structure of religious power (on which I will elaborate later).

Obedience and power are contrasting but also complementary concepts. In the St. Elisaveta Fëdorovna Orthodox Charitable Sisterhood, associated with the same Kazansky Convent,[33] an interview with one of the "sisters" was interrupted and did not take place. My interlocutor did not appear, nor did she call. The reason: I had unknowingly broken the internal hierarchy in the sisterhood. Having heard of the presence of an outside person in the nunnery upon my arrival, the abbess had personally called my interlocutor for an explanation and refused *to give her blessing* (i.e. she forbade the sister) to conduct the interview with me. Later, when the interview took place in a domestic setting over which the abbess had no authority, the sister told me that I should have talked first to the *starosta* [the senior sister] instead of herself: "*There is a senior sister, you should talk to her*".[34]

It is interesting to note how easily I was drawn into the power lines of internal institutional power. The abbess could forbid an interview because we had set the nunnery as the meeting place (actually, this choice was at the request of the interlocutor). Entry within the boundaries of the institutional space transformed both us – the interlocutor and the researcher – into objects of institutional power. It might even seem paradoxical that a disciplinary measure was extended so quickly to Zinaida Anatolievna, whose work in the sisterhood is voluntary. But the value of work done by "volunteers" is often disregarded within the religious hierarchy in favor of discipline and critique.[35]

During a series of conversations with Zinaida Anatolievna, obedience and its opposite – willfulness – were problematized repeatedly. "*I am willful, I am not suited for a nunnery*", she said, and continued: "*All this discipline, obedience – I cannot . . . I have brought up two children alone, I have always made my own decisions. Now I also look after an orphan*".[36] Zinaida Anatolievna implicitly referred to her biographical experience of Soviet times as another, different source for formation of moral patterns. This particular case demonstrates the contradictory and even conflictual nature of the concept of "multiple moralities" (in Zigon, 2011a, p. 8), considering its actual application beyond a purely theoretical construction.

The right to qualify Zinaida Anatolievna as "*willful*", in turn, belongs again to the abbess. It is a serious accusation, since in the language of Orthodox ethics *willfulness* means sin: It is not only the opposite of *obedience*, but also an indicator of *pride* – a severe sin on the scale of Orthodox ethics. That Zinaida Anatolievna so explicitly mentions it with reference to herself is testimony of an internal struggle in the Sisterhood to challenge and define the limits of Christian virtue.

Conflicts in the Sisterhood, only partially examined here, show that it is an arena of struggle for supremacy and power. The discussed concepts of Orthodox ethics, including obedience versus willfulness and humility versus pride, are used as arguments in this struggle. The distinction (borrowed by political anthropology) between normative rules and pragmatic rules is productive for the present analysis. The normative rules are "ultimate and publicly accepted values", while pragmatic rules are "private wisdom" . . . "which lies behind the public face of politics" (Bailey, 2001 [1969], pp. 4, 5–6). The specific Orthodox values commented on here are used as normative arguments in the struggle for power and supremacy in this Orthodox community. From the point of view of pragmatic rules, declarative references to Orthodox ethics are used to discipline an actor (my interlocutor) who is perceived as a threat by the formal religious authority.

Basically, this conflict is also of a moral nature. My interlocutor was, on behalf of the Sisterhood, among the main performers of a voluntary charity project. The construction of a home temple (2006) inside the Nursery Home for the Elderly and Handicapped [*Dom prestarelyh i invalidov*][37] is largely the result of Zinaida Anatolievna's physical work (see Pestova, 2008). Indeed, as a result of the extraordinary workload, she had been seriously ill for months. During her illness, she had been removed from the position of *starosta* [senior sister] and permanently replaced by another person.[38] The project she led did not give her efforts lasting recognition within the Sisterhood. These details begin to fill out a story: *Obedience* and *willfulness* were about longer-lasting relations than a single episode of failing to observe protocol.

More examples can be given in the same direction, but this will not change the main observations that demonstrate the centrality of discipline and disciplinary practices related to the ethics of obedience and submission, both in the monastic environment and among laypeople. Is this Eastern Orthodox Christianity, indeed? What is the reason for this whole "negative moralizing" (Luckmann, 2002, p. 20)?[39]

These questions derive from the analysis and relate to each other. Despite Kathie Rousselet's argument (2011b, p. 216) for "undemocratic Orthodoxy" in modern Russia, careful analysis shows some shades in the overall picture. In order to understand it, the reasons for disciplinary practices in the monastic environment must first be considered. As Talal Asad shows, obedience, humility, punishment, and penance were central concepts for the formation of the virtuous "self" in medieval (Western) Christian monasticism; the similarity with the ideology and ethics of Orthodox monasticism should be no surprise. Along with this, the West-Christian understanding is about the monks' will of obedience to the Catholic orders, which distinguishes the monastery from other total institutions such as the prison and the hospital.[40] In the twelfth century, the obedient monk was not someone who had lost his own will; he was a person for whom obedience was his virtue (Asad, 1993, pp. 125–126, see also p. 135). However, these two elements of medieval Christianity, "the productive role of physical pain and the virtue of self-abasement", are no longer accepted in modern religion. From the point of view of theological modernism, as well as of secular morality, they are both "archaic ('uncivilized') conditions". In the contemporary context, both religious and secular, "humility in the form of self-abasement", is considered to constitute a personality disorder (Asad, 1993, pp. 2, 125–126, 135, 166–167). If all this is so, why do such archaisms find continuation in the restored religious life of Russia after 70 years of aggressive Soviet modernism? How can people who were socialized as "modern" Soviet subjects accept and engage disciplines of obedience, humility, and punishment?

Humble obedience and the refusal of one's own will in Russian Orthodox Christianity are rooted in the traditions of monasticism. In the Eastern Orthodox monastic culture, an experienced spiritual mentor tutors younger inexperienced monks, and precisely within this framework, one must understand obedience. The latter is a central concept in the religious phenomenon, considered a Russian feature – spiritual eldership [*starčetsvo*].[41] Specifically, it is "the people's respect for '*starec*' or '*staritca*' – an ascetic monk/nun to whom believers turn for (spiritual) advice" (Solov'ëv, 2005 [1899], pp. 3–7). Eldership [*starčestvo*] is considered in Max Weber's terms to manifest charismatic power, while priests have "official" charisma (Mitrokhin, 2004, pp. 96, 99–100; Paert, 2010, pp. 7–10; Agadjanian, 2011a; Dubovka, 2017, pp. 37–64). These relations, however, are not considered to have involved violent exercise of power or will by the elder over the novice.

It is out of the question to say that there is some "spiritual violence" or intrusion of their will on the student in the nineteenth century "classical" *starčetsvo*. The unwelcome imposition of one's own will on contemporary believers is characteristic of the so-called "fake-spiritual elders" [*lzhestarcy*] or "junior-spiritual elders" [*mladostarcy*] – self-proclaimed religious leaders who profanize *starčestvo*, led by personal ambition and "leadership" (Sokolov, 2018, p. 37; see also Mitrokhin, 2004).

An indirect testimony to the latter is also found in Dariya Dubovka's observations of a modern community of believers around a small monastery and above all around a charismatic *starec* conceptualized as a "living saint" by his followers. The service of God and the service of man by providing (material) help are the two basic principles of the *starec* (Dubovka, 2017, p. 46), and obviously his ethical "creed", since ministry is work aimed at the good.

Consequently, negative moralizing and the imposition of obedience and humility as ethical categories in modern monasteries is not all encompassing; however, it is due to several factors. These are:

1 the literal perception, interpretation, and application of the principle of monastic discipline (Dubovka, 2015b, pp. 322–344, 2018, pp. 192–211; Medvedeva, 2016b, pp. 92–108);

2 the mechanical transfer of this principle from the monastic milieu to the lay environment (Zabaev, 2007b, p. 59);
3 the insufficient theological competence of a part of the clergy, in the specific conditions of the post-Soviet restoration of religious life, when, especially in the 1990s, a large number of priests had to be educated shortly (Sokolov, 2018, pp. 11–14);
4 the heritage of Soviet culture. The conclusions of Panchenko (2011, pp. 119–145) on the influence of Soviet culture on specific ritual forms in the new religious movement *The Church of the Last Testament* [*Cerkov' poslednego zaveta*] are in principle valid also against the practical ethics of daily communication among Orthodox believers.[42] People who have socialized and experienced life-forming periods under the Soviet era share its habitus, including its communicative aspects;
5 the context of the post-Soviet recovery of church property (primarily church and monastic buildings) and the associated need for a labor force also influence the ethics of obedience and disciplinary practices in the monastic environment (Zabaev, 2007a, pp. 20–21; Dubovka, 2018). The latter problem deepened after the law on the restitution of the ownership of religious organizations came into force. Importantly, as church institutions faced a shortage of resources for the repairs and restoration of the newly returned properties, including manpower (Köllner, 2018, pp. 1–20), a large number of workers (called *trudniki*) coming from marginalized strata (ex-prisoners who have survived drug or alcohol dependence) or people who have lost their homes, entered the monasteries. The presence of such people in large numbers has also been described as a motivation for the application of an "army discipline" (Zabaev, 2007a, p. 25; Dubovka, 2017, p. 46);
6 the theological and dogmatic roots of "negative moralizing". These are related to Orthodox dogma concerning "original sin" (of Adam) and, hereof, the inherently sinful human nature (Knorre, 2011, p. 320).

However, the question remains: To what is the current intentional focus on the archaic layers in Orthodoxy due? Among the most conservative Orthodox circles, the values of active anti-modernism are clearly outlined. One can get acquainted easily with the specific principles of religious anti-modernism held in the complex of concepts of the *pricerkovnyj krug* even from a distance with Internet sites such as *Antimodernism.ru* and *Two Cities*.[43]

To summarize: Among the *pricerkovnyj krug*, periods in Russian history marked by impulses to modernize, such as that pursued under the rule of Peter the Great (1672–1725), are perceived as a retreat from Orthodox identity and as enabling the introduction of "foreign" non-Russian elements into Russian culture (Tarabukina, 2000, p. 1). Other periods of Russian history are idealized when they mark the rise and imperial consolidation of the Russian state without borrowing from the culture of Western Europe, such as under the rule of Ivan the Terrible (1533–1547). The victory of the October 1917 Revolution, in turn, is presented as a consequence of a "Jewish plot".[44] A strong motive in favor of the anti-modern sentiments among the most zealous worshippers is the striving to distinguish themselves from the "renovationists" (the latter were most active in 1917–1924) who were a historic wing of Russian clergy supporting Bolshevism and backed by the Bolshevik wing of the Russian clergy. The renovationists created a parallel church and schism aimed at modernizing Eastern Orthodoxy (Davis, 1995, p. 4; Wynot, 2004, pp. 82–94). Anti-modernism, therefore, and the related archaization among certain currents of contemporary Russian Orthodoxy (including the negative moralizing) are related to the patriotic and nationalistic "reading" of Eastern Orthodoxy and the merging of Russian and Orthodox identities.

"When *matuška* is here, I sing out of tune!": Empowerment of women in contemporary Russian Orthodoxy

In the Orthodox parishes, an informal source of authority exists, which we can compare to a star illuminating with a reflected light: *Matuška*, the priest's wife. Despite the essential role of this figure in the life of the Orthodox parishes, little attention has been paid to it in literature. Both the historical and the contemporary Russian *matuška* is professionally engaged as a religious specialist. She performs a number of activities in the parish to help the ministry of her husband: Usually she sings in the church choir or conducts it, teaches at Sunday schools, and carries out charitable works (Manchester, 2008, p. 22). Additionally, the contemporary *matuška* can administer the parish website and deal with bookkeeping, icon painting, or handicrafts. Her work is assessed as a mission and "sacrificial" ministry (Sveshnikova and Puchkova, 2011, pp. 113–114). In the two parishes that I observed, the employment of the *matuška* corresponds to a great extent with the general parameters. In one of the two parishes, the priest's wife dealt with the publication of the parish newspaper and was considered to be extremely busy. Sometimes other religious activists replaced her on occasions when the presence of a *matuška* was needed.

The *matuška* does not possess religious charisma, unlike her husband who has acquired it through the sacrament of ordination. However, her real position in the parish is a position of authority. My early expectations that female believers would turn to her more often for advice than to the priest were not justified. The attitude to her was comparable to that expressed towards the "boss's wife" in a secular environment. At the very beginning of the fieldwork, I witnessed a *matuška*'s irritation when the priest's conversations with laypeople went on for too long after the end of the Sunday liturgy. She interrupted the conversation, saying, "*I'm leaving!*" This ended the priest's conversation.

In response to my praise for her singing in the same temple, one of the interlocutors said, "*When matuška is here, I sing out of tune!*" [*Kogda matuška zdes', ia fal'šivo poiu!*]. I was surprised: This woman had never expressed a negative reaction to anyone else in my frequent communication with her. Why such tension in her attitude towards the *matuška*? When I asked another woman if she ever consulted with the priest's spouse, the response was more diplomatic: She reported that she "hardly sees" the *matuška* because at church services, priest's wife sang in the *kliros* [choir stalls]. In the second parish, there were similar (if less marked) tensions with the *matuška*, suggesting that the antagonisms cannot be explained with reference to strictly personal qualities or social skills.

Shortly, on certain occasions, *matuška* could be perceived as an exemplary image, as previously mentioned, while on the others she might be a source of covert tensions. The career of a priest depends to a certain extent on his wife. First, he must be married in order to be ordained. Afterwards, he needs her to share in the various ministries of the church. In the historic Russian Church, the possibility that a priest's wife would be unsuited for her role was solved by the principles of the Russian estate system: Priests' wives were, as a rule, daughters of priests (Freeze, 1983, XIII, pp. 144–187). In the nineteenth century, future *matuški* were prepared for their mission in special schools: In nunneries or in religious schools for girls (KEV, 1866, p. 358, 1868, pp. 48–49, 1870, pp. 502–502, 1871, p. 288).

In the current circumstances, the priest does not choose a spouse in a closed estate or professional environment. It is said that the religious school for girls that has been operating in Kaluga since 1996 is meant to prepare suitable wives for young priests and so that they may avoid marriages with unsuitable candidates.[45] I have heard this explanation for the purpose of the school on a number of occasions, and similar things are said of religious schools for girls elsewhere in Russia.

This leads to three conclusions. First, the visible desire to restore the pre-Soviet institutions of the ROC – in this case, schools for girls with a spiritual mission – is confronted with the changed modern social environment in which it is not easy to integrate the institutional patterns of the past, unchanged. The second conclusion is related to the first. Historically, the patriarchal social model set in Christianity must coexist in modern times with gender roles that were altered during socialism. Russian women, who have worked for generations in all professional spheres of the Soviet economy, including as police (*militia*), in trades (such as plumbing), and as scientists (like nuclear physicists), have self-confidence (Ajvazova, 1999, pp. 32–33). Church walls are not a barrier to it. It is no accident, for example, that in the nineteenth century, the charitable societies in the Kaluga diocese were brotherhoods, that is, male associations.[46] In Orthodox life at the beginning of the twenty-first century, however, associations engaged in charitable activities are mainly sisterhoods, such as the Sisterhood of St. Elisaveta Fëdorovna. This fact testifies to the changed gender roles in contemporary Russian Orthodoxy, through the important activities performed by women.

Indeed, women may express significant power and authority through their church-related activities. The *starosta* of the Sisterhood, for example, calls the homeless people that the Sisterhood takes care of a "*team of wards*" [*komanda podopečnyh*]. This commando-administrative phrase speaks for itself. Orthodox discourses on female obedience and submission as virtues are neutralized at the instrumental level. In terms of the authority women achieve through their ministry in various religious communities and structures, they may indeed be "commanders" as well as "commandos".

These facts lead to the third and most important conclusion concerning the empowerment of women in contemporary Russian Orthodoxy, not only in secular environments, through the teaching of religious disciplines (see e.g. Ładykowska, 2018, pp. 96–107), but also in Orthodox parishes and associations, changing the outlines of otherwise traditional status positions.

In search of the good

Despite their significance in a contemporary context, obedience, humility, and discipline are not always dominant, nor the most important moral values and concepts around which religious practices are organized among Russian Orthodox believers.[47] There is a clear distinction between the ethical environment created in the monasteries, on the one hand, and the ethical environment and the moral discourse among laypeople, on the other. In smaller parishes, such as the two Kaluga parishes among which I conducted my field research, the construction of the moral "self" among believers has more complex dimensions. (For comparison, the number of regular churchgoers in the two parishes in Kaluga vary between 100 and 150, while even in the smaller of the two churches studied by Tocheva (2011, p. 70), the churchgoers number about 500–600 people). To put it in an instrumental language, the economic stability of self-sustaining parishes depends on the number of believers, and when they are not numerous, dispelling them with negative moralizing is, to put it mildly, undesirable.

The process of creating the community of Eucharist, which I have witnessed, is the main field of moral communication. The decisive role of the priest as a moral example and a factor in communication as well as the moral "climate" in the parish has been repeatedly noted by the researchers (see e.g. Sergazina, 2006; Agadjanian, 2011a, p. 34; Tocheva, 2017).[48] Although they did so differently, both of the two studied Kaluga parishes turned into communities with internal adherence around the moral example of the priest. The parish of the temple St. John the Warrior has developed its own identity precisely in connection with the priest's personality: "*Our priest is young; with his example, he engages people.*"[49]

Through the shared narrative repertoire of the parishioners, the charismatic reputation of the young priest was created, and the latter was symbolically transferred to the parish as a whole. These are the narratives of miracles (see the next chapter) that occurred on the territory of the temple, defining the positive identity of the religious community. "*The miracles that have happened here, do not happen in every temple*" [*Čudesa, kotorye zdes'proizošli, ne v kazhdom khrame slučaiutsia*], says Maxim in the context of what he said about the priest's kindness and responsiveness.[50] After the ecclesiastical services, a line of believers who need advice or the opinion of the priest is formed, He does not send back anyone and patiently talks with people as long as necessary. At first glance, there is nothing special about this practice. However, given the complete abstinence from food and water in the morning before and during Sunday liturgy, the situation becomes extraordinary. The discomfort of hunger and thirst is overcome in the name of religious ministry. It turns out that the identity of this parish and of its leader as a place of charismatic communication is based on the notions of the good, including its everyday common understanding.

Similarly, the personal moral qualities of the Rector contributed to enhancement of the internal cohesion in the parish community in the Shroud of the Holy Mother. The charisma of this Rector is personal rather than related to the transcendent. His talent for communicating with children and adolescents can be seen in the very fact that in his children's club for scout activities, the Squad of the Young Scouts of St. Andrew the Apostle (the First-Called), there were more than 300 children of different ages, in 2018.[51] The skills of Father A.B. as a spiritual counselor proved to be a decisive factor in at least one believer's complete dedication to the religious life:

> *In* [nineteen] *ninety-four we formed such close spiritual relations with Father A., and I understood that I should be constantly close to this shepherd, who at any given time could give you the advice. And such an attempt to live on a permanent basis according to the advice, I am very much in favor of this, because I said that all that my exaggerated . . . that I had at the Institute when I was a student: Such self-conceit, self-sufficiency, complacency – of course, result in so many mistakes.*[52]

Good is actively sought among the churchgoers of the two Kaluga parishes. Expressed at a normative level, this ethos can be related to the religious concept of *agapé* (Christian Love). Unlike the interlocutors of Rousselet (2011b, pp. 160–161), however, my interlocutors do not often give an explicit expression of their aspiration to good (perhaps also because of the internalized ethics of modesty). Rather, their actions and behavior speak for themselves. One of the believers has taken home and taken care of an elderly sick woman who is not her relative; two other women have adopted children they look after; the third one has housed relatives in her small two-room dwelling, so her household has grown to seven members. Although she was busy and working, she baked bread to ensure that the family was fed and to save on some of the domestic expenses. Another parishioner followed a similar model of generous sharing of limited resources. One of the younger interlocutors worked for six years on a voluntary basis in a children's shelter. The Rector of St. John the Warrior, as well as one of the three priests from the Shroud of the Holy Mother, taught on a voluntary basis the subject *Fundamentals of Orthodox Culture* in some Kaluga schools. Believers visited and cared for elderly and sick members of their parish. There was a shelf in the churches where believers anonymously left modest donations in kind, i.e. food for the people in need. During field observations, I was often invited to get food if I needed it.

Good appears too in the form of charity. It is worth recalling the activity of the St. Elisaveta Fëdorovna Orthodox Sisterhood, mentioned in chapter 1. It works (despite limited resources) among vulnerable groups: The homeless, prisoners, and the sick and disabled elderly in need of care. Nor is the Sisterhood the only Orthodox charity in Kaluga or the region: Dozens of different initiatives existed and exist, with activities of different scale and different levels of regularity.[53] When, in 2019, an Orthodox charitable center opened in Kaluga (Utiatnikova, 2019, n.p.),

Figure 2.3 Influence of monasticism onto parish life: A member of the church choir reads lives of saints during a festive lunch in the parish. Kaluga, July 8, 2007.

Source: Photo: Milena Benovska

the long-standing idea of the Kaluga Metropolitan[54] turned true and a next step towards the institutionalization of local Orthodox charity was made.

Before returning to the subject of the good, it is important to make a few more remarks about charity. That is to say, practices of charity have deep roots in historical Russian Orthodoxy, despite widespread scholarly claims to the contrary. Throughout the nineteenth to the early twentieth century, wealthy citizens and various religious communities in Kaluga (city and the province) engaged in significant charitable initiatives and activities. From 1808 to 1908, five hospitals were built in Kaluga, thanks to the generous donations by local merchants and landlords; a fund of trustees for children's shelters had been established in 1847 (Friedgel'm, 1998, pp. 105–106, 108–115); even a few "church brotherhoods" actively engaged in 1860s and 1870s in the financial support, regular or occasional, for families of the poor in the parishes.[55]

Indeed the practice of ritual charity called "secret almsgiving" [*tainaja milostynia*] is well evidenced in Russian ethnographic literature since the nineteenth century and seems to have been remembered in some regions of Russia during the 1990s (Gromyko and Buganov, 2000, p. 12; Tul'ceva, 2002, pp. 90–100). During the Soviet period, this practice was more or less abandoned, but the same cannot be said about the general ethos of compassion, mercy, and the search for good. While discussing the subject of ascetic practices, one of the interlocutors expressed a brief synthesis of the philosophy of good: "*If you fast, you do good deeds. Fast is not about what you eat, but about good deeds. Do not quarrel with anyone*".[56]

On a normative level, goodness is perceived by believers as an ideal of Russian public life. Exemplary images of Russian holiness, such as that exemplified by St. Sergius of Radonezh, St. Seraphim of Sarovm or St. Ambrose of Optina, embody this idea (Kologrivov, 2010, p. 383). Human empathy and kindness are present in the lives of the two parishes without many words. This is part of morality, understood as unconditionally accepted and unchallenged principles (Heintz, 2009b, pp. 3–4), embodied moral rules that simply are experienced. This is the general moral basis on which the system of specific Orthodox ethical ideas and reasoning builds.

How, however, do the ideal and practices of the good combine with disciplinary practices, negative moralizing, or sometimes even far-right ideologies such as anti-Semitism? Some ideas from the (emergent) "anthropology of the good" can be useful in unraveling this "conundrum" through research on the "cultural construction of the good". The idea is expressed by Robbins:

> The good in this respect is something that must be imaginatively conceived, not simply perceived. . . . It is not that imaginings of the good cannot sometimes be set aside in practice or put to use in ideological projects that support the continued existence of structures of violence and suffering, but if we assume that ideals always and only get either ignored or deployed in nefarious ways, then the anthropology of the good can never get off the ground.
>
> (Robbins, 2013, p. 457)

In the sense outlined, good can be construed as an overarching concept capable of bringing together the conflicting ideologies and practices of "multiple moralities".

The social practices belonging to different spheres of public and private religious life and discussed in this chapter are united by the concept of "multiple

Figure 2.4 Orthodoxy is rather rediscovered and reinvented instead of being "dug out of ashes". Baptisterium built in post-Soviet conditions, for baptisms of adults with full immersion of a body. Kaluga, August 8, 2007.

Source: Photo: Milena Benovska

moralities", along with notions of power and national consolidation. Led by a striving for a more prominent presence in the Russian public sphere, the ROC plays the role of a moral mentor and "entrepreneur" at the international, national, and local levels. A basic moral area in which the church fights for supremacy in public debate is the question of the philosophy of the human body, "traditional values", and the family. Together with the secular institutions of the central government, the ROC is a major actor in initiatives, both secular and religious, for new "invented traditions". Orthodox family values, state pro-nationalist politics, and nation-building are in synergy, forged by the historical imagination.

The rise of monuments of saints in Russian cities is also an aspect of another policy: Transforming the public space by saturating it with religious symbolism. The policy of enhanced public presence visibly takes priority over the strict respect of historically inherited aesthetic canons in Eastern Christianity, such as not allowing the representation of sacred images in a three-dimensional form. As Russian Orthodoxy is turned into a public religion, Eastern Christianity is rediscovered and reinvented instead of being "dug out of the ashes" by literally copying the patterns of the past. Beneath the slogans of continuity with the past, new practices are being introduced.

In another configuration, the combination of break and continuity is also revealed in personal moral narratives and discourses. The conversion – personal change from disbelief to zealous religiosity – is related to the crossing of the boundaries between secular and religious moral domains. Crossing the boundaries in everyday human interaction and in narratives through multiple "ethical affordances" testify to the predominantly secular character of the Russian public milieu. Believers approach religion to tackle their own spiritual and moral quests. As a result, moral reasoning, with the help of moral imagination, collides with contradictory ethical notions. The ethic of Orthodox virtue is entangled with and disputed by the humanist ideas and principles inherited from socialism. Personal ethical reasoning also testifies to the heterogeneous nature of the social practices in contemporary Russian Orthodoxy.

The religious power is the foundation upon which ethical discourses, negative moralizing, and disciplinary practices unfold in Orthodox communities. The appeals of part of the clergy to obedience and humility as an aspect of Christian soteriology reflect the strong influence of monastic religiosity on the laity. Monasteries are a complex and contradictory social field where, together with calls for Christian humility and self-denial, disciplinary practices, internal conflicts, and struggles for supremacy unfold. These "archaisms" are similar to the medieval Christian practices of monastic discipline (Asad, 1993), but there are complex reasons for their existence in a modern Orthodox environment. Apart from the material context – the post-Soviet restoration of church property – they also consist of the canonical Orthodox tenet of the incurably "fallen" human nature. Negative moralizing is due to the literal interpretation and direct transfer of ascetic monastic values into a lay environment. The struggle for power and discipline in contemporary Orthodox communities is also related to the empowerment of women through their active participation in important liturgical and charitable practices. This, in turn, is the result of a meeting between the respected traditions of Orthodoxy (patriarchal models) and the changed contemporary gender roles.

The empowerment of women in parishes and other religious communities, however, is in clear contradiction with the appeals (sometimes internalized by women themselves) for wifely submission. Ethical "archaisms" and anti-modernism among certain circles of the most conservative Christians are explained by a patriotic and nationalist reading of Orthodoxy. The latter symbolizes Russian traditions and uniqueness; modern developments symbolize the deviation (perceived negatively) from the particular Russian historical path.

Under the conditions of ongoing social change, the aspirations of the clerics to impose a unitary Orthodox morality inevitably face the contemporary "multiple moralities". Moralities, however multiple, are disputed and contradictory in both the cultural domain and as an analytical tool in emic and etic levels. Beyond all this, we can still detect that striving for the good is the main ethos at the emic level and an overarching concept that reconciles the uneven and contradictory character of the multiple moralities. The good is supported by the charisma (spiritual or personal) of an ecclesiastical leader, priest, and it is on his moral axis that the identity of an Orthodox parish is consolidated. These are the unconditional and undisputed principles of shared morality.

Notes

1 See the lessons of the *spiritual elders* canonized as saints from Optina Hermitage: www.optina.ru/nastavl_uchashchimsja. Last accessed: 2.09.2018.
2 For an in-depth discussion on the moral imagination, see Johnson (1997, pp. 185–216).
3 See a concise review in the Introduction.
4 Highlighted in the original. Keane relies for this concept on the philosopher Bernard Williams.
5 A considerable body of literature has accumulated on religious education in Russia. See e.g. Mitrokhin (2004), Glanzer (2005, pp. 208, 215–216), Willems (2006, pp. 288–291), Mulders (2008, pp. 7–9), Ładykowska (2011, pp. 27–47), Ładykowska (2018), Ładykowska and Tocheva (2013, pp. 55–74), Köllner (2016, pp. 366–386).
6 Alexii II (2008): "*Etot prazdnik prizvan sodeistvovat' utverzhdeniju v Rossii vysokih nravstvennyh cennostei i ukrepleniju instituta sem'i* [This holiday is intended to promote the establishment of high moral values in Russia and the strengthening of the institution of the family]." On the Day of Family, Love, and Faithfulness in all the churches of the Russian Orthodox Church will be held celebratory worship. Announcement of the Information Agency *Russkaja Linja*, July 8, 2008 – https://rusk.ru/st.php?idar=177565. Last accessed: 3.09.2018.
7 The Sculpture of Sts. Pëtr and Fevronia of Murom. 2012, http://smilekaluga.ru/discover/skulptura-svyatyih-petra-i-fevronii-muromskih/. Last accessed: 3.09.2018.
8 A monument to Sts. Pëtr and Fevronia will be mounted in Yaroslavl. Announcement of the Information *Agency Russkaja Linija*, 05/30/2009.- https://rusk.ru/newsdata.php?idar=183110. Last accessed: 3.09.2018.
9 Novosti eparhii (2014, p. 2).
10 Novosti eparhii (2015, p. 2).
11 http://petripavel.tomsk.ru/openArticle.php?number=96. Last accessed: 25.09.2018.
12 www.parad-nevest.ru. Last accessed: 14.09.2018.
13 For criticism of the latter term, see Keane (2016, pp. 133–135).
14 In Russian:

> *Ja k pravoslaviju prišla čerez muzha. Mne nravilos', čto on menia k etomu ne podtalkival. A potikhonečku ja stala sama – on pomogal.*
>
> – Interview with Nadezhda Sidorovna, 32, university education, a housewife. 30.06.2007, Kaluga.

15 In Russian:

> *A kak tiazhelo – idti po ulice i ne osuzhdat' [drugikh]. Eto samoe tiazhëloe. Kak ot etogo izbavit'sia? Eto tiazhelo. Kogda čelovek načinaet borot'sia – eto tiazhelo. Khristianin – eto imenno tot, komu nuzhen Khristos – izbavit'ot nas samih. Esli proverit'eto na praktike: „Segodnia ne budu dumat'plokhogo!" – Kak čelovek vidit, čto sam ne mozhet – ne polučaet'sia: togda načinaeš'Gospodu molit'sia, kak Spasiteliu, a ne kak podateliu zemnyh blag.*
>
> – Interview with Nadezhda Sidorovna, 32, university education, a housewife. 30.06.2007, Kaluga.

16 In Russian:

> *Ob'jazannosti pionera – oni ot Evangelija, tol'ko nazvany po drugomu. I togda mnogo horoših liudei bylo, tol'ko ne znali.*
>
> – Interview with Nadezhda Sidorovna, 32, university education, a housewife. 30.06.2007, Kaluga.

17 In Russian:

> *'Smirenie – eto ne zabitost', a videt'svoi grehi. Eto ne nesoprotivlenie zlu. Smirenie – videt', čto ty greshnyi. Nesoprotivlenie zlu, eto kogda ne otvečaeš': "Raz on nagovoril na menia, značit, ia na samom dele takoj". – Smirit'sia.*
>
> *A esli kto-to topčet ikonu – nado ëë zaščtit'. Mal'čik poidët v školu – vidit, čto b'jut drugogo: nado zaščitit'. Ili esli b'iut ego samogo – nado zaščitit'sia. Eto čisto moë mnenie.*
>
> *Serafim Sarovskii – on byl sviatym: na nego napali razbojniki. On rubil drova. Kogda ego napali, on brosil topor. Byl krepkim, a ego izbili, udarili. Hristianin dolzhen byt'voinom. Borot'sia, prezhde vsego vnutri sebia.*
>
> *Kazhdogo čeloveka nado prinimat'kak obraz Bozhii. Eto očen' tiazhelo, no k etomu nuzhno stremit'sia. Samye glavnye zapovedi: "Vozliubi Gospoda" i "Vozlyubi blizhnego kak samogo sebia".*
>
> – Interview with Nadezhda Sidorovna, 32, university education, a housewife. 30.06.2007, Kaluga.

18 Seraphim of Sarov (1759–1833), see: Kologrivov (2010, pp. 385–407).

19 *The Moral Code of the Builder of Communism* was adopted at the XXII Congress of the Communist Party of the Soviet Union (CPSU) in 1961. For its influence among believers, see Benovska-Sabkova, Köllner, Komáromi, Ładykowska, Tocheva, Zigon (2010, p. 19).

20 27th Congress (1986).

21 Prof. Alexei Osipov's lectures are available on the Internet (https://ok.ru/lektsiipr), as well as in TV programs (http://tv-soyuz.ru/peredachi/lektsii-professora-a-i-osipova). Last accessed: 1.09.2018.

22 "By ethical affordance I mean any aspect of people's experiences and perceptions that they might draw on in the process of making ethical evaluations and decisions, whether consciously or not. . . . Anything at all that people can experience, such as emotions, bodily movements, habitual practices, linguistic forms, laws, etiquette or narratives, possesses an indefinite number of combinations of properties. . . . Ethical affordance refers to the opportunities that any experiences might offer as people evaluate themselves, other persons, and their circumstances" (Keane, 2016, pp. 27, 30, 31).

23 In Russian:

> *'Vse idut [*v hram*], čtoby čto-to polučit': rabotu, nevestu, zhenikha. I k starcam s etim khodyat: mne zhenit'sia, ili net . . . po zhiteiskim voprosam. Polučaetsia, čto liudi ne staraiutsia ispravliat'svoyu zhizn' . . . a nikto ne khočet meniat sebya.' . . . 'Kogda prišli k pravoslaviju* [v 1990-yh], *eto byla obriadovaya storona. A samoe tiazhëloe, čto my pravoslavnye, veruyuščie, a ne znaem. Obriadovaya storona k etomu vedët: ya vypolnil, značit ia molodec – ia praveden!' . . . 'Khristiane my vse – tol'ko na slovakh. Samoe glavnoe očistit' čeloveka ot strastei. Vnešnie ispolneniia [obriadov] mogut gordost'prinesti, a ničego ne otdelyaet čeloveka bol'še ot Boga, čem gordost'.*
>
> – An interview with Nadezhda Sidorovna, 32, university education, a housewife. 4.08.2007, Kaluga.

24 For this case, see Pitirimov (2002).

25 "*Russkii narod čuvstvuet, čto nado k Bogu obratit'sia. Tiazhelo bez very! Zhivëš' - I dlia čego zhivëš'*" – the same interview, 4.08.2007, Kaluga.

26 In Russian:

> *I kak ona tol'ko vedët sebia! On ej govorit: 'Matuška!' – a ona emu: 'Da, batiuška! Kak skazhete, batiuška!' Takoe povinovenie! Ni v čëm emu ne protivorečit'! Ja hoču, čtoby moja doč' eë videla i naučilas'u neë.*
>
> – Interview with Larissa Makarovna, 50, medical education, a paramedic. 4.08.2007, Kaluga-2.

27 ibid.
28 See Tarabukina (2000), Mitrokhin (2004).
29 For such practices of "humility" through open humiliation, see Mitrokhin (2004, pp. 134–144).
30 In Russian:

> *Opyta v monastyrskoi zhizni dukhovnoi net. V Optinu [pustyn']preemstvennost'est', tam starčestvo bylo. U etikh opyta ne bylo. Nastoyatel'*[monastyria] *dolzhen byt'dukhovno bogatym: ne byt'administratorom, a čelovek, kotoryi liudei ne pogubit.*
> – An interview with Vadim Nikitič, 41, higher medical education, a doctor. 9.08.2007, Kaluga.

31 In Russian, there is just one word (monastery) for male or female monastic communities. Here, the priest is generalizing, indicating that "normal" priests prefer to serve in a parish rather than a monastic community.
32 The same interview, see the note above.
33 For more information on the Sisterhood and the nunnery in chapter 1.
34 In Russian:

> *Est'staršaja sestra, s nej nado razgovarivat'.*
> – Interview with Zinaida Anatolievna, 66, university education, an engineer/ pensioner. 2.08.2007, Kaluga.

35 Ivan Zabaev writes about the rude attitude of a monastery hegumen to a volunteer woman who helped to provide food for the monastery at a time of financial difficulty: "I was very surprised: the woman did something [good], and there was no gratitude. Isaiah spoke with all of them as though he was not obliged to be grateful for the fact that they were working for free at the monastery, [it was] they [who should be grateful] to him now that they had a place where they can save their soul" (Zabaev, 2017a, p. 24).
36 In Russian:

> *Vsia eta disciplina, podčinenie – ja ne mogu. . . . Ja vyrastila dvoe detei odna, vsegda sama prinimala rešenija. Teper'vyraščivaiu sirotu tozhe.*
> – An interview with Zinaida Anatolievna, 66, university education, an engineer/ pensioner. 2.08.2018, Kaluga.

37 Nursery home care for the elderly and handicapped in Kaluga – www.kdi40.ru. Last accessed: 28.08.2018.
38 Interviews with Zinaida Anatolievna, 66, university education, an engineer/ pensioner. 23.07.2007 and 2.08.2007.
39 "Moralizing is either positive, as in praise, or negative, as in condemnation, and it may consist both of the evaluations of the behavior of others as well as of one's own actions" (Luckmann, 2002, p. 20).
40 Asad refers here to Goffman (1961).
41 Solov'ëv (2005 [1899]), Kuchumov (2002, pp. 223–244), Mitrokhin (2004, pp. 92–115), Gorbacheva (2006), Paert (2010). Linked to an ancient fourth-century ascetic tradition, in Russia this phenomenon was fully formed in the nineteenth century, and its homeland was Optina Hermitage (Solov'ëv, 2005 [1899], pp. 3–7; Kuchumov, 2002, pp. 223–244; Mitrokhin, 2004, p. 102; Gorbacheva, 2006, pp. 5–23; Paert, 2010).
42 Similar are also some of Kathie Rousselet's observations (2011a, pp. 160–161) on the moral notions consolidated by the worship to the family of the last Russian Tsar Nicolas II.
43 https://antimodern.ru/; https://dvagrada.ru/wiki/Заглавная_страница. Last accessed: 24.09.2018.
44 An informal conversation with Zinaida Anatolievna, also an ex-member of the Communist party. 24.08.2007, Kaluga.

45 Initially, the school was called The School of Kaluga Diocese and only girls attended it; after 2002 it changed its statute and was called The Spiritual School of Kaluga and it also accepted boys.
46 Female charity societies become possible in Russia only at the end of the nineteenth and at the beginning of the twentieth century (Wagner, 2007, pp. 119–145).
47 Knorre (2011, p. 320) shares the opposite view.
48 Virtually all authors in the Agadjanian and Rousselet, 2011 edited book confirm this.
49 In Russian:

> *U nas batiuška molodoj, svoim primerom liudej uvlekaet.*
>
> – An interview with Nadezhda Sidorovna, 32, university education, a housewife. 30.06.2007, Kaluga.

50 An interview with Maksim Andreevič, born in 1985, a student. 11.07.2007, Kaluga.
51 See the Internet site of the church: http://kaluga-pokrov.cerkov.ru/voskresnaya-shkola/ Last accessed: 20.08.2018.
52 In Russian:

> *V 94-m godu u nas sformirovalis' s otcom A. otnošenia takie dostatočno tesnye duhovnye i ia poniala, čto nuzhno byt' postoianno riadom s tem pastyrem, kotoryj vsegda v nuzhnyj moment mozhet dat' nuzhnyj sovet. I takaia popytka zhit' postoianno po sovetu, ona menia očen' ustraivaet do sih por, potomu čto ia poniala, čto vsë moë vot eto napusknoe, čto ia imela v institute, kogda učilas', takaia samonadeiannost', samodostatočnost', samodovol'stvo takoe, ono konečno očen' mnogo ošibok za soboj vlečët.*
>
> – An interview with Ekaterina Viačeslavovna, 36, university education, a teacher/ religious activist. 12.07.2007, Kaluga.

53 http://social.diaconia.ru/search?eparchy_id=56. Last accessed: 18.09.2019.
54 A couple of interviews with priests mentioned the plans of the Metropolitan to establish sustainable charity institutions: with Father V. K., 34, university education, a priest. 18.08.2007, Kaluga; Father E. K., 34, university education, an engineer/ priest. 30.06.2007, Kaluga.
55 KEV (1864a, 22, pp. 170–174, 406–411, 1864b, 12, pp. 222–223, 1866, 2, pp. 37–50, 1866, 21, pp. 650–653, 1867, 7, pp. 197–200, 1870, 5, 153–157).
56 In Russian:

> *Esli ty postišsia, ty delaj dobrye dela. Ne v ede post, a v dobryh delah. Ne rugajsia ni s kem.*
>
> – Interview with Lidia Vassilievna, 67, university education, a bibliographer. 26.09.2006, Kaluga.

3 In search of salvation

Narratives of conversion, "moral torment", and miracles

Introduction

The topic of ethical reasoning connects chapters 2 and 3. In the previous chapter, the ethical quests and manifestations of multiple moralities were presented through various ethical affordances or expressions: Policies, materialities, symbolic forms (new rituals and traditions), and narratives. The different social environments of their implementation were also shown: Central state projects (secular and religious) and bottom-up initiatives or personal individual perceptions and beliefs. In this third chapter, a different approach is suggested. It explores personal autobiographical stories recorded during the 2006–2007 fieldwork, firstly, as a testimony of the processes of conversion from non-belief or indifference to belief and practice of Orthodox Christianity; and secondly, as specific narrative forms giving voice to "ethical reasoning" and religious experience. It is the main purpose here to address moral quests and moral dilemmas of contemporary Russian Orthodox believers through the study of personal narratives. It is by no means my intention to present here a representative "picture" of conversion in Russia; I would rather present significant narrative strategies that voice the main moral concerns among the most devoted believers.

In other words, here I base the study on the theoretical approaches that underline generic relationships between morality and narratives. The study of moral principles, predispositions, and ethical reasoning is based on the analysis of narratives that structure the moral nature of a person. "*Any adequate theory of morality will have to explain the central role of such narratives and other imaginative structures in moral deliberation.* A central task for any moral theory, therefore, must be to understand how we narratively construct our lives and how our deliberations are framed by those narratives" (Johnson, 1997, p. 152, original emphasis).

This chapter demonstrates, through the study of narratives, the links between conversion, moral imagination, and moral perceptions, on the one hand and a radical personal transformation, on the other. Perceptions of sin and religious salvation will be central to this analysis. I will compare the peculiarities of the stories of Orthodox conversion with similar narratives in the Protestant environment to outline the similarities and differences between them. Within the framework of the same task, I will also examine the narratives of the miracles I recorded or heard at the two Orthodox parishes in Kaluga in the context of the immediate religious communication of the religious communities. Theoretically, the third chapter relies on the concepts of conversion, "moral torment" (Robbins, 2004), and "moral lazarets" (Hann, 2010).

Conversion and its narratives: A theoretical framework

The concept of conversion is used in a remarkable multitude of contexts and research approaches. It is therefore necessary to clarify the meaning it serves in these analyses. A relatively simple definition claims that "conversion is affiliation of a person to a new religious group, conceptualized as positive transformation of the nature and value of [the] person" (Stark and Bainbridge, 1996, p. 197). Still, this definition hardly offsets the inconveniences of dealing with the concept. These inconveniences include the practical impossibility of finding a universally applicable definition of conversion, as well as its relationship to Christian symbolism with the paradigmatic conversion of St. Paul as recorded in *Acts* [9: 3–8, 13–20] (Asad, 1996, p. 264; Stark and Bainbridge, 1996, p. 195; Spilka et al., 2003, p. 344). Thus, attempts to define this concept tend to be linked with the various cultural and historical contexts in which "it" is being studied (Comaroff and Comaroff, 1991, p. 250; Pelkmans, 2010, pp. 114–115; Rambo and Farhadian, 2014, p. 10).[1]

Despite these difficulties, many authors unite around similar conceptions of conversion as change or transformation (Rambo and Farhadian, 2014, p. 9; Stromberg, 2014, p. 118) or a passage (Austin-Broos, 2003, p. 9). It is well known that religious conversion, and even more narratives of it, have been studied mostly in the Protestant environment, and research observations and conclusions bear the footprint of this environment. This is largely the case of post-Soviet and postsocialist conversion research (see e.g. Pelkmans, 2009; Vallikivi, 2009, pp. 59–83; Wanner, 2009, pp. 163–182). Conversion to Orthodoxy is much less studied (Rambo and Farhadian, 2014, p. 10), and even less so – the narratives of conversion. Rather, the great body of literature, Russian and foreign, on the post-Soviet rediscovery of Orthodoxy testifies that this process is rarely conceived and conceptualized as a conversion. This, in part, explains the near absence of research on contemporary Russian Orthodoxy in comparative study of religious conversion. Indeed, as such a small part of the literature on contemporary Russian Orthodoxy makes uses of narrative research, it would be hard to capture conversion.[2] The analysis of autobiographical narratives in this chapter will show that, despite the specificity of the Russian Orthodox context, some similarities with the narratives characteristic of the global evangelical circles are found in the Orthodox conversion stories.

The legacy of Soviet atheism means that the most useful theoretical models are those that include a shift from indifference or non-belief to devotion (Nocks, 1933, p. 7, Hervieu-Léger, 1999b, pp. 120–125; Pelkmans, 2010). Indeed, the situation for much of the Soviet period might better be described as "indifference" to religion rather than "atheism". While atheism refers to policies, it is much harder to grasp individual convictions or ideas. Various religious phenomena did continue to exist throughout the Soviet period: For example, in the religious practices among the rural elderly, as well as in beliefs in magic and in New Age-type beliefs in late socialism (Linquist, 2006; Panchenko, 2011). Moreover, "religious" ideas seem to have been channeled into communism itself: "[T]he success of communism as quasi-religion has contributed to the process of de-Christianization, which in the majority of the population has not been linked to the abandonment of orientation to the supernatural at the level of consciousness" (Andreeva, 2003, p. 98). Rather than an atheist "spiritual home", socialist and postsocialist Russia seems rather a "fragile" spiritual home with a generally low level of religious knowledge and weak institutional connectivity to Christianity (Nocks, 1933, p. 7; discussed in Pelkmans, 2010, pp. 115–118). Religious expression in Russia, as elsewhere in the post-Soviet space, manifests with "interrupted continuity" "between contemporary religious forms and their pre-socialist referents" (Pelkmans, 2009, p. 5).

The definition of conversion to Orthodoxy as a form of "interrupted continuity" would be incomplete if we do not mark the perception of an intimate, personal relationship of the individual with Orthodoxy. It is not only about the political alignment of Orthodoxy with the Russian national identity, but about the personally experienced relationship with Orthodoxy as an intimate and one's "own" value. According to sociological observations, a significant proportion of Russian citizens with Orthodox identities who rarely or never attend church services, sacraments, or practices, still "consider Orthodoxy as something unconditionally native and important to themselves" (Ipatova, 2006, p. 422). Such a view is shared by the active believers I spoke with in Kaluga: "*Orthodoxy is in the heart of every Russian person*". "*It's all from our roots*". I heard variations of these statements from most interlocutors during the field study.

These statements show that for people with an Orthodox identity in Russia, continuity has an incomparably greater symbolic importance than a break. This is essential in the plan of perceptions and values. However, the high place of Orthodoxy in the scale of symbolic values does not alter the fact that a significant part of religious knowledge was lost during the Soviet period. The political, temporal, and cognitive boundaries outlined by the breakup of the Soviet state, and the loss of associated collective identities, gives literal as well as figurative meaning to Pelkmans' description of conversion as a border crossing (2010, pp. 115–118).

In the Introduction, I presented the peculiarities of my fieldwork in Kaluga and discussed, in particular, the recording of autobiographical interviews. Here I will add that interviewing is practically indispensable in the study of conversion. During fieldwork, I did not witness personal conversions, and it seems hardly feasible to do so if judged by Simon Coleman's assertion that he never witnessed the "getting" of personal conversions despite long-term participant observation among charismatic evangelicals in Sweden (Coleman, 2000, p. 12; Coleman, 2003, p. 18).[3] Contrary to the tendency to present conversion as a sudden, momentary event (by analogy with St. Paul's spiritual transformation), most contemporary authors unite around the conclusion that conversion is marked by a continuous and gradual character (Coleman, 2003, pp. 15–28; also Austin-Broos, 2003, p. 9; Baer, 2014, p. 25; Rambo and Farhadian, 2014, pp. 5–6). Because of its lengthy nature, conversion cannot be recorded through (non-continuous) ethnographic observations, and stories about it are an appropriate means of studying it.

Conversion trajectories

The large-scale conversion processes that take place in much of today's world are a response to global economic, social, and political insecurity, and social distress (Austin-Broos, 2003, p. 9; Pelkmans, 2009, p. 5). In the postsocialist spaces, the destabilizing forces of the turbulent changes that accompanied the collapse of socialism and the intrusion of predatory capitalism without rules were added to this. The overall process of modern Russian religious revivalism can be viewed (at a collective level) as a change from non-belief or indifference to religion to acceptance of religious devotion. At the individual level, conversion can be seen as "a strategy for social adaptation that a person chooses, based on the conditions of his/her social/biographical situation as part of the biographical project" (Ipatova, 2006, p. 11). But what are the trajectories of individual conversions: sudden, gradual, or temporary? The very term "conversion" does not answer this question (Pelkmans, 2010, p. 25). The exploration of autobiographical narratives will shed more light in this respect.

Narratives and the narrative patterns of religious conversion

Since the 1980s, it has been widely accepted that narratives are a powerful means of forming individual identity and self-perception (Ricoeur, 1992). Known in Protestant environments as "testimonies", such narratives are part of the conversion itself and are a central element of the ritual life of Pentecostal parishes (Coleman, 2000, pp. 117–142; Stromberg, 2008, p. 3; Rambo and Farhadian, 2014, p. 8).

In contrast, the Russian narratives of conversion to Orthodox Christianity that I analyze here do not have clearly outlined ritual functions. Autobiographical narratives are derived in the context of fieldwork, tailored to the perceived audience and "the story that emerges is co-created in the socially contingent event of an interview" (Ammerman and Williams, 2012, p. 121). In this sense, the recorded oral texts are the result of unique communicative situations that could not be repeated in the same way, even with the same interviewer and the same narrator. Alternating the monologue with the dialogical form of the autobiographical interview, both the overall life story and the smaller narratives, whether or not connected to the overall thread of the narrative, are defined as an autobiographical narrative. The religious experience has been embedded in the plot of the narrative. This is achieved through a preliminary conversation with the interlocutors[4] who are encouraged to tell about themselves without omitting the story of their commitment to Orthodox religious life.

The analysis of autobiographical narratives inevitably faces the question of their credibility. That is, to what extent do they actually reflect social reality? "*Does Jim tell the truth?*" asks Peter Stromberg (2008, p. 2), like other authors. Stromberg does not question the integrity of narrators but discusses the question of the relationship between language and religious experience. Assuming that the narrator constructs his own identity through the autobiographical narrative, we also recognize the subjectivity of the narrative. Comparison of individual autobiographical texts, however, reveals certain (repetitive) patterns or regularities in stories, and then subjectivity ceases to be a problem of credibility.

In this chapter, I look at contemporary conversion to Orthodoxy in Russia by analyzing the sample of 32 autobiographical narratives. Only one of the interlocutors firmly declares herself as an atheist. Twenty-one out of the remaining 31 narratives contain a story about personal conversion, and it often occupies a central place in them. Another ten of the texts are not about a change in religious affiliation. Instead, they rather present the stages of a personal religious socialization with no dramatic dimensions. Most of these are the accounts of people from families with a strong religious tradition. The narratives from such individuals are less clearly definable as narratives of conversion because they do not present a change or crossing of a border. They rather outline personal religious biographies that deserve a separate analysis. Due to this reason, they are not explored in this chapter. The rest of the 21 stories show three main conversion trajectories: a sudden conversion following "the model of St. Paul"; conversion as physical pain; and conversion as "moral torment".

Sudden conversion: "The model of St. Paul"

The interview with Ostap Kirillovič, remarkable in various respects, was held in a place where an intimate conversation about personal religious devotion could be least expected: in the open city space in the ideal center of Kaluga, on a bench in the garden in front of the Theater Square, in the immediate vicinity of the large urban fountain. As I mentioned in the Introduction, the tape recorder caught the murmur of the fountain-, and the voices of many passersby.

I contacted Ostap Kirillovič, then 50, on the advice and advocacy of one of my main interlocutors. Like Ostap Kirillovič – the person who referred me to him was closely related to the local clerical elite. This, apparently, was not enough to establish confidence; the meeting was delayed for a long time and the negotiation for it lasted almost a month. During the telephone conversation in which Ostap Kirillovič agreed to meet, I heard clearly Orthodox chants in the background of the conversation. Extremely embarrassed by the thought that I had disturbed him during a church service, I apologized. It turned out, however, that he was at work. It was just that he listened to church singing while he was working! For some reason, he did not accept meeting either at his workplace or in other nearby places (such as the Belinski Library) and offered the Theater Square as a meeting place.

I recreate these details from the fieldwork to give an insight into the amazing personality of Ostap Kirillovič and the extent of his immersion in Orthodoxy and its history and culture. The text of the interview, which had to be autobiographical, spoke eloquently in that direction. The interlocutor mentioned the facts of his personal story in a very laconic way. As a compensation, the whole story was a series of stories of martyrdom in the name of faith and of miracles related to the interlocutor's activity as a member of the Kaluga Diocese Canonization Commission.[5] In the context of this, it is not surprising that the account of his transformation follows the emblematic model of the conversion of St. Paul: from a hardline atheist to a passionate follower of Orthodoxy, a church activist, and a religious entrepreneur. I quote verbatim:

> *I'm 50 years old, I was born into the family of an engineer, my mother is a medical doctor. I was born in an atheistic family. And I stayed for a long time* [in the condition of an atheist] . . . *well. I received higher education, well, I graduated from Donetsk University – also being atheistic. After the university, I graduated from a more specialized one – such were the years – the University of Marxism-Leninism at the Department of Atheism and Religion.* (Question: In Kaluga or elsewhere?) *In Kaluga.*
>
> *And then, so to say, with God's help, by His great mercy, He, so to speak, directed my mind to the right side, overturned me, upside down – put me on my feet. Here is my consciousness and my mind . . . it may take a long time to tell how this happened. But I think that I am a little chosen, everything has happened according to God's grace.* (Question: Can you tell a little bit more about how this happened?)
>
> *Well, if only briefly. My wife intended to baptize the children, my two children. I, then, resisted. But then, in order not to be . . . so to speak, not to be ignorant, unfamiliar, what is going to take place or not . . . I did not go to be baptized, and I myself decided to read the Gospel entirely to find out what it was, why I should be baptized. And when I finished the last line of the Revelation of John the Theologian: there all these letters, I read everything. Then I had a . . . moment, unmistakably everything turned upside down, instantly. It was such an indescribable state – and bliss, and I suddenly changed my worldview, the worldly understanding. Suddenly everything changed, and I firmly decided myself – I was not baptized – to be baptized. I went myself, I got baptized – I pushed myself.*
>
> *Then, little by little, with God's help, I began going* [to church] *and getting deeper and deeper. Then the Lord brought me here: there is a training here in the Kaluga Seminary, it is called the Theological School. I started going. We were the first class; I finished it with God's help. I began to deal with the martyrs during the training, at the blessing of Bishop Georgii, I was dealing with the martyr Aleksii.*
>
> *I was baptized in 1996, I started going to the* [Theological] *school in 2001.*[6]

The similarities with the paradigmatic transformation of evangelical Saul into St. Paul the Apostle cannot fail to be noticed. Like Saul, the persecutor of the first Christians, Ostap Kirillovič, who graduated in scientific atheism, was hostile to the rise of Orthodoxy that infiltrated his own family in the mid-1990s. Again, like St. Paul the Apostle, Ostap Kirillovič experienced a moment of spiritual revelation and radical transformation. This indisputable culmination of the narrative is described in both intellectual and emotional-ecstatic terms: the way to the turning point is intellectual, by reading the Gospel. This "learning of the truth", however, unleashes an instant, lightning reaction to euphoria ("*indescribable state – and bliss*") simultaneously with the radical spiritual transformation ("*everything turned upside down, instantly,*" "*suddenly my worldview changed*"). Religious language penetrates this narrative by repeatedly mentioning *God's Will, Help, Grace, Great Mercy*, and also an idea of being chosen: "*But I think that I am a little chosen*". The analogy with St. Paul's transformation is not just a narrative reflection of the evangelical episode. The incorporation of the religious language, the series of episodes that fill the whole narrative and are devoted to particular neo-martyrs (or candidates for new martyrs), speaks of the overall influence of hagiographic imagery, moral imagination and "canonical language" (Stromberg, 2008, p. 9) on the narrative. In other words, the story recreates both personal experience and certain cultural conventions.

Along with this, the interlocutor controls his story well. The written transcription of the verbal narrative that I quoted earlier cannot give an idea of this control. The intonation and the breaks in the oral narrative (which transcription does not capture) express the narrator's effort not to succumb to the temptation to enter into detail (the phrase "*it may take a long time to tell*" and the attempt to "close down" the episode by invoking the "*grace of God*"). All this shows that this story has been narrated repeatedly, though not in a ritual context.

Ostap Kirillovič's narrative confirms the relevance of one of the few attempts to establish a model of Russian religious biographies. The main points of reference in these are the moments of conversion, baptism, and *vocerkovlenie* or, at least one of them. Conversion is related to changing the worldview, baptism – to changing of identity. "If conversion and baptism are separated into narratives as chronological points, as specific events of life, then '*vocerkovlenie*' will be described as a process" (Tupahina, 2012, pp. 191–192).

These are actually three stages of conversion. It can be presented narratively as a lightning event, as in the aforementioned story, however, the overall trajectory of *vocerkovlenie* is a continuous process that unfolds to the incorporation of the set of Orthodox beliefs and practices. From the change and baptism to the complete enchurchment [*vocerkovlenie*] of Ostap Kirilovic, years passed: from 1996 to 2001 (when he graduated from theological school) or even until 2003 (when he joined the work of various diocesan committees and initiatives).

The narrative is also indicative of the socio-historical context of conversion. The radical personal transformation of Ostap Kirillovich was triggered under the influence of external forces. His wife's initiative to baptize their two children (a ritual which normally requires that the parents have been baptized) dates to 1996 when the Orthodox revival in Russia was gaining momentum. In the interviews, but also in the scholarly literature, the initial elemental and massive religious enthusiasm, with which thousands of people filled the churches in the early 1990s, has been repeatedly mentioned. Most of the buildings of Orthodox temples in Kaluga which had survived, for example, were returned to the Russian Orthodox Church around 1994. At the same time, the construction of new temples began.[7] Then the mass wave (unleashed at the end of the 1980s) continued to involve people in sacraments banned during the Soviet era, and baptism was the first one.[8] In other words, although conversion is individual, there are external, social impulses to it: the liberalization of religious life after 1988 (an opportunity to get acquainted with the text of the Gospel), the mass implementation of ecclesiastical sacraments, and the gradual restoration of the institutional life of the Russian Orthodox Church. Particularly, collective conversion – the transition of large layers of Russian society from non-belief or indifference to religion to (different degrees of) religiosity – is a context and an external stimulus for personal conversion.

Conversion, sin, redemption, and moral torment

Sensitivity to the subject of sin is present, to some extent, in a significant number of the interviews. For some of the interlocutors, however, this is a central moral concept, around which they not only construct their biographical narratives but also orient their overall behavior in the present. These narratives link the theme of sin to the theme of suffering: moral and physical.

Conversion as physical pain

The link between conversion and suffering is characteristic of the second main narrative strategy to present conversion. This strategy is presented in two main varieties. In the first variant, conversion, or at least its initial phase, is described as a memorable physical challenge in terms of pain and acute physical suffering. The second variant emphasizes the connection between sin, redemption, and moral suffering. The latter condition is also described in bodily, physical terms, in the form of severe suffering and pain. I will examine these two varieties in turn.

One of the narratives is central to understanding the relationship between physical suffering, conversion, and the path to good. Larissa Makarovna tells of the culmination of her conversion, of her state of neophyte, when she turns from a baptized Christian into a regular worshipper. I quote in full this episode of biographical narrative because of the unusually convincing and detailed description of the painful bodily experience and the physical dimensions of conversion:

> *And here too, I had a very strong temptation . . . I will not say exactly what, what a strong temptation that I could fall into sin. And knowing that it was a great sin, I was afraid and asked my acquaintance – I was not so close* [to her], *I did not go as often to the temple . . .*
>
> *When I started going to the temple, I could not stand the full liturgy in the temple. I always went out. I cannot . . . I gasped. I felt sick. I was nauseous. I wanted to do this: just go out under any pretext, but just go outside. I knew that this should not be done, and I did my best not to.*
>
> *And once, I promised myself that I would not go out now. It was the evening service. And I said, "No, I will not go out. I will not go out!" But I felt very sick, and then I was going to fall and then, as if mechanically, I grabbed the woman in front of me by the shoulder, I touched her while I was falling. . . . She looked around, put me beside the wall, and said, "Say 'Let God Arise!'"*
>
> *And I cannot lift my hand to cross myself. I had such a weakness. And I could not, I could not even speak.*

She hurried, took some holy water. She raised my hand, made the sign of the cross with my own hand, and said [the prayer] *"Let God Arise". She gave me that drink of water, and I sprinkled my face with holy water from the same cup. And here at this point, I felt something falling down from the root of my hair. But I could not breathe, I gasped. I could not breathe deeply. I tried to exhale, but I could not inhale either. And I felt my face was getting blue, because I could not breathe. And I felt that something like that was coming out of me: here I felt how something was falling down from the forehead, lower – down my nose, my mouth, my neck – and when it got lower than my heart, I immediately breathed.*

And I still felt it had not come out yet, here was another thing below, here . . . I took deep breath, exhaled, and when I exhaled, it came out of me. I felt it went out straight through my legs, here, it came out through my heels. And I exhaled again, and I felt very light! And I did not seem to be sick. I felt such a weight. I felt terrible. And here it was so good that I even started smiling.

And I said "thank you" to this woman, and that's when my temptation . . . I was coming back – it came up, I wanted to be friends with her, with this woman. I came to her and said, "Help me! Pray for me! I'm afraid I'll be tempted!"

She said, "Read the Akathistos of the Mother of God from Kaluga".

And I began to read [the Akathistos] *for 40 days. And I was saying this Akathistos, and so it came, so God's Mother helped me, and it all passed. And my soul was fine, and everything was resolved as if nothing had ever happened. This is how God's Mother has helped me a few times.*

And now whenever I feel bad, I always turn to and read the Akathistos of God's Mother from Kaluga. So, she listens to me and helps me! It happens when you turn to her. There were several, many times, when I was reading the Akathistos and everything was being solved – as I had been praying for, so it happened. Well, this is the case I had, and here I am even telling about it so that everyone should know that God's Mother from Kaluga is such.

Question: "*Did all this happen in Kaluga?*"

Yes, it did happen here. I started going to the temple in Kaluga.[9]

This narrative cannot be understood without an analysis of the meanings implied in the context.

The Orthodox prayer "*Da voskresnet Bog*!" [Let God Arise] is, along with its other meanings, aimed at evicting the devil and demons.[10] It was precisely in this prayer that supernatural help was sought because of the idea that when neophytes tried to join the church, they were attacked by the devil who wanted to separate them from God.

This perceived "attack" is experienced by a person as physical suffering and pain that impedes participation in liturgical life. The latter idea is well known and shared both among *cerkovnye liudi* and among clergy. Thus, when I apologized for my suffering and my finding it very hard to withstand the lengths of the three and one-half hours of liturgies, I heard from one of the priests (later also from some believers) that I was attacked by the devil because I was trying to do a good deed.[11] Or, as in the following narrative, in which a priest explains that the physical tests, as bodily pains, suffered by neophytes, as well as by children, and even himself,[12] are the result of satanic interference:

> *How to teach children to participate in church services, to evict the demons that conquer the child? Some children cannot stand the service at all: they fidget, faint. They have to learn to endure. Here's a boy who always wanted to go out during the service to go to the toilet. Finally, his mother says, "Piss in the church!" – "Somehow I do not want to". The boy endured the urge and then calmed down. And I myself – in the summer, when it's very hot, I'm dying for some water during the service. But I force myself to wait till the end, and when the service is over – I'm no longer thirsty.*[13]

The similarities between this narrative and the similar episode of Larissa Makarovna's narrative cannot go unnoticed. "Satanic attacks" are one of the standard explanations offered in connection with the topic of physical and moral sufferings in the initial phase of conversion and religious socialization. Possibly, this view is based on the medieval theology literature, namely to the popular medieval reading *Lestvica* [*Ladder* of Divine Ascent], by St. Joann Letvičnik [John Climacus]: "In all deeds by which we try to please God, demons dig for us three pits" (Lestvica, 1862, pp. 26, 8). It is related to the more common belief, deep-rooted among the people of the *pricerkovnyi krug*, that places of Christian holiness, like churches, monasteries, and the people connected with them, attract the attacks of the "dark power" against the divine powers of light and good. As Arina Tarabukina (2000, 1) convincingly demonstrates, this is part of a more general feature of the "world view" that is typical of the people of *pricerkovnyi krug* (see also chapter 1). The eschatological expectations that have dominated this world view since the beginning of the twentieth century are related in particular to the belief in an asymmetric relationship between the powers of divine light and those of satanic darkness, in which the latter are gaining strength and territory. Because the *pricerkovnyi krug* preserved these beliefs during the Soviet period, the beliefs are reproduced today by those who join it:

> *There, you know, where it abounds with grace, there is always too much dark power. It wields; it does not linger. This, you know, when there is light, a lamp, and around it the shadow merges into darkness. This is a law that works a total hundred* [percent]. *Here's how, in Optina* [Hermitage], *you probably know that in* [nineteen] *ninety-three a Satanist killed three monks there. And, in principle, there periodically, there – whether a trudnik* [worker at a monastery] *or someone else –* [someone] *is killed. Because there, that's the place* [of light]. *Naturally, every devilry tries to settle there. It cannot go without it. But what to be afraid of? If you can't stand the heat, get out of the kitchen.*[14]

The narrative expresses certain beliefs showing its function as an explanatory matrix in which real life events are introduced. The murder in the Optina Hermitage of three monks, which was committed during Easter 1993, is such an event. The late monks were canonized in 2000, and books and numerous publications have been devoted to their doom.[15] The same narrative approach is revealed in a prominent dialogue (quoted by Boris Knorre) between a laywoman (who complains of negative changes in her own character as a result of her participation in the church life) and the priest:

> While you were a non-believer, the devil did not worry about you. You were totally in his nails; he knew that you could never hide from him and allowed you to live and develop naturally. And now he started to worry – and he tempts you, trying to get you out of the way of salvation. Consider this as a trial; pray and be patient.
>
> (Knorre, 2011, pp. 328–329)

The quintessence of the same idea was expressed by a statement I already quoted in chapter 1: "*If laymen are followed by a horned one, then there will be ten horned ones after the monks: when a person strives for spiritual perfection, the enemy attacks him more*".

In Larissa Makarovna's narrative, her spiritual and physical experience at the same time is associated with something else. There is a second reason for her vulnerability as a neophyte: her temptation to commit a sin. The links between cause and effect that explain the demonic presence are not explicitly named, they are implicated in the context and the intersubjective knowledge shared among believers. The latter means in practice that, with the help of ethical ideas shared by believers about the intrigue of demonic power against the good (i.e. ideas of Christian piety), Larissa Makarovna was cognitively prepared for her suffering. When she experienced it, she already had an imaginative, cognitive, and narrative matrix with which it was conceptualized. Although it sounds paradoxical, in this way the unknown and the frightening are transformed into something familiar so that she can deal with them. With the help of "moral imagination", the narrator gives meaning to painful bodily experiences. The "moral imagination" also gives her the narrative means to construct the experience itself (for example the systematic way in which she describes the emergence of the "demon" from her body in the top-down direction: from the roots of the hair to the heels).

This story also shows how the "ethically saturated" world (Keane, 2014, p. 318) of the regular worshippers is governed by the rules of a specific semiotic ideology, where things and events are signs of an inner, second plan of action beyond the external events. These "semiotic phenomena make it possible for people to take their experiences of things and events as evidence of a hidden agent with intentions . . . constructed in ethical terms" (Keane, 2014, pp. 318, 314). In the narrative, the holy water, the sign of the cross, and prayer play the role of ethical affordances. She can expect her listener to understand them as ("properties of something in light of what those properties offer to someone who perceives them" – Gibson,

1977, after Keane, 2014, p. 315) agents of the divine power of good and sacred against total evil.

The biographical narrative of Larissa Makarovna expresses in extreme form the moral conviction that sustainability, patient tolerance of physical pain, and prayer are embodied means to counteract the effects of the demonic "hidden agent with intent". The same idea and the same "ethical affordances" with clear physical dimensions, recommended as a strategy to deal with suffering, can also be found in the quotes from the two priests.

It is the linking unit with another variant of the narrative strategy representing the conversion in the terms of pain and physical suffering. This variety is most clearly demonstrated in a master narrative, part of a long, multi-hour interview. I include a more extensive quote from it because it presents with remarkable openness details that interlocutors usually do not wish to share. I give the highlights of the story, but due to its length, I do not include the entire Russian text in original.

"Moral torment"

I was baptized in the Optina Hermitage [in 1991]. *Now they don't do baptisms there. And I just found myself among those lucky ones who went to the Optina Hermitage and were baptized. In this temple, where the relics of [St.] Ambrose are. It's just a miracle of miracles. Even then, they did not baptize by full immersion, the temples were still without baptisteries, without these fonts. And I was fully immersed! And the Father showed so much attention to me. . . . He paid so much attention to me, supplying me with books, everything . . . .*

I saw the sky completely different. But as far as I was a human being who was uneducated spiritually, I thought everything spiritual was from God. And I fell into a very clever man's clutches. He is educated, clever, charming, but he is an occultist!

And for three years I was under the charm of this occult influence. . . . He all too, all the time [he used to say]*: "We are at the crossroads of all religions, where Christianity is also recognized".*

Generally, we were dealing with Agni-Yoga and transpersonal meditation. Generally, there were so many things there. Well.

And when he found out that there was a grandmother in my family who was a sorceress. [He said], *"Listen, you should give lectures on occult medicine!"*

And I said, "Well I do not know how!"

"And to you" – he says, "the dark power there, everything will reveal to you!"

"How the dark power? How? No, that's not what I'm doing! The dark power – it is not ours".

Here, I brought to a logical conclusion everything that he read to us. I went to the woods. According to tradition, I spent one night in the woods – I did all this. Well. And one more interesting thing: I was in the woods not far from the Optina Hermitage, in the woods. That is, I did all this in good faith. I stayed there alone, honestly – no one accompanied me. Out of the jet-black darkness, in the thicket of the forest, there are wolves howling and foxes there. There are beasts there. The Father says, "Devils live there in great numbers, here in the woods, and they start screaming at night".

I heard everything. Because I went too far. . . . And how I did not get into that pit there, how I did not step into a wolf trap, that's amazing.

I used to follow this D. for three years. He was a talented man. Well. He took me to an international theosophical seminar. I met there such people – you can go mad! All this happened, it was horrible!

And, in general, I visited Holotropic Breathwork therapy . . . this is a psychotechnique, with the help of special exercises a man acquires occult abilities. Some superpowers. I started to paint there. They painted in a mandala circle. There was an exhibition of these paintings, [the people] *came to watch me. And I had only one passion: to paint, to paint, to paint! I have never been gifted with such talents in my life. Never. I was a musician, but I was not an artist. Here I have some interesting images, everything.*

Now, it is not easy to remind myself of all this, but I'm just telling you what difficulties the intelligentsia have before they come to God. In our country, many people have gone through these Eastern cults, because this sort of thing is like an intermediate stage. This is exotic, but it is not so strict. Buddhism, for example, there is no figure of the Creator. And that's why many people were stuck in this. Buddhism. Well. And so far, many people have been attracted to this. But some, as they tried from this rotten thing [gnil], *they went further. They realized that they were not sitting in the Divine light here, but in a pitiful rottenness.*

It was scary. I watched the sky, the stars. D. had told me: "If you're afraid, watch the stars". And suddenly – as if I can see the crucified Christ among the trees – I knew I was a Christian, that I should not be in these places. . . .

But this year, fortunately, it happened that after the theosophical seminar I wanted to cleanse my soul. . . . And I just rushed to [the priest]. *Something called me.*

And I had some terrible problems, all this cannot go unpunished ['darom ne prohodit']. *The Demon* [bes] *so clung to me that they sent me to the The Trinity Lavra of St. Sergius for an exorcism prayer* [otčitka] *to expel the demons. Because I did not manage myself. Because it just managed to get hold of myself for these three years.*

Here. And I see there, during exorcist prayer [na otčitku], *in the John the Baptist* [Ioann Predteča] *Temple, the "elder" was cleansing a lot of possessed people* [besnovatye] *from all over the country. My God! What was going on there during the exclamation of prayers: some people were wheezing, others were hissing like snakes, and still others were quarreling with an invisible interlocutor, and others were howling like wolves – and here I am in this company! Just imagine!*

You have to go through this three times. Then you confess, receive Holy Communion, participate in the anointment [posoboruesh'sia].[16] *And then you will be released from this, from what is in you.*

Because it's a terrible thing. Holotropic breath therapy – this is the most terrible invasion of the demonic powers [vlaganie besovskih sil] *in the heart. Some say that whole sessions go to this holotrop; it is held for whole days and nights. . . . Such lustful passions* [bludnye strasti] *start, you know, such things. Well, all the horror is what I saw there! Then they need a nursing caregiver because a person starts to rave* [besnovat'sia], *drops into a state of altered consciousness, to unconsciously pee, to roll like a ball, a total horror.*

And it was not that simple to overpower it. It had to be forcibly expelled. But I traveled up there, everything, I found it difficult because there was no hotel, you were just sleeping on the floor in the temple.

Well, I had to redeem my sin. Then somehow, it became a bit easier for me. I got better.[17]

This narrative contains two plans of meaning. The first plan tracks the sequence of events and their biographical logic; it is entirely analytical. The second one is entirely conditioned by the context of the Orthodox understanding of sin. The latter concept is central to the meaning of narrative: it is about "travelling" from error and sin, through moral viewing and revelation, repentance, and redemption. The narrative is not just about continuous conversion but also about what some authors call an awkward conversion or a conversion career (Coleman, 2003, p. 17).[18] It passes in three stages: conversion to Orthodoxy by baptism; a second conversion to an esoteric religious doctrine of the New Age type; and reconversion to Orthodoxy, followed by a long, many-year process of redemption and moral cleansing. Sin is represented by two narrative strategies: directly, through the narrative of delusions and transgression of moral boundaries ("*because I have gone too far*"); and second, through the contrasting motives of the signs of God's mercy and grace that the protagonist has not understood and ignored.

Sin and the defilement of the soul are represented by the extreme negativism against the enthusiasm of "occult" (including the techniques of holotropic therapy). The complete immersion in this doctrine and practice is presented, firstly, analytically: as the collective enthusiasm of the intelligentsia for Eastern teachings and the "intermediate stage" of a collective quest for spirituality after atheism. The second narrative strategy uses the language of Orthodox demonology: occult practices are perceived as the bodily possession of the protagonist by the devils ("*the most terrible demonic invasion of the heart*"). In order to intensify the negative perception of engaging in "occult" practices, the latter is also described in terms of bodily impurity and disease state ("*lustful passions*", *uncontrolled urination)* and temporary insanity *("man begins to rave*", "*to roll like a ball*"*)*. Moral imagination serves here with the repertoire of Christian imagery. The "ethically saturated" world built in the narrative is represented by the semiotic ideology. This is expressed in the second logical plan of the narrative, which reveals the presence of the "hidden agent" – the divine presence as a hidden motor of action (Keane, 2014, pp. 318, 314).

The initial episode of the narrative should be understood in this sense, which testifies to the "hidden agent" – God's grace – through the privileged place and unusual baptism. It occurs in a sacred topos with special significance for Russian Orthodoxy: in Optina Hermitage, and even in the temple where the relics of an emblematic saint rest. Baptism involves a full immersion of the body, which had not been practiced elsewhere yet, and with particular attention given by the priest.

The undisputed climax of the story is the moment of enlightenment: the vision of the crucified Christ in the night forest, echoed by the wild beasts' wailing. This image is relativized by the expression "as if" ("*As if I can see the crucified Christ*"). Despite the narrative strategy of relativization, here is the point of twist and moral rift. Here comes awareness of the Christian identity and the depth of the perception of sin. This is where the second conversion of N.N. begins: the start of a multi-year integration into an active Orthodox life – *vocerkovlenie*.

It should be noted too that the story bears a striking coincidence with the classical Protestant narrative of Sampson Stanforth, recorded in 1748. As one scholar pointed out, it was [Stanforth's] midnight vision of the crucified Christ that he selected when he wrote his autobiography years later, and he emplotted this account to Aristotle's narrative syntax of beginning, middle, and the end. This vision was the turning point in his story that moved from his beginning in irreligion to his end as a servant of God (Hindmarsch, 2014, p. 346).

For all of its specificities, the Orthodox moral imagination follows some of the same patterns that determine Western Christianity too. Texts from the Gospel, as well as other classical and early modern texts, have crucial significance for the imaginative tradition of the Christian world (Hindmarsch, 2014, p. 346).

This prolonged process also involves radical personal transformation. This narrative tells about the gradual transformation of N.N. into the religious activist she was at the time I interviewed her. By 2007, her activities were semi-professional within the Church: teaching in Sunday schools and in the Theological School; working as an Orthodox guide; singing in church choirs. At the same time, her efforts towards the redemption of sin do not end with all this: they continue. Despite the remorse and the experiences of exorcism, (which she repeated, even during my stay in Kaluga), the perception of sin does not leave N.N. In her narrative, she fully motivates her desire to enter a convent in search of a religious salvation ("*How to find salvation*?" [A kak spastis'?], she asks rhetorically). Publications in the religious press in Kaluga testify that in 2014 N.N. entered a convent as a neophyte.

Her narrative presents both types of conversion: the pattern of the sudden and lightning event (according to St. Paul's model with the night vision), which unlocks moral rift and a cognitive change; but also the model of the continuous process of complete personal transformation, moral and behavioral, passing through different stages. It also shows connections between conversion and exorcism that Tünde Komáromi draws attention to, but it does not confirm the thesis that conversion may be unlocked by exorcism (Komáromi, 2017, p. 47). The latter is presented here as one of the phases of the continuous process of personal conversion. The contradictory nature of the exorcism practices, perceived with disapproval by part of the Orthodox clergy, is worth noting (Mitrokhin, 2004).

Conversion as a "moral torment", but also as an acute physical suffering, is a unifying feature of some of the narratives, among which is the one previously presented. The suffering expressed in them is due to the retrospective assessment of the past life, through the prism of Orthodox concepts of sin, adopted and internalized during and through conversion. In other words, conversion also contains a moment of "learning", when the criteria of today's believer are applied to the past life as a non-believer. From this rethinking and reassessment of past life experience, the "moral torment", which has clear physical aspects, is unlocked. The ignorance of the moral norms of Orthodoxy during a life without faith, or with indifference to it, is understood as motivating past life choices that are now perceived with the help of an Orthodox moral imagination as sins. In N.N.'s narrative, ignorance is said to have motivated her engagement with Eastern and occult religious practices. In three other narratives, interlocutors mentioned former marriages to Muslims as a great transgression. In fact, in two of these three narratives, the major sin is not even a personal one: it is the interlocuter's parents who contracted the sinful marriage between a Christian woman and a Muslim man. According to their current perceptions, the "new" believers consider their transgressions to have been punished with hard suffering (severe illnesses and related misfortunes) but not yet redeemed despite their repentance and zealous Orthodox dedication. In another interview, the narrator presents as a sin her adoption of a child. The adoption was motivated by her infertility, itself caused by illness, which she should have understood as a sign of God's will that she should have no children. Instead, by pursuing adoption, she (unconsciously) disobeyed God's will.[19]

In all cases, the assessment of the sinful past is a source of moral sufferings with clear physical dimensions. The extremes of this suffering are represented as a state of demonic possession, as in N.N.'s narrative. The question, "How to find salvation?" thus attains a dramatic dimension when former sins are regarded as unredeemed. Then too, the search for religious salvation becomes a major motive for integrating one's own everyday life into the requirements of Orthodox canons.

Moral sensitivity and suffering, in some cases, also manifests against collective misdemeanors and guilt, such as the indifference to faith among their relatives or the appearance of the consequences of Soviet atheism:

> *I was in the village where our grandfather lived. And the temple in which he had served was destroyed now completely. Even when I was a little girl, the temple was without a cross, no bells, but it was still standing. And the grain was kept there. And now there is no temple. Now in this place, on the base of* [the temple] *they have built a large shop. . . . Not only this, but the store is also deserted. When I saw all of this, it was just like a knife stubbed into the heart. . . . How we all, including myself, how we're all guilty of letting that happen.*[20]

The narrator "extends" her consciousness of guilt and moral responsibility not only to her personal negligence and transgressions, but also to collective actions and to events over which she has no control. The ruin she describes is located in a place she has not visited for 30 years.

But to what extent is moral suffering a spontaneous manifestation and how much can it be considered a cultural convention? "Russians have been said to have 'need to suffer', and Russia has been called a country of suffering", remarks Pesmen (2000, p. 40). The notion and experience of suffering have been discussed extensively[21] and this tradition has been often linked with Dostoevsky and his influence on popular imaginary.

The source of Dostoevsky's own moral beliefs, however, was Russian Orthodoxy. They were formed, moreover, in the midst of the ascetic Russian monasticism that was thriving in the nineteenth century. It is enough just to examine the moral teachings of the canonized emblematic spiritual elders [*starcy*] of Optina Hermitage Monastery to have no doubt about the direction of influences between literature and the Church.[22] In other words, the inherited peculiarities of Russian Orthodoxy are at the root of the Russian "cultural" moral environment, in which suffering can be an anticipated response to the perception of one's own moral imperfection.

Despite the existence of cultural conventions (even formalized to some extent – Ries, 1997, pp. 83–125), the genuine character of moral suffering is beyond doubt. A detail of the fieldwork provides a key to understanding these dramatic stories of a painful personal experience. Some of the interlocutors explicitly define the autobiographical interview as an informal means of confession. Such advice is given by some priests: "Confess to one another" [*Ispoveduytes' drug drugu*].[23] The difference between the communicative situation of confession in its usual ritual context and the autobiographical interview does not require long explanations. The emotional tenors within the interviews, as well as the prayers that preceded them (sometimes the performance of religious songs as well), are evidence that some of my interlocutors (but not all) viewed the elicitation of these narratives as more than just a simple conversation or an interview.

The autobiographical narrative, however, when deliberately articulated with confessional openness and sincerity, brought an unintended result. This is the complicity of the researcher in the "pain of the other" (Stevenson, 2009, p. 59). Simply put, the interviewing elicited empathy from me. Without exaggerating the importance of the affective aspect of the fieldwork, it is important to make this note. Perhaps in another era, I would not need to make it, but since the 1990s anthropology has been "changing its relation to those it studied from one of analytic distance and critical comparison focused on difference to one of empathic connection and moral witnessing based on human unity" (Robbins, 2013, p. 453). Relatedly, sustained reflection on my personal emotional experience in the field helps to understand how the suffering expressed in autobiographical narratives is as much based on cultural conventions as it is a spontaneous expression of moral crisis. Radical personal transformation is patterned, however acutely felt.

The understanding of "moral torment" proposed by Joel Robbins (2004, 2013) in a Protestant environment is an appropriate definition of the state of ethical reasoning contained in the narratives I am discussing in this section of the third chapter. I apply this concept in a Russian context with a clear awareness of the obvious differences between the Urapmin from a remote Pacific region and Russian Orthodox believers. However, the comparison is valid within certain limits: in both cases, "moral torment" is a reaction to personal transformations in the context of conversion; in both cases high levels of moral sensitivity are found which determine the status of "moral torment".

Moral sensitivity is expressed in both cases through the constant self-observation of believers. They give high levels of attention and strong emotional responses to their actions and (perceived) transgressions. Examples of this sensitivity among contemporary Russian Orthodox believers expressed through ethical reasoning have also been presented in chapter 2; placing the focus on narrative analysis in chapter 3 continues and deepens these observations.

The comparison also shows that Robbins' interlocutors share similar millenaristic expectations for the end of the world, defining the worldview of the most devoted Russian believers in the *pricerkovnyi krug* since the beginning of the twentieth century. In the context of the tense eschatological expectation, the fears of salvation of the soul, related to self-judgment of sinfulness, become more understandable. Robbins presents convincing arguments about this:

> Achieving salvation in what they understood to be Christian terms became their primary individual and collective project. Another fundamental feature of Urapmin Christianity is the way it defines salvation as almost wholly dependent on moral self-regulation. People need to avoid sin as much as possible and to atone through confession and ritual cleansing for sins they do commit. The Christian moral code the Urapmin have adopted is a difficult one that not only forbids acts such as physical violence, theft, and adultery, but also interdicts all intense desires and strong emotions such as anger, which is never morally justified in any circumstances, and jealousy. Given this moral emphasis on emotional regulation, it is fitting that most Urapmin constantly monitor their hearts – the seat of all thought and feeling – and keep careful track of all of their moral breaches. This constant self-monitoring is supported by a final key feature of Urapmin Christianity: its strong conviction that Jesus could return at any moment, and that people therefore have always to be morally ready for his arrival.
>
> (Robbins, 2013, pp. 451–452)

Being anxious about the anger he felt at his own children, one of Robbins' protagonists spent the night in prayers – and not in his home, but in the church. "Given these lapses into anger and violence, he doubted he had much chance of being saved when Jesus returned, and this would mean separation from his family for eternity" (Robbins, 2013, p. 452).

It is a strong temptation to compare this example with the moral watchfulness of some of my interlocutors and their anxiety about the salvation of their own souls. One of the storytellers is convinced that at night the Lord hears her prayers (spoken out loud) better, and she wakes up at night to pray in the corridor of her little home for forgiveness of her sins and of her relatives' sins as well. She had to endure the reproach of her husband, who considered her becoming a "fanatic" ['*Ty stala fanatkoi*!'].[24]

How to find salvation? Most of my interlocutors ask this question feeling alarmed. The difference between the latter and Robbins' protagonists relates mainly to the time scope in which some and the others have their reflections on sin, redemption, and salvation. It is characteristic of some Russian Orthodox believers that their concerns about personal religious salvation are largely retrospective. In other words, "moral torment" is related to past sins committed in ignorance of Orthodox canons and morals and to the radically different way in which one's own actions are assessed as a result of the radical personal change that occurred after the conversion. The new religious "self" finds it difficult to reconcile with its former state, judged to be deeply sinful.

In contrast, Ostap Kirillovič's narrative does not imply remorse concerning his transgressions of the past (i.e. his own past engagement with "scientific atheism"): "*such were the years*" is his laconic comment legitimizing his choices of behavior. Moreover, this narrator considers himself as "slightly chosen" (by God). In this, his narrative is also reminiscent of the "testimonies" in Protestant environments stressing the triumphant victory of the light of conversion over the darkness before it. It seems, therefore, that rather (perceived) intimate personal transgressions trigger the condition of "moral torment", unlike consciousness about the past political errors or delusions.

The comparison here between the Pacific Protestant believers and Russian Orthodox believers, based mostly on the notion of "moral torment", is not due to extravagance or premature conclusions. My intention is to show, through these examples, that there are more similarities between the different strands of Christianity than researchers usually mark or recognize.[25] I will return to this issue later.

Moral lazarets, semiotic ideology, and continuous conversion

It is not surprising that conversion is very often achieved through experiencing a life crisis. As I noted earlier in this chapter, researchers have found a more general connection between social and economic instability in the modern world, on the one hand, and the widespread distribution of conversion in its various forms, on the other. Interviews testify to severe social and life collisions that some of the interlocutors experienced in the 1990s: the loss of close people or severe incurable illness, the loss of housing or any source of income due to long-term unemployment, disintegration of family and kinship relationships, and sometimes, all of these together. For these people, who lost their orientation, including cognitive, in the rapidly changing postsocialist world in the 1990s, faith turned out to be a factor in the quest for stability and, last but not least, for building a new moral identity. Faith offers a cognitive model through which a perceived stability and an opportunity to discover patterns beyond the life chaos can be brought into the personal worldview. However, representing conversion as a response to a life crisis is not the basis of a specific model or its variety but rather a culmination in stories that follow otherwise different narrative patterns.

In the outlined context, it is appropriate to use the phrase "moral lazarets", to characterize the postsocialist rise of religiosity in different regions of the world (Hann, 2010, pp. 1–21). Like a lazaret meant to hold and treat people with contagious diseases, religion offers care and comfort for souls suffering from moral afflictions. As a metaphor, "moral lazaret" is open to a wide range of empirical phenomena. Moreover, the "moral lazaret" expresses the idea of trauma and the search for a new morality after it in a way that sometimes finds direct matches (at an emic level) in autobiographical narratives:

"*I was sick of sin and I did not know the way out. . . . The enemy overpowered me*", says Andrej, a typical representative of the *pricerkovnyj krug*, when he talks about the period of his life that has passed under the sign of drug addiction.[26] Representing addiction as a disease caused by sin and, ultimately, by Satan, is a narrative strategy by which our own transgressions are objectified. In other words, the Orthodox language provides the narrator with a linguistic arsenal by which personal responsibility is separated from the narrator's personality and transferred to external forces: the actions of the perceived demon agent. This narrative strategy is also found in other stories. However, at higher levels of moral sensitivity, as presented earlier in this chapter, the reference to Orthodox demonology is coupled with the painful recognition of personal responsibility for one's own mistakes.

Andrej presents the complete merging of his life with Orthodox canons as healing, and the healing unlocks a radical personal and moral transformation. Turning to religion in this case turns out to be a "moral lazaret". Similarly, N.N., a protagonist in the master narrative, seeks healing in Orthodoxy: she "ran like blazes" to the priest when she understood the depth of her mistake. The transition from non-belief to faith can often be portrayed in narratives as passing through a "moral lazaret". Conversion, which occurs as a consecutive and regular engagement with Orthodox practices, can therefore be defined as an agency, as a form of active managing of one's own life.

An interesting detail sheds light on this issue. In some of the aforementioned narratives, the conversion is also described as the beginning of the narrators solving material difficulties: finding work, housing, or additional income. This understanding – that real agency begins with conversion – is, in turn, an integral part of the concept of religious revivalism. The possibility to attain agency through conversion should thus be considered an important element in the analytical framework for understanding the Orthodox resurgence in modern Russia (see chapter 1).

The narrative does not always present the conversion in connection with dramatic crises, according to my interlocutor Vadim Nikityč (41). Sometimes these are more trivial difficulties, but you cannot see a quick or easy way out "when you feel miserable":

> *I do not know how I turned to God, but the first, perhaps, such sensations, and the first conversation with God was probably in the army – it's always complicated, it's always hard. And the man's first experience when he feels really miserable is probably still in the barracks. . . . I even spoke not to God – I spoke to my dead ancestors.*[27]

The decision to baptize made after this episode led Vadim to accept immediately the Orthodox way of life. He began to fast and receive Holy Communion; he gave up smoking. Then, he gradually became an Orthodox activist. Conversion, as in the aforementioned cases, led to a radical change of personality. During his initial steps of integration into church life, one of the interlocutors re-evaluated his own perceived moral inferiority in contrast to the moral exemplarity of the believers: "*These are humans, and I am not*".[28] Another interview also mentions a similar motive of personal transformation while getting to know a community of believers that he perceived as a moral model.[29]

Another part of conversion narratives outlines the trajectory of external events of the believer's life and interprets these events as signs of God's guidance. They mark the narrator's path from non-belief to faith. In one of the interviews, this principle of "semiotic ideology" (in the terms of Keane) is explicitly stated:

> *I had, perhaps, many such moments when the Lord showed me. That I had to turn to him. But I did everything in my own way . . . I could not understand. That . . . that the Lord was calling me.*[30]

Some narratives are built as a chain of episodes, each of which is a sign of God's presence. The "hidden agent" is not named, but it makes itself felt through the outline of biographical events. The shared intersubjective knowledge of Orthodoxy and the moral imagination related to it make it possible for the listener to understand these narratives. Characteristic of the storytelling of this type is the accumulation of similar episodes and the gradation of the signs they contain. At the same time, narrators contrast their spiritual "blindness" and misunderstanding with the signs' transcendent presence. This strategy emphasizes the ignorance and darkness in which the protagonist resides, so that God's grace and glory stand out. The chain structure of the narrative, built up by the accumulation of similar episodes-signs, also achieves the retardation effect, which distances the narrative from its culmination, and thus emphasizes the effect of the latter. This is characteristic of some of the narratives that represent conversion as a lengthy process.[31]

The stories of miracles

Some of the stories of miracles that I recorded during the fieldwork can be seen as a variation of the last narrative model. I have included these narratives in the analysis of conversion because the perceived miracles are most often presented as part of the gradual cognitive process that unlocks or accompanies the conversions. Moreover, these stories are also important from the point of view of the reliability of the analysis: they also exist outside the context of interviewing. They are not extracted by the researcher but are part of the autonomous narrative repertoire of the studied Orthodox parishes.

I do not discuss the question of the "authenticity" of the miracles. At least, it is not important for my analysis. However, due to the controversial nature of the concept of a miracle, I must clarify that I adhere to the two senses in which it is used by my narrators. The first is more strictly religious: "Most theists . . . do conceive of the miraculous as an unusual, unexpected, awe-producing observable event due in part to the intentional activity of a benevolent God". This definition excludes the perceived actions of malicious supernatural beings because the miracle is a desirable event that the believers are grateful for (Basinger, 2011, pp. 43, 21–22, see also Basinger, 2018). Some events can be defined as miracles only when they are accepted and recognized as such, and the story of "divine interventions" is an essential aspect of their examples (Pelkmans, 2015, p. 9). Besides the narrowest and most important understanding in a religious context, there is a second, broader discursive use of the term miracle: then it is used more simply in the sense of an unexpected, unusual event from the realm of everyday life (such as an unanticipated job offer or discovery of lost heirloom) (Basinger, 2011, p. 19).

Both of the discursive varieties of the concept of miracles are presented in the narratives I study. I will show that the difference between them does not affect such perceptions of miracles. It refers mainly to the character of the patterns around which the narrative is structured: whether these are models inherited from historical Orthodoxy (hagiographic literature or religious folklore), or are the result of a religious interpretation of unexpected events that do not interfere with natural laws.

Miracles of everyday life

Stories about unusual but otherwise not inexplicable events are present in most of the interviews. They turn into stories of miracles by direct naming them as a "miracle" – as an expression of God's will, or through the intonation of the narrator, which emphasizes the second plan of the event presented. Certain narratives contain more examples than others. The most general narrative scheme contains the confrontation between the state of the life crisis and the unusual, unexpected way of its beneficial solution. To give a clearer idea of this model of religious narrative, I will present one of them.

Zinaida Makarovna builds her narrative of conversion as a chain of episodes, each of which represents a stage in her conversion and strengthens her belief. Some of them are stories of deliverance from a sure death: her sister recovered from a state of illness, and the narrator herself survived a severe illness. "*I had a surgery in Saratov. I was almost ten years old; I lay there for two years without leaving the hospital*".[32] Each subsequent episode strengthens the idea of a second hidden plan beyond the external events:

> *And even before I was baptized, how many cases there were that I did not know why, what was my purpose.*

But when I was still not baptized, I studied at the institute. Or maybe I was already baptized – I do not remember. During the vacation, I arrived at my grandmother's sister; the vacation was over, I had to go back. I said: "I'll be going".

But we were at my grandmother's cottage [na dache] *and my grandmother said: "You'd better not travel, we'll take you to the workers' bus tonight, free of charge".*

The workers' bus went from the city to our posëlok.[33] *And I did not go. I wanted to go, but I thought – not to offend them, as if obedience, the respect of the adults was very strong, and I stayed.*

This bus, which I had to take first, turned over and fell into the abyss. Fifty-four people died. This is how the Lord took this trouble away from me, incomprehensible in what way.[34]

In this well-organized narrative, with distinct introductory, central, and concluding parts, the word "miracle" is not mentioned. Instead, the Lord and His will are explicitly named, as well as the characteristic humility by which the narrator reflects on the reasons of God's mercy.

One of the episodes related to Zinaida Makarovna's mother is again associated with healing, thanks to the help of God, called upon through prayer. This episode of narrative marks a decisive stage in personal conversion: a baptized Christian, Zinaida becomes a zealous believer. The narrator explicitly defines it as the moment of complete faith. I present the abridged version of the text:

How did I turn to faith? Also, there when I was, we lived with mom. The most precious to me is Mom. It was through Mom He brought me to Himself. [In a domestic incident, her mother temporarily loses her memory and behaves like a "mentally ill person".]

She began shaking, what a shake, her teeth were chattering, throwing her in chills. It was then that my teapot boiled. I had some hot water. I poured some into the hot water bottle, made her some strong sweet tea. I put a blanket on her and tucked her in, I said, "Mom, it will all pass". I helped her to bed, and I went out. I helped my mom to bed in the living room, and there was a small icon in the kitchen – Mom always prayed. And I thought: what if Mom went mad – what would I do with her? I was all alone – no one else but me. And I fell on my knees and said, "Lord, if you exist, bring back Mom's memory. I will pray".

You will not believe it. A minute had not passed, Mom came to her senses, though ten minutes past, she was in such a state as if mentally ill. Only then, as I said so, she immediately came to her senses.

I have been praying ever since.[35]

The strategy to present events for which there is a rational explanation [i.e. domestic accident] as if they are the fruit of transcendental interference reaches its culmination in another biographical episode of the same narrative. The narrative is about an everyday event but at the same time a vital case.

In the next episode, Zinaida Makarovna faced bureaucratic obstacles and disrespect when she sought accommodation in a [state-owned] flat. The flat was vacant, but another person, a neighbor, had it registered as his legal address [*propiska*],[36] and Zinaida Makarovna could not get it. On her request for help, she received an explicit refusal from the head of the passport bureau.

> *At first, I was desperate. And then I thought, what if it should be? So be it, it is all God's will, nothing is done without the will of God. I calmed down, began to say prayers: "Lord, send me the meekness of David and his wisdom; the meekness of Solomon and his wisdom". And as I was saying this, the accountant went out and said: "You know, I felt sorry for you, let me help you".*
>
> *She went to the passports officer, then brought a report saying that I lived with my daughter so as to form a subsidy* [to get dwelling]. *She said: "[Do you know] where should you bring it?" But this is on 47, Lenin* [Boulevard], *it is far away. "You do not have to go anywhere, I'm there every day, I'll take it there tomorrow. You do not have to go; the subsidy will be finalized".*
>
> *Immediately, instantly.*
>
> *You will not believe how shocked I was. While I was relying on myself, I was not getting anything, they looked daggers at me. Only when I turned to Lord for help: he* [the neighbor] *must have been registered with me – that is the Lord's will; let it be as the Lord wants". Immediately everything was resolved. Then it turned out that it was all wrong, that they* [neighbors] *did not even have a registration, and everything was solved by itself. That's a miracle! How not to call it a miracle?*[37]

This episode is the only one of all that builds a chain of narratives about miracles, where the word "miracle" is explicitly spoken. In the course of the narrative, the narrative strategy gradually changes, along with the growing excitement of the interlocutor. The initial episodes are "semiotically saturated" with references to God as the invisible agent. Here are episodes in which God's presence is explicitly named in the closing part as the engine of the action. The last of the episodes does not simply refer to God's will, but also explicitly defines the events as a miracle.

The two narratives (about the healing of the mother and about the mitigation of the bureaucrats' hearts) contain another rhetorical technique, which aims to reinforce the expectation and the perception of a miracle in the listener. The happy outcome of the crisis is presented as immediate intervention and termination: expressions "instant", "immediately", "after a minute" are used in both texts to highlight the unusual and unearthly nature of the event. The perceived intercession of God takes place in both cases after a prayer. Moreover, in the second case, the prayer and moral attitude of the protagonist expressing reconciliation with what was happening and accepting the will of God are forms of personal dialogue with the transcendent power. The miracle is the answer that the narrator receives as an echo of her requests and prayers, as well as an implicit moral suggestion. In the spirit of Christian ethics, humility is rewarded.

Another important feature of the narrative should be noted, too. The interlocutor speaks of her sinfulness as a contrast that must emphasize God's mercy: "*I do not even know why the Lord is so gracious to me. With my sins, as I am sinful, and Lord – here you are. What purpose have I not yet fulfilled?*"[38] However, this does not lead to a re-examination of her life, unlike narratives expressing the state of moral torment. The state of ethical reasoning in this case is not experienced as suffering. Instead, this story is filled with the perception of God's mercy and grace. Probably these are individual differences in the perception of sin.

The written version of the oral narrative cannot render the narrator's intentions to gradually convey to the interlocutor – in this case, to me – the perception of a miracle. During the narrative, I clearly perceived through intonation this deliberate conduction of the narrative on a trajectory that led to the conclusion of a miracle. When, after some time, I reread the textualized interview, I was surprised that this effect was harder to detect in the written text. The conclusion is that this type of narrative relies on the effect of impulse and empathy on the listener, not only through the means of moral imagination but also through intersubjectively shared expectations in a religious environment that make explicit explanations unnecessary.

That the narrative transitions from the purely implicit suggestion for a second plan of the narrative, relating to the hidden transcendent agent, to a clearer reference to this invisible subject-God is most characteristic of this narrator. Other narrators adhere entirely to the approach of "semiotic ideology": the implicit suggestions of God's presence. Perhaps the fact that Zinaida Makarovna's narrative was recorded in the church, albeit confidentially, further reinforced the affective charge of the narrative, making her religious messages sound more direct and open.

The cultural conventions that form the basis of this type of narrative are related to a peculiarity of the narrative repertoire of *pricerkovnyj krug*: the presentation of unexpected but otherwise rationally explicable life events as miracles (Tarabukina, 2000, 3). Perhaps this is also one of the strategies for building an environment of people with the same mindset, in other words, to homogenize this environment and build adhesion within it. Adhesion is a factor for its reproduction and survival.

"New wine in old barrels": Narratives about miracle-working icons

Here I present contemporary narratives about perceived miracles that are related to tangible material symbols such as icons. They follow narrative patterns well known from the history of Orthodox Christianity, mostly in their oral, but also in written versions. Typically, it is about the "actions" of icons that are represented as seemingly independent agents. The icons (are said to) provide healing; they stream myrrh; they smell sweet; they disappear or the opposite, they appear unexpectedly. The analysis here focuses not on the perceived miracle, but rather on the narratives about it and their capacity to express and highlight the identities of the communities of believers.

Veneration of miracle-working icons is an important part of the history of Christianity (not just of Orthodoxy).[39] The most common such icons are of God's mother. There are well-known historical precedents, described as miracles and the result of divine interference, which are fundamental in the history of a country. Such examples include the Vladimirskaja or Kazanskaja icon of the Mother of God in Russia, and the Virgin of the Monastery of Jasna Góra Częstochowa in Poland.[40] With respect to Russian Orthodoxy, what is most remarkable is the vast number and "extraordinary spread" of the miraculous images, whose names vary between 200 and 4,000 (Krasilin, 1996, p. 392; Lidov, 1996b, p. 5).

At the same time, the attitude of Christian institutions towards miracles is ambiguous in all three strands of Christianity.[41] The recognition of the miraculous nature of an event and, moreover, the divine origin of the miracle in an Orthodox setting requires official recognition by the church institutional authority (Shevzov, 1999, p. 38; Worobec, 2007, p. 23).

It is no surprise, therefore, that the perception of events identified as miracles is associated with a state of uncertainty. The observation of the inherently unstable character of the charisma (Pelkmans, 2015, p. 188), although formulated in a slightly different context, is also valid here. The feeling of insecurity is important for the way the narratives discussed here are built. Without the understanding of this perception, performative fluctuations in their presentation would remain unclear.

Here I present two types of narratives about miracles. I have chosen them because of their relatively fixed narrative form and because of their importance to the ecclesiastical communities that created them. They are an important part of the shared narrative repertoire of ecclesiastical communities through which they express their specific identity, strengthen their faith, and, as we shall see, express their moral convictions. These are narratives for perceived transcendental interference – miracles – with the help of a miracle-working icon. They follow two well-known and established models in the Orthodox setting: the icon heals, and it was lost and rediscovered (i.e. the icon is epiphanic [*javlennaja*]) (Shevzov, 1999, p. 29). Both types of stories have been heard and recorded in different versions during the fieldwork by various interlocutors, which shows that they are not the result of individual creativity but form the discourses that are emblematic of a particular religious community.

The stories of miracle-working icons are part of a common Orthodox tradition found not only in Russia. In the Russian environment, however, they are known in oral form and as written (and printed) "stories" [*skazaniia*].[42] Such narratives are evidenced in the Russian Church literature (Shevzov, 1999, pp. 26–31) and periodicals, including in the local magazine *Kaluga Diocesan News* [Kaluzhkie eparkhial'nye vedomosti], published from the middle of the nineteenth century until the October Revolution of 1917.

The narratives about healing that I recorded during the fieldwork are related to a contemporary copy (1991) of the icon of the Kaluga God's mother, later officially recognized by the Russian Orthodox Church as miracle-working. From being locally venerated in the eighteenth century, it gradually "became associated with events that concerned the Russian nation as a whole, specifically with the victory of Russian over French troops at Maloiaroslavets in 1812, during Napoleon's invasion" (Shevzov, 1999, p. 33).

The "popular" understanding of miraculous images treats each copy as possessing charisma equivalent to that of the original, regardless of the artistic qualities of these works (Shevzov, 1999, p. 39; Krasilin, 1996, p. 392). In the context of the latter, we also have to interpret the expectations of miracles connected with the many copies.[43] The copy around which healing stories are constructed is located in Church of St. John the Warrior in the Silikatnyj suburban district of Kaluga. Their structure is not a complex one. I quote two of them in a version first recorded during the interview with a parish priest:

> *The icon of the Kaluga God's mother was newly painted in 1991, and it has already created several cases of apparent healings. In 1999, on the first Sunday of the St. Peter's fasting* [Petrov post] *was the feast of the Kaluga's mother – a woman, Zoia, aged about 65, came on crutches. She had been to most of the Moscow hospitals, the doctors told her she would never walk. She came to the temple and for the first time in her life, she confessed her sins and received Holy Communion. She went home, fell asleep the whole day, and felt some strength. In two weeks' time, she started to walk. Being blessed by Starec Ilii, she has been travelling around Russia and telling her story.*
>
> *Since then, the icon-lamp in front of the icon has been burning.*[44]

The last sentence testifies to a change in the status of the icon: the icon-lamp before it is a sign that it has received (by the decision of the Kaluga Metropolitan) a special statute of locally venerated [*mestnočtimaja*].

The second story is similar to the first one, with the difference that it is about the healing of drug addiction. It is remarkable, however, due to the fact that the main character was among the most devoted faithful in the parish when this interview was taken. His identity was not revealed by the priest, in order not to violate the seal of confession.

However, the story was familiar to the people of the parish. Guided by ethical considerations, my interlocutors declined my attempts to learn his name, but they carefully directed me, and that led me to the hero of the story. He agreed to a conversation provided that he would not reveal what his sins were before he became a fully devoted man. His autobiographical narrative mentions years of struggle with the "sin", and healing is shortly referred to as "miracles", as a triumphant manifestation of God's mercy and will. Thus, his story, which avoids naming the traumatic subject directly, is split into two: a story of suffering and misfortunes before turning to faith, and a narrative of enlightenment, grace, and solution to life's problems after the miracle of healing. The same storyline – for the healing of drug addiction under the influence of the icon of Kaluga's Mother of God – is fully depicted in the parish priest's narrative, as the narrator is a witness and participant in the events:

> *During the whole service, a man stood crying in front of the icon of God's Mother. I asked him what had happened. He had been a drug addict for five years, and he'd been taking heroin – a heavy drug.*
>
> *The next day he came. And next week he received Holy Communion, he confessed his sins. In the morning, he felt he had the strength to give up drugs.*

So, he gave up the drugs. Since then he has been a parishioner, regularly attending the services. I cannot say who he is, because I would violate the seal of confession.[45]

Miraculous healing is related not to the materiality of the icon but to its charismatic "biography" and the transcendent mediation of the sacred image. In this sense, the icon in the narrative brings "ethical affordance". The listener is expected to understand that (because the man had been crying by the icon) the icon was responsible for the man's ability to change.

The crying, however, is also to be understood as an indicator of a moral rift within the man, and of his moral reasoning (Wanner, 2013, pp. 376–383). The story is at once also a narrative of conversion. Though it is unlocked under the influence of the miracle-working icon, the conversion narrative proceeds through church sacraments. The narrative contains clear temporal markers ("the next day", "the next week"), but the overall impression is still of instantaneous moral transformation. In this sense, the text converges with the narratives about instant, miraculous conversion on the model of St. Paul.[46] Along with this, it also confirms the observation that one basic model of narratives about conversion is the one that portrays religion as a "moral lazaret".

The presentation of these two narratives will be incomplete if I do not say that they were told one after another. They were preceded by another story presenting an event from 2003 and devoted to a precedent with the myrrh-streaming icon of St. Seraphim of Sarov in the temple of St. Nicolas in Kaluga (known as *Nikolo-Kozinskii* temple).[47] The three episodes were told one after another. Such a serial presentation of the same type of texts is known in narrative studies and characterizes not only the performance of religious stories[48] but also of other oral and folk narrative genres. The serial stories in this case show that for the narrator they have a common meaning: these are stories of miracles. The very word "miracle", however, was not pronounced: it was carefully avoided by the priest. From the eighteenth century until the first two decades of the twentieth century, the highest levels of the Russian Church hierarchy conducted a careful policy of controlling the authenticity of messages about miracles. "There were legitimate concerns about fraud, profiteering, and superstition". Referring to a special law of 1722, the high clergy refused to recognize as miraculous numerous icons that were commonly perceived as miracle-workers. The discrepancy between the "popular" and the clerical understanding of miracles was also the basis for conflicts between laymen and high clergy, especially in the early twentieth century (Shevzov, 1999, pp. 38–48). In the context of this historical experience of the Russian Orthodox Church, it is understandable that the priest was restrained in presenting the stories of miracles that had taken place in his church.

Predictably, however, this caution is completely absent in the stories told by parishioners. Here are the extraordinary cases associated with the icon of the Kaluga Mother of God, through the eyes of one of the most zealous believers in St. John the Warrior parish:

Our icon is a miraculous icon, of which there were healings. That is, a woman came on crutches, sick – and walked. Then I personally saw: a girl was brought, aged 7. She could not walk until then. And after the liturgy the girl rose to her feet and walked. For the first time. Everyone was so excited, and the priest immediately handed her a great prosphora.[49] *Due to the prayers to the Holy Mother of God. We have a miraculous icon. It heals from drug addiction, from drunkenness. Miraculous.*[50]

The narrator collects several significant events into one by briefly mentioning them, but she does not develop them as complete narratives. In return, however, the word "miraculous" is mentioned three times and without any hesitation. The firm belief in the miraculous nature of the events described is even more categorically summed up by another believer: "*The miracles that have happened here – do not happen in every temple*".[51] This is also an expression of the positive identity of the religious community based on moral terms: in the interview with the same interlocutor, the parish is described as a community full of Christian spirit and solidarity. Probably the perception of moral dignity is conceived in a hidden connection to miracles: signs of God's benevolence.

Another story of an unusual spiritual sign, fully comprehended in the spirit of "semiotic ideology", provides an additional meaningful "key" to the stories of miracles and their morally assertive function. This is part of the priest's personal biography: the beginning of his career as a religious "shepherd". At the time, still a student, the future priest decided to turn to a spiritual career after meeting a respected spiritual elder from a monastery near Kaluga. But this happened in an unusual way: Although they were total strangers, the monk greeted the young man by name, welcomed him as if he were an acting priest, and commented on events in his life that a stranger should not have known. In reply to the young man's statement that he did not intend to become a priest, the monk insisted repeatedly: "*You will be, you will be. You will become, you will become*".

This narrative of self-fulfilling prophecy is familiar to the parishioners, and it is also part of the narrative repertoire of the community; the priest recalled it once during his Sunday sermon. Years later, the story was published in a Kaluga religious periodical (Slabova, 2010). It is the basis of the charismatic reputation of the priest, which is projected on the whole parish. It is also a key to the general meaning of this series of stories of miracles and their apologetic and morally assertive function.

Again, the image of the Kaluga Mother of God is at the center of another miracle story related to another religious community: The Orthodox Charitable Sisterhood St. Elisaveta Fëdorovna. I heard and recorded three oral versions of the narrative; the fourth version was published in Kaluga religious periodicals. I quote the most complete oral version in its entirety:

A year ago, we were blessed to build a small home temple. I will now tell you what miracles we had. When the bishop blessed the place where a temple should be built, we did not know which . . . they would give us. It so happened that one year before that, our Mother Superior gave an icon of the Kaluga God's mother to the librarian [in the home for seniors]. *Not large in size, about 20 to 30* [centimeters]. *And they put it in such a rough frame, you see. She* [the librarian] *put it behind the glass of the library cabinet. Well, she went there and prayed.*

And then, one day, she went there, and the icon was gone. She was worried sick; she did not know what to do. Who could have stolen the icon? You know how the saying goes, "It is one sin to steal something. But if something is stolen from you, then these are 100 sins." Because she does not know who to think about. Whether the patients have stolen from her – who else? But who knows?

Some time passed, the bishop blessed, that is, the temple. The director with this librarian went looking for a room, in which room this temple could be built. They came in . . . and at first it was not for a temple, at first, they just decided to build a prayer room.

They come to the lobby on the first floor and the director says: "Let's make a prayer room here, moreover, there is an icon on the wall".

And our librarian looked up and bit her tongue – for fear! Her icon was hanging on the wall.

And here's what's amazing: in two years, instead of a prayer room, we built a home temple. Here this icon is hanging on the wall . . . on the iconostasis [ikonostas]. *And we come and pray to it, we worship it. And it is amazing: and the temple is called in honor of Kaluga God's Mother. This was God's providence!*[52]

The story recreates real events that took place in the Home for Seniors [*Dom prestarelyh i invalidov*] in Kaluga, which is the most important object of the Sisterhood charity. The event, perceived as a miracle, can have a fully rational explanation, as a work of a human hand. Nevertheless, the narrator's intention is to present a miracle: through the vocabulary she uses ("miracles", "God's providence") and by emphasizing the extraordinary, "amazing" character of events.

Stories about epiphanic icons are particularly well known and most common among oral and published *skazanija* in imperial Russia (Shevzov, 1999, p. 29). Stories of this type were also published in the Kaluga diocesan magazine from the middle of the nineteenth century until the first decades of the twentieth century.[53] There can be no direct link and continuity between texts published in the nineteenth century and today's stories, but I can assume that the memory of these narrative models has been preserved in the community of the *pricerkovnyj krug*.

The transformation of this story into a story of a miracle and miracle-working icon is possible due to two factors: first, the moral imagination that lies at the heart of the narrative and second, the perception of the narrative that is decisive for the affirmation of its meaning.

"Moral reasoning is a constructive imaginative activity that is based, not primarily on universal moral laws, but principally on metaphoric concepts at two basic levels: (1) our most fundamental moral concepts . . . are defined metaphorically, typically by multiple metaphoric mappings for a single moral concept. (2) The way we conceptualize a particular situation will depend on our use of systematic conceptual metaphors that make up a common understanding of members of our culture. . . . Moral reasoning is imaginative" and it is grounded in embodied structures of meaning (Johnson, 1997, pp. 1–2).

In this context, the miracle can be seen as a moral metaphorical concept. It gives meaning to charity, to the voluntary work of a group of women, not very young, aimed at relieving the suffering of elderly people, often severely ill, in a social institution. Mentioning the modest little icon in a rough wooden frame highlights the intimate meaning of well-known moral accents in Orthodoxy: sensitivity to modesty, poverty, and suffering as a basis for the development of moral virtue.

The disappearance and re-appearance of the icon, along with the fright of the librarian when she beheld its re-appearance, give rise to the "semiotic ideology" that saturates the narrative, directing it to the "hidden agent": God's presence and mercy. The intention of building a small temple by one's own efforts is given a moral sanction through the miracle – a sign of God's benevolence.

The religious community constructs the meaning of a miracle. It is the community that associates events with icons and attaches importance to the stories then told. Miracles transpire through the policy of recognition. The miracle must be recognized first by the community itself and secondly (but critically) by the ecclesiastical hierarchy (Shevzov, 1999, pp. 38–39; Worobec, 2007, p. 34; Coleman and Hackett, 2015, p. 24; Pelkmans, 2015, pp. 184–187). Similar to the stories heard at St. John the Warrior, the narrative about the miracle-working icon in the home for seniors strengthens the positive identity of a particular religious community. The Orthodox Sisterhood needs this positive symbol, especially in contrast to the internal rivalries and tensions of its "profane" daily life mentioned in the previous chapter. A miracle is a symbolic "tool" for sacralization of a community, despite the challenges of everyday life.

The comparison between contemporary Russian narratives about conversion and the long established, but today globalized, Protestant narrative tradition leads to some important conclusions. There are differences as well as similarities. Narratives about conversion have a long-standing tradition in Protestantism. At first written, they can be documented from the seventeenth century in English-speaking environments (Hindmarsh, 2014, pp. 345–346). The established sustainable patterns of religious narrative (Coleman, 2000) are constantly reinforced by the ritual functions of the narrative, i.e. the use of personal stories – the so-called *testimonies* – during Protestant worship. Conversion is represented as a path from sinful darkness to triumphal enlightenment, the birth of a new moral "self", and a radical personal transformation.

Unlike the Protestant tradition, personal stories have no ritualistic role in Orthodox liturgical life. These narratives remain outside its "scene"; the contexts of their implementation are rather informal and not so common, which explains the absence of an established structural pattern of narrative. In the modern Russian Orthodox environment, the narratives about conversion can hardly be reduced to a common pattern. They represent differing trajectories of conversion from non-belief to religiosity. This is also a sign of the diverse personal motivations for conversion and of the social and cultural heterogeneity of Russian society.

The differences, however, do not diminish the similarities between Protestantism and Orthodoxy. In both, the narrative of a sudden, lightning-like awareness and conversion akin to that of St. Paul's is known. Most narratives of conversion, however, show that even after such a moment, conversion is a continuous and rather controversial process. Pain, moral torment, and breaks or ruptures with a past self and way of life are also common to both Protestant and Russian Orthodox narratives of conversion. Here, it is important to note the modulations.

One type of Russian Orthodox narratives describes conversion overwhelmingly in terms of pain and acute physical suffering. These testify to the juggernaut of the self, prompt a re-evaluation of one's past life as deeply sinful, and press the person with the challenging need to save the soul. In this chapter, I have picked up Robbins' (2004, 2013) concept of "moral torment" to prove that a model of "break" and "rupture" is neither exclusively Protestant nor Pentecostal. The "moral torment" forged in Protestant environments is also associated among Russian Orthodox believers with a radical personal transformation, with millenarian expectations, and with anxiety about personal religious salvation. The condition of "moral torment" is a sign of high moral sensitivity among the most committed Russian believers.

In general, Russian narratives represent conversion as a cognitive process in which the believer learns to recognize the signs of God's presence and grace ("semiotic ideology"). Such recognition is possible with the help of shared intersubjective knowledge. Like conversion narratives, stories of miracles are built on shared intersubjective knowledge. Both are evidence of intense ethical reasoning, searching for the meaning of its own purpose and place both in the world and at the ontological level. The perception of a miracle, moreover, is a product of power relations; it must be recognized by a religious community and cannot be proclaimed officially as a miracle without the recognition of the ecclesiastical hierarchy. Even without official recognition, narratives about miracles and miracle-working icons are central to the construction of a positive identity for and the sacralization of religious communities.

As elsewhere in postsocialist space, the conversion to Orthodoxy in Russia is also an expression of the search for stability in the uncertain world of late modernity. The seven decades of atheism determine the character of today's conversions through the concept of "interrupted continuity". The social environment of the most dedicated believers of the *pricerkovnyj krug* and the *vocerkovlënnye* has a central role in conveying the religious knowledge and moral aspirations as an intimate "personal" heritage.

Notes

1 For a systematic review of literature on conversion in various scientific disciplines see Rambo and Farhadian (2014, pp. 1–22); for a review of anthropological literature on the subject see Gooren (2014, pp. 85–110).

2 Some exceptions: see Ipatova (2006), Tupakhina (2012, pp. 185–197), Divissenko and Divissenko (2016, pp. 24–37).

3 Simon Coleman's first field study in Sweden lasted for 15 months and was followed by several periodic returns to the same field (2000, p. 12).
4 For this interviewing technique for eliciting religious narratives by recording autobiographies, see Ammerman and Williams (2012, p. 121).
5 For this commission and its activity, see chapter 4.
6 In Russian:

> *Mne piat'desyat let, rodilsia ia v sem'e inzhenera, mat'medik. V ateističeskoi sem'e rodilsia. I dovol'no dolgo prebyval . . . značit, obrazovanie polučil vysšee, značit universitet zakončil Donetskiy, tozhe ateisticheskoe. Posle universiteta zakončil eščë specializirovannyj takoj, takie gody byli, Universitet marksizma-leninizma, na Otdelenii ateizma i religii.* (Vopros: V Kaluge ili gde?). *V Kaluge.*
>
> *Nu potom tak skazat', s Bozh'jy pomoščju, po ego velikoj milosti, on menia, tak skazat', moj um napravil v nuzhnuiu storonu, perevernul menia, s golovoj na nogi postavil. Vot moë soznanie i um . . . mozhno dolgo rasskazyvat' kak eto proizošlo. No ja tak dumaju, čto čut' ja vybrannyi, vsë po blagodati Bozh'ej proizošlo.* (Vopros: Vy mozhete nemnozhko rasskazat', ob etom kak eto proizošlo?).
>
> *Nu, esli korotko, moja supruga namerevalas' krestit' detey, dvoih moih detej. Ja, znachit, soprotivlialsia. No potom čto by ne byt'. . . tak skazat' ne byt' neznajuščim, nevedujuščim, čto tam vesti – ne vesti.*
>
> *Ja ne pošël krestit'sia, a sam rešil pročest' Evangelie polnost'iu, chtoby poniat' čto zhe takoe, začem zhe krestit'sia. I kogda ja zakončil posledniuiu stročku Otkrovenija Ioanna Bogoslova, tam zhe vse eti pis'ma, vsë pročital. Togda u menia byl . . . moment, odnoznachno vsë u menia vdrug golovoj perevernulos', momental'no. Bylo takoe neopisuemoe sostojanie – i blazhenstva, i srazu i ves'ma pomenialos' mirooščuščenie, miroponimanie. Vdrug srazu vsë izmenilos' i ja rešil tvërdo sam – byl nekreščën – krestits'ia. Sam pošël, krestilsya, zastavil sebia.*
>
> *A potom ja tam tak potihon'ku, s Bozh'ej pomošč'iu, sam načal hodit'* [v cerkov'] *i bol'še i bol'še uglubliat'sia. Potom menia Gospod' privël, zdes' u nas u pri seminarii Kaluzhskoi učëba, Bogoslovskaja škola nazyvaemaja. Ja pošël, pervyi vypusk byl u nas, ja zakonchil ego. S Bozh'ej pomoščiu. (Stal zanimat'sia mučenikami vo vremia obučenija, po blagoslovleniju vikarnogo episkopa Georgija; zanimalsia mučenikom Aleksiem). . . .*
>
> *Krestilsia v 1996 godu, v školu postupil v 2001 godu.*
>
> – Interview with Ostap Kirillovič, 50, university education, customs officer. 16.08.2007, Kaluga.

7 This is the case with the two temples – Shroud of the Holy Mother and John the Warrior – among whose parishes I have done the fieldwork. The first was returned to the Russian Orthodox Church in 1994; the construction of the second began in 1994. For more on the subject see the Introduction of the current work.
8 See chapter 1 for the initial stage of restoration of religious life after 1988 in the then Soviet Union and in post-Soviet Russia.
9 In Russian:

> *I zdes' tozhe u menia bylo odno iskušenie očen' sil'noe . . . nu ne budu govorit' čto imenno, kakoe sil'noe iskušenie, čto ia mogla vpast' v grekh. I ia znaia, čto eto bol'šoj grekh, ia ispugalas' i poprosila svoiu znakomuiu zhenščinu, ia eščhëe ne tak byla blizka, ne tak často khodila v hram. . . . Kogda ia načala khodit' v khram, ia ne mogla vystoiat' v khrame polnuiu liturgiiu. Ia vsegda vykhodila. Ia ne mogu . . . ya zadykhalas'. Mne bylo plokho. Menia tošnilo. Mne khotelos' čto-to vot – lish' by vyjti na ulicu pod liubym predlogom, no tol'ko-by vyti na ulicu. Ia znala, čto etogo nel'zia delat' i ia staralas'. I odnazhdy ia dala sama sebe slovo, čto ia sejčas ne vyjdu. Byla večerniaia. I ia govoryu: „Net, ia ne vyydu. Ia ne*

vyydu". No ia tak čuvstvuiu, čto mne plokho-plokho i čto ia seyčas upadu i vperedi ia vziala zhenščinu kak by mašinal'no za plečo, dotronulas' uzhe padaia. . . . Ona oglianulas', postavila menia k stenke i govorit: „Čitaj: "Da voskresnet Bog". I ia ne mogla ruku podniat', perekrestitsia. U menia byla takaia slabost'. I ne mogla ničego, ja dazhe ne mogla govorit'. Ona pobezhala, vziala sviatoi vody. Podnimayet moiu ruku, krestit menia moej rukoj i čitaet „Da voskresnet Bog". Daet mne etu vodu pit' i potom iz etoj zhe kruzhki na menia v lico . . . mne bryzgaet. I zdes' ia v etot moment čuvstvuyu kak ot koreškov volos u menia načinaet čto-to spuskat'sia. No ia ne mogla dyšat'. Ia zadykhalas'. Ia ne mogla vzdokhnut' polnoj grud'iu. Ia vydokhnula, a vzdokhnut' ja ne mogla. I ia čuvstvuiu, čto ia uzhe sineiu, ia ot togo čto ja zadykhaius'. Ia čuvstvuiu kak čto-to takoe kak by u menia ukhodit – vot ia čuvstvuyu kak vot oto lba, vot nizhe – nos, rot, šeja i vot kogda spustil, nabrala polnuiu grud' vozdukha, ia vzdokhnula i kogda ia vzdokhnula, ono iz menia vot ia počuvstvovala kak priamo čerez nogi, vot čerez piatki vyšlo. I ia polnost'iu vzdokhnula i mne stalo tak legko-legko! I kak budto by ia i ne bolela. To u menia byla takaya tiazhest'. Tak mne bylo plokho. A zdes' vse tak bylo khorosho, čto ia dazhe zaulybalas'. I ia iej skazala „spasibo" etoi zhenščine i vot kogda u menia eto iskušenie u menia . . . ia vozvraščalas', ia s nej stala druzhit', s etoj zhenščinoj. Ia priekhala k nei i skazala: „Pomogi mne! Pomolis' za mena! Ia boius', čto ia vpadu v iskušenie!" Ona skazala: „Čitaj akafist Kaluzhskoi Bozh'ej materi. I ia načala čitat' sorok dnei. Ia čitala etot akafist i tak polučilos', tak mne Bozh'ja mater' pomogla, čto vsë proshlo. I na duše bylo khorošo i vse tak razrešilos', kak budto ničego i ne bylo. Vot tak vot Bozh'ia mater' neskol'ko raz mne pomogala. I teper', kogda mne plokho, ia vsegda srazu zhe obraščaius' i čitaiu akafist Kaluzhskoy Bozh'ei materi. Ona tak slyšit i tak pomogaet! Imenno kogda k ney obratiš'sia. Neskol'ko, mnogo slučaev bylo, togda kogda ja čitala akafist i vsë razrešalos', tak kak ia prosila – tak i bylo. Nu vot takoj vot slučaj u menya byl, ja vot dazhe rasskazyvaiu ob etom, čtoby vse znali, čto Bozh'ja mater' Kaluzhskaia takaja.

– Vopros: Vse uzhe v Kaluge eto slučilos'?

– Da, uzhe zdes' eto slučilos'. Ja v Kaluge načala khodit' v khram.

– An interview with Larissa Makarovna, 50, medical education, a paramedic. 4.08.2007, Kaluga-2.

10 See the full text of the prayer at: www.molitvoslov.com/content/molitva-Chestnomu-Krestu. Last accessed: 14.09.2018.

11 The same demonological idea is also reported by Komaromi (2017, p. 132).

12 At the time of the interview, the priest was still in the early years of his career as a clergyman. Earlier in life, he had pursued another worldly professional career. Interview with Father E.Č., 55, university education, teacher/ priest. September 22, 2006.

13

Kak naučit' detei učastvovat' v cerkovnye sluzhby, vygnat' ot tuda besy, kotorye ovladevaiut rebënka? Nekotorye deti nikak ne mogut vyterpet' sluzhbu: krutiatsia, padaiut v obmorok. Ikh nado naučit' stojkosti. Vot odin mal'čik vsega hotel vyjti vo vremia sluzhby, potomu čto khotel pisat'. Nakonec mat' emu skazala: "Pisai v tserkov'" – "Kak-to ne hočetsia". Mal'čik sterpel i s tekh por uspokoilsia. Sam ia letom, kogda očen' zharko, vo vremia sluzhby mne očen' hotelos' pit' vodu. No ia sebia zastavlial zhdat' do kontsa, a kogda sluzhba končitsia – vsë, uzhe ne hočetsia pit.

– An interview with Father E.Č., 55, university education, teacher/priest. 22.09.2006, Kaluga.

14

Tam, znaete, tam, gde očen' mnogo preizobiluet blagodat'ju, tam vsegda mnogo i temnaja sila oruduet, ona ne dremlet. Eto, znaete, kogda svet, lampa, a vokrug – ten' sguščaetsia. Etot zakon, on rabotaet na vse sto. Tak zhe vot kak Optina [pustyn']. Vy navernoe znaete, čto v devianosto tret'em godu, tam trëkh monakhov ubil satanist. I v principe tam periodičeski vot tam, to li trudnika kakogo, to eščë kto-to – ubivajut. Potomu čto vot tam, takoe eto mesto. Estestveno, tam vsiakaja nečist'pytaetsia tam obosnovat'sia. Ne bez etogo. No čego etogo boyat'sia? Volkov bojat'sia – v les ne khodit'.

– An interview with N.N., 52, university education, an author. 13.07.2007, Kaluga. I refer to the interlocutor by random initials to protect her anonymity.

15 See more on the Internet site of Optina Hermitage. – www.optina.ru/martyrs/.

16 The word given here, posoboruesh'sia, is derived from *soborovanie* [anointment], which is one of the seven sacraments in Orthodoxy. Anointing with sanctified oil is used for healing the sick and especially for cleansing oneself of unconscious sin. The Orthodox understanding of this sacrament differs from the Catholic one, according to which anointment is the last mortal anointing. See Dudchenko (2011).

17 An interview with N.N., 52, university education, an author. 13.07.2007, Kaluga. Because of the most sensitive nature of the information, I mention her with random fictitious initials to protect her anonymity.

18 This trajectory of crossing through more than one conversion is also present in one of the other narratives.

19 An interview with Zinaida Makarovna, 43, university education, teacher/ religious activist. 24.07.2007, Kaluga.

20 In Russian:

Ja byla v sele, gde deduška naš zhil. I khram, v kotorom on sluzhil, razrušen uzhe teper' polnost'ju. Uzhe kogda ja i devočkoj byla, khram byl bez kresta, bez kolokola, no on eščë stojal. I tam khranilos' zerno. A sejčas tam khrama net. Sejčas na tom meste, na fundamente, postroili bol'shoy magazin. . . . Malo togo, magazin kak zapustel. Ja kogda vse eto videla – vot nozhom po serdcu. Kak my vse, i ja v tom čisle, vinovaty, čto my dopustili do takogo . . .

– An interview with Zinaida Anatolievna, 66, university education, a pensioner. 2.08.2007, Kaluga.

21 See for example Ries (1997, pp. 83–125).

22 See the official site of the monastery: www.optina.ru/lection/86/#2. Last accessed: 17.05.2019.

23 An interview with Natalia Emelianovna, 55, secondary education, a housewife/ pensioner, 16.08.2007, Kaluga.

24 An interview with Natalia Emelianovna, 55, secondary education, a housewife /pensioner, 16.08.2007, Kaluga.

25 For some exceptions, see Hann and Golz (2010, pp. 1–29), Hann (2014).

26 In Russian:

Ja bolel grekhom i ne znal vykhoda. . . . Vrag sdelal svoë.

– An interview with Andrej Mikhajlovič, 32, secondary education, a religious activist. 4.08.2007, Kaluga. I do not mention the profession of the interlocutor, to protect his anonymity.

27 In Russian:

Ja ne znaju kak prišël k Bogu, no pervye naverno vot takie oščusščenija i pervyj razgovor s Bogom naverno byl v armii, kogda sluzhil. Potomu-čto armija – eto vsegda slozhno, eto vsegda tiazhelo. I pervyj opyt muzhčiny, takoy opyt, kogda emu deystvitel'no tiazhelo naverno, vsë taki v armii. . . . Ja dazhe ne s Bogom razgovarival, ja razgovarival so svoimi umeršimi predkami.

– An interview with Vadim Nikityč, 41, university education, a doctor. 9.08.2007, Kaluga.

28 In Russian:

> *Eto liudi, a ja ne čelovek.*
>
> – Interview with Father V. K., 34, university education, a priest.

29 Interview with Sviatoslav Denisovič, 52, university education, an engineer/manager. 1.08.2007, Kaluga.

30 In Russian:

> *U menia bylo, naverno, mnogo, mnogo takikh momentov, kogda Gospod' pokazyval. čto ja dolzhna priiti k nemu. No ja vsë po svoemu... nikak ne mogla poniat'. čto... Gospod' k nemu prizyvaet. Vot.*
>
> – An interview with Zinaida Anatolievna, 66, university education, an engineer/pensioner. 2.08.2007, Kaluga.

31 These are, for example, some of the narratives mentioned: Larisa Makarovna, Natalija Emeljanovna, Ekaterina Viačeslavovna, Zinaida Makarovna, and some others I have not explicitly referred to in this chapter.

32 In Russian:

> *Mne delali operatsiju v Saratove, počti v desiat' let. Dva goda ja tam lezhala bezvyezdno.*
>
> – An interview with Zinaida Makarovna, 45, university education, a teacher/religious activist. 24.07.2007, Kaluga.

33 '*Posëlok*' (Rus): an urban settlement, intermediate between an urban and rural layout.

34 In Russian:

> *Da i do togo kak krestili, skol'ko slučaev bylo, čto ja ne znaju dlia čego, kakovo moë prednaznačenie bylo. No kogda eščë nekreščënnaya byla, v institute učilas'. Ili mozhet uzhe kreščënnaya byla – ne pomniu. Na kanikuly priekhala k babuškinoj sestre v gosti, kanikuly zakončilis', nado bylo vozvraščat'sia. Ja govoriu:*
>
> *– Ja poedu.*
>
> *A u babuški na dače byli i babuška govorit:*
>
> *– Ne ezdi lučše, my tebia na rabočem avtobuse večerom otvezem besplatno.*
>
> *Rabočij avtobus khodil iz goroda do posëlka našego. I ja ne poekhala, ja khotela poekhat', no dumaiu, čtoby oni ne obidelis', kak by poslušanie, počitaniye vzroslykh bylo očen' sil'no razvito i ja ostalas'.*
>
> *Tot avtobus, na kotorom ja dolzhna byla poekhat', perevernulsia i upal v propast'. Piat'desiat čeloveka pogiblo. Vot tak Gospod' otvël menia ot bedy etoj, nepostizhimo kakim obrazom.*
>
> – An interview with Zinaida Makarovna. See note 33.

35 In Russian:

> *Kak prišla k vere? Tozhe tam eščë kogda byla, zhili my vdvoëm s mamoj. Samoe cennoe dlia menia eto mama. čerez mamu On menia i privël k sebe.... Eë stalo znobit', oznob takoj, zuby triasutsia, vsiu eë v drozh' kinulo. Khorošo, čajnik tol'ko vskipel, u menia byla goriačaja voda, ja nalila grelku, sdelala krepkogo čju ej sladkogo, ukryla eë odejalom, govoriu: «Mama, eto vsë projdët». Ulozhila eë, a sama vyšla. Mamu v zale ulozhila, a na kukhne ikonočka, mama molilas' vsegda. I ja dumaju: čto budet, esli mama s uma sojdët, čto ja budu delat' s nej? Odna ja i nikogo. I ja vstala na koleni i skazala: «Gospodi, esli ty est', verni mame pamiat'. Ja budu molit'sia». Ne poverite. Minuty ne prošlo, mama prišla v sebia, khotia do etogo minut desiat' ona byla v takom sostojanii kak umališënnaja. Vot tol'ko posle togo, kak ja vot tak vot skazala, momental'no ona prišla v sebia. Vot s tekh por ja stala molit'sia.*
>
> – An interview with Zinaida Makarovna. See note 175.

36 *Propiska*: according to Russian (and Soviet) legislation, address registration at the place of permanent residence. *Propiska* defines the access to accommodation, jobs, and education. For details, consult The Law of the Russian Federation "On the right of citizens of the Russian Federation to freedom of movement, choice of place of residence within the Russian Federation" dated 06.06.1993 N 5242-1 (latest edition) [Zakon Russkoj Federacii "O prave grazhdan Rossijskj Federacii na svobodu peredvizhenija, vybor mesta prebyvanija i zhitel'stva v predelakh Russkoj Federacii"], 25.06.1993, № 5242-1. – www.consultant.ru/document/cons_doc_LAW_2255/. Last accessed: 1.12.2019.

37 In Russian:

> *I ja snačala otčajalas'. A potom dumaju: čto zh ja tak eto . . . Esli tak nado, to vsë po vole Bozh'ey, ved' ničego ne delaetsya bez voli Bozh'ey. Ja uspokoilas', stala čitat' molitvy: «Gospodi, pošli mne krotost' Davida i mudrost' ego, krotost' Solomona i mudrost' ego». I čitala vot eto i momental'no čerez piat' minut vykhodit bukhgalterša i govorit: «Vy znaete, mne Vas zhalko stalo, davajte ja vam pomogu». Pošla k pasportistu, vynesla mne ottuda spravku, chto my zhivem vdvoyem s docher'ju, chtoby mne subsidiju oformit'. Govorit: «Vam kuda eë nesti?» A eto na Lenina 47, eto dalekovato. «Ne nado vam nikuda khodit', ya kazhdyj den' tam byvaju, ja zavtra eë tuda otnesu. Vy mozhete dazhe ne khodit', subsidija vam budet oformlena». Tut zhe momental'no.*
>
> *Vy ne poverite, u menia takoe shokovoe sostoyanie bylo. Poka ja vsë nadejalas' na sebia, u menia ničego ne polučalos', vse v štyki bylo mne. Kak tol'ko ja polozhilas' na Gospoda. Nado, chtoby on byl u menia propisan, značit volia takaja Gospoda, pust' budet tak, kak Gospod' khochet. Srazu momental'no vse razrešilos'. Potom okazalos', čto eto bylo ošibočno, čto u nikh dazhe i propiski-to netu i vse samo soboj razrešilos'. Vot takoe vot čudo bylo. Kak kak ne čudo nazvat' vot eto?*
>
> – An interview with Zinaida Makarovna. See note 33.

38 In Russian:

> *I ja dazhe ne znayu za čto Gospod' nastol'ko byvaet milostiv ko mne. Po moim grekham byvaet, naskol'ko ja grešna byvaju, a Gospod' – vot. Kakoe prednaznačeniye ja ne vypolnila eščë?*
>
> – An interview with Zinaida Makarovna.

39 For the miracle-working icons in Byzantine and Russian Medieval Orthodoxy from an artistic and historical point of view, see Lidov (1996a). For the veneration of icons in Russian Orthodoxy, see Tsehanskaya (2004).

40 See Shevzov (1999, 2007, pp. 61–93), Vusheva (2009, pp. 108–135).

41 Concerning the understanding of miracles in the Protestant environment and its transformation in different historical periods, see Mullin (1996).

42 For medieval Russia, Byzantium, and Serbia, see Lidov (1996b, p. 9). For similar Bulgarian stories related to the activity of Bona Velinova, the Bulgarian village prophet from the first half of the twentieth century, see Valchinova (2003, p. 160).

43 The original icon of the Kaluga God's mother (discovered in 1748) is most likely lost. Two icons, located in two of the Kaluga temples (St. Troitsky and St. Georgievsky), are regarded as equivalent to the original (Shevchenko, 2015, pp. 628–634).

44 In Russian:

> *Ikona Kaluzhskoj Bozh'ej materi novopisnaja, s 1991 goda, a ona uzhe sotvorila neskol'ko slučaev javnykh iscelenij. V 1999 godu, v pervom voskresenii Petrova posta – prazdnik ikony Kaluzhskoj Bozh'ey materi – prišla zhenščina, Zoya, let okolo šestidesiati piati, na kostyliakh. Ona obošla moskovskikh gospitalej, jej vrači skazali, čto ona nikogda ne pojdët. I ona prišla v cerkov', v pervyj raz v svoej zhizni ispovedovalas' i pričastilas'. Prišla domoj, prospala celyj den' i počuvstvovala silu.*

V tečenii dvukh nedel' ona stala khodit'. Po blagoslovleniju starca Ilii ona ezdit po Rossii, rasskazyvaet. S tekh por pered ikonoj gorit neugasayuščaja lampada.

– An interview with E. K., university education, an engineer/priest. 30.07.2007, Kaluga.

45 In Russian:

Muzhčina stojal na vsiu sluzhbu, plača pered ikonoj Bozh'ej materi. Ja sprosil, čto slučilos'. On byl narkomanom v tečenii pyati let, pri tom on prinimal geroin, tyazhëlyj narkotik.

Na sleduyuščjy den' on prišël. I na sledujuščej nedele pričastilsia, ispovedovalsia. Utrom vstal, počuvstvoval, čto u nego est' sily otkazat'sia ot narkotikov. Tak on otkazalsia ot narkotikov. S tekh por on u nas prikhozhanin, reguliarno poseščaet sluzhby. Ja ne mogu skazat', kto on, potomu čto polučitsia narušeniye tajny ispovedi.

– An interview with E. K., university education, engineer/priest. 30.07.2007, Kaluga.

46 Regarding narratives about miracles, which include a narrative about conversion, see Worobec (2007, p. 37).

47 The case is also described in publications in the local press in Kaluga (Yushina, 2007).

48 For this type of narrative among *pricerkovnyj krug* see Tarabukina (2000).

49 *Prosphora* – in Orthodox Christianity, a small communion (piece of) loaf.

50 In Russian:

Naša ikona – eto čudotvornaja ikona, ot neë byli iscelenija. T.e. zhenščina prišla na kostyliakh bol'naja – ušla. Potom ja videla eščë sama lično dazhe: devočku prinosili na rukakh v khram, semiletniaja. Vot do semi let ona ne khodila. I posle liturgii devočka pošla svoimi nogami. Pervyj raz. Vse byli tak rady i batiuška srazu ej prosforku vynes bol'šuju. Po molitvy Presviatoj Bogorodice. Čudotvornaja ikona u nas. Ot narkomanii ona isceliaet, ot p'ianstva. čudotvornaja.

– An interview with Zinaida Makarovna, 45, university education, teacher/religious activist. 24.07.2007, Kaluga.

51 In Russian:

Čudesa, kotorye zdes'proizošli – ne v kazhdom khrame slučajutsia.

– An interview with Maksim Andreevič, 22, secondary education, a university student. 11.07.2007, Kaluga.

52 In Russian:

U nas god nazad, značit, blagoslovili postroit' malen'kij domovoj khram. Ja sejčas Vam rasskazhu kakie čudesa byli u nas. Kogda vladyka blagoslovil tam postroit' khram, u nas, značit, my ne znali kakuju-to komnatu nam dadut. U nas tak polučilos', čto za god do etogo, matuška naša igumenija podarila bibliotekariu ikonočku Kaluzhskoj Bozh'ej materi. Nebol'šogo razmera, tak primerno dvadtsat' na tridtsat' razmer. I oni eë, značit, v grubuyu ramku takuyu pomestili tak. Ona [bibliotekar'] *sebe za steklo postavila v knizhnyy shkaf v biblioteke. Nu i prikhodila tam, i molilas'.*

I potom v odin prekrasnyj moment prikhodit tam – ikony net. Ona strašno perezhivala, ona ne znala chto delat'. Kto mog vziat' ikonu? Znayeš' tam kak govorit'sia: „Kto ukral – eto odin grekh. A u kogo ukrali – eto sto grekhov". Potomu-čto ona ne znayet, na kogo podumat'. To li bol'nye ukrali – kto eščë? No malo li?

Prokhodit nekotoroye vremia, vladyka blagoslavlcaet, značit, khramik. Direktor s etoj-zhe bibliotekarem pošli iskat' komnatu. V kakoj komnate mozhno postroit' etot khramik. Zakhodiat oni . . . a v načale ne do khrama delo bylo, v načale prosto molel'nuju komnatu rešili postroit'.

Prikhodiat v foaje na pervom etazhe i direktor govorit:

Nu davajte budem delat' zdes' komnatu molel'nuju, tem bolee ikona zdes' visit.

I naša bibliotekar' posmotrela i jazyk prikusila – ot strakha! Eë ikonočka visit na stenke!

I vot čto udivitel'no: togda čerez dva goda vmesto molel'noj komnaty postroili my domovoj khramik. Vot eta ikonočka visit na stene . . . ikonostasa. I my prikhodim i uzhe ej molimsia, poklaniaemsia. I čto udivitel'no: i khram tot nazvan v čest' Kaluzhskoj Bozh'ej materi. Vot takoj byl promysel Bozhij!

– An interview with Zinaida Anatolievna, 66, university education, an engineer/pensioner. 2.08.2007, Kaluga.

53 Story, 1863, № 13, pp. 223–234; Story, 1863, № 18, pp. 309–317; Story, 1867, № 18, pp. 457–466; Story, 1870, № 2, p. 63; Story, 1870, № 20, pp. 571–574.

4 Politics of memory and religious nationalism

Martyrs and heroes[1]

Introduction

While the analysis of conversion narratives reveals personal moral trajectories in chapter 3, the manifestations of the politics of memory show collective ideas marked by religious nationalism and by synergy between the secular and the religious. This is the central concern in chapter 4. This chapter addresses the way in which the past is lived and understood in and through the religious identity of observant Russians.

An orientation to the past, whether idealized or imagined, is a particularity of social practices connected to the religious life in contemporary Russia. Besides, this orientation implies not just Orthodox Christianity, but certain social practices of secular character as well. How to explain the focus on the past that is imprinted on various aspects and manifestations of the symbolic practices that are projected over the complexities of everyday life? Which are manifestations of the politics of memory in both the religious and secular milieux on the local level? These questions intrigued me during my fieldwork in Kaluga and are, respectively, the research questions to which the present chapter answers. It is the aim here to provide an analysis of the politics of memory as an aspect of 'religious revivalism'. In particular, I am going to address: (a) the project of *kraevedenie* [writing on local history and culture]; and (b) the veneration of the "special dead" (i.e. martyrs and heroes) (see Brown, 2002 [1981], pp. 69–85) as an intersection of symbolic practices in the religious and secular spheres of life.

Politics of memory: Theoretical framework

Certain influential authors conceptualize memory as pivotal in defining religion (Davie, 2000, pp. 36–37, 58–60, 70–79, 142–167; Hervieu-Léger, 1999a, pp. 4, 124–130). From the other side, as it has always been during historical periods of dramatic political changes, a process of intensive production of practices and places of memory is taking place in postsocialist countries (Pine, Kaneff and Haukanes, 2004, p. 1), and Russia is far from being an exception. The politics of memory bridge the religious and secular aspects of change. As a theoretical point of departure, I support a notion of politics of memory which unites "official or government sponsored efforts to come to terms with the past" and "unofficial and private initiatives emerging from within society to deal with the past" (Barahona de Brito, Gonzales-Enriquez and Aguilar, 2001, p. 1). According to the same authors, the politics of memory are in correlation with the historic legacies of past repressions.

Additionally, it is worth noting that "forgetting is automatically linked to what it negates: that is, to historicism" (Connerton, 1989, p. 61). Remembering and forgetting likewise are part of the complex puzzle of the politics of memory.

The politics of memory exist in different spheres and develop on different societal levels in Russia. They could also be described in terms of interplay between different institutions and different social actors both at the local and the national level. The examples analyzed in the following section confirm the observation that "political and religious movements often involve the same processes, particularly evocations and appeals to the past" (Pine, Kaneff and Haukanes, 2004, p. 2). But let us look more closely at the problem of the politics of memory surrounding the "special dead".

As Verdery noted, the postsocialist developments in Russia and Eastern Europe were accompanied by activities around the dead aiming at "reassessing or rewriting the past and creating or retrieving memory" (Verdery, 1999, p. 3). Actually, long before the end of socialism, similar practices of "civil religion" took place in countries such as Japan and the United States (Kearl and Rinaldi, 1983, pp. 693–708). Scholars point at the discrepancy between modern "segregation" of the dead "from the affairs of the living" and the political "practice of maintaining the memories and citizenship rights of its deceased members" (ibid., p. 693). What is specific in the postsocialist context is the intensity and widespread character of a (political) veneration of the dead.

Hence, the worship of the dead is not a Russian particularity, nor even a postsocialist one, yet I argue that its sweeping character, combined with specific temporal and spatial contexts, makes it distinct.

The project of *kraevedenie*

The project of *kraevedenie*[2] is one important branch of the politics of memory, and it can be defined as an intersection of: (a) the central state political project; (b) the work of local authorities and institutions on projects of strengthening local identity through the politics of memory; and (c) genuine and spontaneous individual initiatives "from below". *Kraevedenie* was shaped at the edge of the nineteenth and early twentieth centuries among erudite scholars. It has been conceptualized since the early Soviet times. It experienced its heyday in the 1920s, political repressions in the 1930s, and subsequently, a post-Stalinist renaissance thereafter (Johnson, 2006, pp. 157–176; Donovan, 2012, pp. 379–387; Mel'nikova, 2012, 2013).[3] It has spread not just in the Soviet Union but also in other socialist countries. In earlier Soviet decades (1920s), leading university professors were actively involved in *kraevedenie* (Mel'nikova, 2012, pp. 214, 2013, pp. 46–47). In the postsocialist period, *kraevedenie* is engaged mostly by representatives of the local *intelligentsia* (see further in this chapter). There are remarkable similarities between what has been called in German "local historical writings" (*Heimatkunde*) and Russian *kraevedenie* in the Putin era (Johnson, 2006, pp. 4, 118). As Eidson notes for the German case:

> The term local historical writing refers both to relatively naïve compositions by amateurs, usually concerning organisations to which they belong and to more ambitious works by those amateurs or semi-professionals who seek public recognition as authoritative local historians. [. . .] In fact, public events of different kinds are often accompanied by historicising gestures and presided over by local historians, that is, librarians, teachers, school directors, civil servants and priests who research and write about local history in their leisure time or after retiring. Local historians are organised in local committees, in state commissions for public history and in regional historical societies.
>
> (Eidson, 2004, pp. 62, 67)[4]

In this section I will address several specific questions regarding Russian *kraevedenie* after the 2000s and its manifestations in Kaluga, in particular. In which ways has it gained momentum since 2000? What is the social status of *kraevedy* (the people involved in *kraevedenie*) as social actors? How to define the status of their occupation in terms of the dichotomy professional-amateur? How to define the social and economic mechanisms that are the vehicle of *kraevedenie* as a politics of memory?

As previously mentioned, *kraevedenie* was conceptualized during the early Soviet epoch as a form for the production of knowledge and even as a social movement. It was turned to a specific expression of "Soviet patriotism" (Donovan, 2012, p. 380) or of "ethno-nationalist spirit of the time" (Shnirelman, 2011). We can follow this process from the local Kaluga perspective. As an example, Optina Hermitage [Pustyn]' was transformed (for a relatively short time, 1919–1927) into the Museum of Kraevedenie according to the testimony of its director, A. Pavlovich (Pavlovich, 1980, p. 88). Then, the Museum of Kraevedenie in the town of Kosel'sk opened a branch in Optina three decades later, in 1957; the department of literature of the same museum still exists on the grounds of the monastery.[5] As they did in other big Russian monastic centers, these small museum units of *kraevedenie* became niches where a few monks could act as museum workers while still living in the monastery. While the small-scale survival of monastic culture meant that it did not spread the values of Christianity very widely under socialism, the museological and historiographical niches associated with monasteries became important sources of religious expertise during the revivalism of the 1990s.

The Museum of History in Kaluga (established in 1922) was renamed the Museum of Kraevedenie in 1930; it existed under the latter name until 2013 when it was reorganized and renamed (see note 7). Moreover, pre-revolutionary practices and publications of ethnographic and/or historical character that focused on particular regions (i.e. were not national in scope) and met academic standards were reconsidered and re-conceptualized later as *kraevedenie*. Respectively, their authors were accorded the status of *kraevedy*. For instance, Malinin (1992 [1912]) is an author on whom the *kraevedy* of Kaluga rely very often for information. Though trained as a geographer, currently he is labelled as a *kraeved*. Pre-revolutionary church literature and periodicals of the nineteenth and twentieth centuries are currently also being labelled as belonging to "church *kraevedenie*" (Bauer, 2001, p. 3).

According to some local opinions, *kraevedenie* has been promoted strongly in Russia since President Putin came to power in 2000. A quotation from a slightly sarcastic interview provides a good insight into that phenomenon:

> *Kraevedenie has become a fashion just after the President [Putin] said that children should be patriotically educated, and the subject of kraevedenie had been introduced into the schools. Until then, no one even knew what sort of subject it was. Nobody had paid attention to kraevedy, they used to write, but [their books] had not been published. But now they [kraevedy] publish, they started organizing conferences and printing books. Actually, the problem is that there are lots of fairy-tale tellers among them. That is why they have been fighting at conferences. There will be many such conferences in September and in October [2006]*.[6]

This (skeptical) opinion is informative concerning some important peculiarities of *kraevedenie*: the semi-professional or amateur status of the *kraevedy* (many have non-academic professions), the "patriotic" overtones, and sometimes completely fictitious additions to the facts and their interpretation. To be more specific, the literature in question counts numerous books, booklets, newspaper articles, albums, etc. Church *kraevedenie* is already a separately marked category on the shelves of church bookshops and parish libraries. It is no surprise that *kraevedenie* often serves as a vehicle for the appropriation of a national narrative as a local asset.[7]

In the following, I will explore in more detail the social and professional profiles of local church *kraevedy*. Most often, they belong to the local intelligentsia and are rather close to the background of the local community: teachers, librarians, local writers, museum workers, civil servants, and, in one prominent exception, a specialist in cars. In principle, the contemporary *kraeved* is an amateur or semi-professional occupation. The fact that teaching church *kraevedenie* in Sunday schools might be either on a paid or on a voluntary basis (depending on personal negotiations or agreement between the rektor [*nastoiatel'*] and a given teacher) confirms the validity of that observation. The amateur or semi-professional character has prevailed until recently, when professional museum workers got involved in church *kraevedenie* exploring the original locations of abolished churches and organizing exhibitions dedicated to the history of Orthodox religion (Bauer, 2001, p. 3). Church *kraevedenie* is certainly not a permanent occupation for museum experts. Their involvement is indicative of a certain development in the direction towards more visible engagement of professionals in *kraevedenie*.

There are variations in the degree of personal commitment of church *kraevedy* to religion. For some of the writers, it is a "patriotic" interest in both Orthodoxy and in the cultural heritage connected to it which is the leading motivation for their efforts. One may define their participation in church life as rather sporadic. For others, their preoccupation with church *kraevedenie* brought them to the internalization of religious values and to a change in their behavior: being atheists in Soviet times, they eventually converted to being believers and active participants in church life. There is also a third type of *kraevedy* in Kaluga. These have a religious motivation as their main priority, and their infatuation with *kraevedenie* follows. These people could be defined not just as rigorists (see Makrides, 2004, pp. 511–521) but rather as church activists who are closer to *pricerkovnyj krug*.

Kraevedenie was institutionalized in Russia, notwithstanding the intermediate status it obtained in terms of "amateurism – professionalism". In particular, the Museum of Kraevedenie is referred to as an important cultural institution in Kaluga.[8] In the Belinskii District Scientific Library of Kaluga there is a special department and reading room for *kraevedenie*. Courses of *kraevedenie* are taught in Sunday schools (Razumovskaja, 2002, pp. 12–13). But there are also exhibitions, seminars, and numerous conferences provide occasions where *kraevedenie* gains momentum in the public's attention and imposes its claims of "scientific occupation". It is worth noting the important institutional role played by the district library in the promotion of *kraevedenie* in Kaluga. The library has its special department, but it also endorses and organizes various conferences and edits and publishes books. One of the most popular *kraevedy* in Kaluga, the late Genrietta M. Morozova, was a prominent librarian (see Morozova, 1993), and the subsequent director of the library, S. Mironovich, has kept contributing to *kraevedenie* (Berestov and Mironovich, 2003).

The analysis of all the *kraevedenie* publications dedicated to Kaluga, the city and the district, would be beyond the scope of this chapter. (Their impressive number alone would indeed demand a separate study of subgenres). Thus, I rather focus on the so-called church *kraevedenie* [*cerkovnoe kraevedenie*] as a specific phenomenon, which has been recently discerned. There is indirect evidence in favor of this assumption: publications on the subject date back as early as 2000.

Church *kraevedenie* is involved in discovering the locations of abolished churches; exploring chronicles of existing or vanished temples (Bauer, 2001, p. 3); providing archival information concerning biographies and genealogies of prerevolutionary clergy (Legostaev and Pautova, 2004, pp. 132–210); and collecting data about activities of the parishes in the past, the history of important icons, etc. These activities have practical aspects in the process of religious revivalism, especially if one takes into consideration the significant loss of Orthodox cultural knowledge in Russia during the Soviet period.

The first person to start searching for locations of abandoned churches in Kaluga (in 1992) and erecting crosses at these locations, was perhaps Vitalii Legostaev. The interview with him demonstrates that this is not just an archive and library research but an investigation involving serious efforts in exploring *in situ* different locations, which are often not easily accessible:

> *Well, I have worked on it since [nineteen] ninety-two. . . . I have studied this county [*uezd*]*[9] *of Kaluga for more than ten years. [There are about] 60*

temples, and they are all listed in a register. We erected a cross in place of a destroyed temple for the first time in this Eparchy. The cross looks quite nice, made from iron and concrete. Well, respectively I visited the sites of all these 60 temples. That is, I have made an itinerary and marked them on the map I have, and such ancient maps. That is, in the winter, I made the itinerary; and during the summer I travelled there [by car] and put the crosses up. I also photographed all the sites. It turned out that I needed to travel several times.[10]

We can learn from the same interview that this work has been a voluntary one for a long time. Since the first publications of Vitalii Legostaev gained local popularity and recognition after the year 2000, he started receiving offers to work on particular projects. It is in this way that his amateur work was transformed into something semi-professional. Moreover, his different projects have been gradually involved in a network of exchanges. Legostaev supplemented a database consisting of about 3000 names of priests (mostly pre-revolutionary ones) with short personal data about each of them. When one of the local priests decided to commemorate his late fellows by reading all their names during the course of church services, he turned to Legostaev's database. Legostaev was also approached by monks from one of the local monasteries for data on persecuted "black clergy"; he agreed to provide it in return for sponsorship in publishing his database. Publishing is sometimes financially supported by public funds, but it is sometimes sponsored by local businessmen (see Legostaev and Pautova, 2004, p. 236).[11] One can see how church *kraevedenie* might become a source not just of personal prestige and recognition but also a resource for building social capital and potentially even transforming the latter into economic capital.

The very term "church *kraevedenie*" aims to differentiate the particular profile of the subject, to stress its specificity and thus to achieve its higher social recognition and symbolic status. Yet, it is difficult to discern church *kraevedenie* on any independent criteria. For example, a book of church *kraevedenie* usually is a mixture of different genres:[12] histories, descriptions and chronicles of churches, publications of archival documents, memoirs, manuscripts, genealogies, etc. It is also difficult to distinguish whether it, like all kinds of *kraevedenie*, is more a construction of local significance and uniqueness or a testament of public national-affirmative discourses. This is clearly observed in social practices of the implementation of church *kraevedenie* as a discipline taught in Sunday schools. I have been personally involved in an event which (unintentionally) demonstrated the gap between the concept of church *kraevedenie* and its practical implementation. It happened during one of the periodically organized "excursions in the temple" (on August 8, 2007) at Shroud of the Holy Mother. It is the aim of these excursions to familiarize the audience with the history of the temple, with its internal settings, with complications in its reconstruction after 1994, and with its present-day spiritual treasures: relics, icons, church utensils. The director of the Sunday school (a teacher by profession) skillfully took the part of a guide and kept the attention of the children up for two hours.

Excursions like this one are part of education in church *kraevedenie* in Sunday school, but they are open for visitors too. While the excursion focused on the temple (i.e. strictly on the local cultural history), the ideas expressed by the church activist-teacher-guide concerning teaching church *kraevedenie* focused on the importance of teaching national history. This publication reveals the hardship church *kraevedenie* faces in the efforts to define its own profile:

> *The native countryside is a small image of the Fatherland – Russia. For that reason, we need to talk about kraevedenie. . . . Following the rather short experience of our [Sunday] school (the school opened in 1998, thus three years ago), I would like to note a different kind of experience we made during the implementation of the elements of kraevedenie. . . . From the beginning, the work of kraevedenie has been conducted fragmentarily, with no particular system, at four levels: at the level of the history of the parish, of the city of Kaluga, of the Eparchy, and of the native land. Yet, the necessity to study the native countryside according to the history of the Fatherland has only taken shape over time. But it is impossible to teach Orthodox kraevedenie without knowledge and understanding of national history.*
>
> (Razumovskaja, 2002, p. 13)

Apparently, memory and history overlap, the same is valid regarding the sacred and the secular, and the local countryside and the native country turn out to be functionally equivalent. The fact that the most active church *kraevedy* do not originate from Kaluga (although spent most of their lives in this city), whose cultural heritage they glorify, may suggest that the national bias is stronger than the local one. Some forms of appropriation of national history and imagery as local assets lead to this conclusion. This is valid, for instance, regarding the exaggerated attention which is locally paid to an important event of Russian medieval history, known as the "Great Stand on the Ugra River" [*Stoianie na Ugre*]. It took place within the territory of the contemporary district of Kaluga, on the bank of the river Ugra. It was the decisive confrontation between troops of Russians and Tatars in 1480, which turned out to be victorious for the Russians and is considered, at least by some Russian historians, as the final act in the shaping of Russian statehood. This historic episode is a moment in time when Kaluga turns out to be in the focus of fateful events of all-Russian significance. Therefore, the local community periodically has commemorated it and symbolically reproduced it through different – as Eidson (2004, p. 67) puts it – "historicising gestures".

One can clearly follow the trajectories of the politics of memory to 1980, when the 500-year jubilee of the event was celebrated. New "places of memory" were produced: an impressive monument near the river, tourist routes in the Ugra National Park, pilgrimage travels including visits of the temples located near the bank of the river Ugra (see Makarova and Kalašnikova, 2006, pp. 351–352). Meanwhile, numerous publications remembered and celebrated the event: popular, journalistic, *kraevedenie*, and historical literature.[13] In 2005, the commemorative style was reinvoked, and the peak of these practices was marked by the publication of a prestigious collection dedicated to the 525-year jubilee of the event; it is titled *1480 in the History of Russia*, and it consists of articles, documents, and reprints.

Here, *kraevedenie* is in collaboration with professional historians. The publication was sponsored by the local and central authorities and under the auspice of the head of the city administration of Kaluga (sees Chaikina and Chaikin, 2006).

Historic narratives about the Great Stand on the Ugra River have been coded also in the language of religion, and this aspect is strongly represented in the literature of church *kraevedenie*. One may find a medieval historical legend about the victory of the Russian troops thanks to the miraculous intervention of the Holy Mother. Due to that legend, locations near the bank of the river Ugra were called "The Belt of the Holy Mother". Similar historical legends are widespread in the Christian world, of course, and this narrative pattern could neither be considered a trademark of Russia or of Orthodoxy. What is significant here is that church *kraevedenie* actively reproduces the legend (see Makarova and Kalašnikova, 2006, pp. 343–344), and accordingly, the legend has become well known among the local community. Moreover, the perception of the territory of Kaluga and the district as being specially chosen, protected, and sacred, has gained popularity.

These manifestations of the politics of memory are obviously constructed "from above", with direct involvement of central and local state institutions. One may claim that *kraevedy* play the role of mediators, transmitting important messages between different strata of Russian society. This intermediary role is clearly visible when mediating between the middle social level and the larger societal background. The case of a small school museum in Kaluga, called the Ugra Museum, and dedicated to the events of 1480 and the rule of Ivan the Terrible, provides a good example. The teacher, who was also the initiator of the museum, is actively involved in (church) *kraevedenie*: she is one of the two editors of the collection *1480 in the History of Russia* (Chaikina and Chaikin, 2006). Furthermore, she was a pioneer in the teaching of *Fundamentals of Orthodox Culture* in Kaluga as a school subject. The museum surprises its visitors with a wax statue of Ivan the Terrible located in a classroom (Arsent'ev, 2007, pp. 18–19). Obviously, local and national, as well as religious and secular, are unalienable, and the messages of *kraevedenie* are directly transmitted to the school students.

Returning to the question of the appropriation of national history as a local asset, one has to note the paradoxical character of this trend. While in some other countries, it is the local community that stands behind the invention of memory and the appropriation of national heritage aiming to outrun neighboring communities (see Forbess, 2005, pp. 49–51; Benovska-Sabkova, 2007, pp. 295–296), the practices observed in Kaluga should be interpreted as working in a different direction. Texts of *kraevedenie* and *lieux de mémoire*, like the school museum, give me reason to assume that what we see here is a symbolic operation in which the local is not just a belittled version of the national, but in which the local is an epitome of the national.

Yet, it would be simplistic to claim that church *kraevedenie* has been completely constructed top-down. Some of the most active *kraevedy* in Kaluga have spontaneously developed their amateur interests in and infatuation with the subject. Their initial motivation was far from any religious commitment. Vitalii Legostaev, mentioned earlier, was a passionate amateur photographer. But the pictures he made of the churches in Kaluga provoked his intellectual curiosity. In 1984, he started investigations in the local state archives, which led to the creation of his database, books, and booklets (Legostaev, 2000a, 2000b, 2000c, 2001, 2003; Legostaev and Pautova, 2004). An obvious split between commitment to religion and passion for photography marks his life-history narrative. Nonetheless, the autobiography eloquently demonstrates the spontaneous nature of Legostaev's early commitment to *kraevedenie* and reveals how the existing social and political order framed and disciplined spontaneity. It also provides an insight into how *kraevedenie* functioned on an amateur or semi-professional basis during the late Soviet period:

> *[Since the 1960s] I have taken pictures wherever I was: I have been taking pictures in the open air, I have been taking pictures in the army, and when I was still a child, and when I came to Kaluga [1972]. I have photographed it all. [And then, already in Kaluga] I had so many photographs that I started sorting them out. I compiled different albums, domestic photos in a domestic album, photographs of workplaces* [. . .], *nature, sketches, butterflies, starlings . . . and also of monuments and temples. And this particular album I started in 1984: Temples of the City of Kaluga. It is in black and white. I have photographed everything I could find; there are also memoir plaques, and I added annotations concerning the temples. For the ones I had no [information on], I went to the library, and this ultimately started my interest in the literature of* kraevedenie. *It is from there that everything started . . . with that album. I decided to show it to somebody. In these days, the luminaries of* kraevedenie *were Aleksandr Sergeevič Dneprovskii and Genrietta Mikhailovna Morozova. I first met Dneprovskii. There was a club named Good Will, and they used to meet there on Wednesdays for tea and conversations, discussing opinions, etc. Then I approached Morozova. Genrietta Mikhailovna used to work here [in the district library], in the department of bibliography. She said: "Young man, you have to go to the archive". It was complicated to get into the archive. A letter [of reference] was required, on behalf of the department of culture. "I am going to provide it", she said, "and you are going to go to work".*[14]

Similarly, the hobby of photography was also what brought Semën Kondratievič, a middle-aged engineer, writer, and manager of a large local enterprise, to compile and publish several annotated albums of local churches and monasteries just recently. One should note, however, that photography is by no means the only inspiration for *kraevedenie*.

The current development of church *kraevedenie* could be defined as an intersection of initiatives from the "bottom-up" and politics from the "top-down". The latter is the decisive factor that has transformed *kraevedenie* from peripheral individual infatuations into a socially visible and significant project.

One may assume that *kraevedenie* aims to strengthen the significance of the past in shaping both local and national identities. Forging symbolic bonds between the individuals and their native countryside, *kraevedenie* could suggest more answers to the popular question: "What does Fatherland begin with?" [*S čego načinaetsia*

Rodina?], if one refers to the famous Russian song under the same title. *Kraevedenie* has the capacity to provide local dimensions for the "national sentiments" (Bendix, 1992, pp. 768–790). By giving strong religious connotations to this initially secular project, the church *kraevedenie* provides further instances of the synergy between state and church. It supports the sacred aura of both local and national identities.

The "special dead": The religious and secular veneration of the dead

Kraevedenie overlaps with another manifestation of the politics of memory: the interest in and veneration of the "special dead" (Brown, 2002 [1981], pp. 69–85). Some social actors actively involved in *kraevedenie* have also become a vehicle for the symbolic practices expressing the veneration of the dead. As Verdery noted, the postsocialist developments in Russia and Eastern Europe were accompanied by activities around the dead aiming at "reassessing or rewriting the past and creating or retrieving memory" (Verdery, 1999, p. 3). In the following section, I will try to analyze certain interrelated manifestations in the veneration of the dead, in which both religious and secular institutions are involved.

Since 1988, the ROC has initiated a large-scale project of canonization of martyrs and "new martyrs".[15] While certain authors explore canonization and the veneration of the new martyrs as central politics of the ROC, constructed and implemented from the top-down (Rock, 2011; Christensen, 2018), my approach privileges a local perspective and focuses on bottom-up initiatives. The concept of "new martyrs" implies its political connotations: the "new" martyrs are those who suffered and died "in the name of the faith" predominantly during the time of socialism.[16] A second category of confessors [*ispovedniki*] involves those who suffered but died "without bloodshed" (Anonymous, 2003, pp. 265–272).

Both central and local institutions of the ROC are involved in the canonization. The central level is represented by the Synodal Commission of Canonization of Saints (established in 1989),[17] and the local one, respectively, is the Commission of Canonization of the Eparchy of Kaluga.[18] It is important to note that not all locally recognized martyrs acquire all-nation validity. Only the central Synodal Commission is entitled to grant the highest status of saint. Canonization "is an exercise of power" (Christensen, 2018, p. 5).[19]

The Eparchial Commission of Canonization in Kaluga is in charge of investigating the biographies of people of local origin (and/or church affiliation) who suffered severe persecutions and of verifying the testimonies for their martyrdom. The local commission consists of ten members, all of them men, drawn from the clergy (both priests and monks) and the laity. (Two of the latter define themselves as *kraevedy*.)

The canonization of new saints is a significant aspect of Russian religious revivalism, symbolically and politically loaded, as far as it resumes an important institutional activity of the ROC, which was almost completely abandoned during the Soviet era. Building all-Russian memory about new martyrs is a sweeping project in which a monk, Damascin (Orlovskii), had played and still plays an important role. He is a pioneer of research on the martyrdom of the clergy and his activity began in the 1970s. Hegumen Damascin is the author of an impressive series of documentary books on the subject (Damascin, 1992, 1996, 1999, 2000, 2001, 2002a, 2002b). Since 1997, a large web resource (The Public Resource [fond] "Memory of the Martyrs and Confessors of the Russian Orthodox Church") has been established to provide information (including icons, photos, video films, etc.) concerning numerous new martyrs.[20]

One should briefly note that canonization is also a subject of violent disputes between the different factions of the ROC clergy, involving mostly the so-called church liberals and their opponents, the rigorists. The latter are often emotionally referred to as "fundamentalists" (Mitrokhin, 2004). The canonization of the royal family (i.e. the family of the last tsar of Russia, Nickolas II) in 2000 was a clear example of disagreement between these factions, but it was also the exemplary case of canonization of new martyrs (Knox, 2004, pp. 125–128).

The canonization of prominent *starcy* (who lived during the second half of the nineteenth and the beginning of the twentieth centuries) from the monastery of Optina Pustyn' was a process in which local and national dimensions overlapped. Because Optina Pustyn' is located on the territory of the district [*oblast*] of Kaluga, the Eparchy of Kaluga provided the territorial aspect of the first stage of the transformation of memory about *starcy* into national sanctuaries. It was announced that 12 of the *starcy* of Optina Pustyn' were to be "locally venerated" [*mestnočtimye*] martyrs and confessors on July 26, 1996. The announced veneration prompted Patriarch Aleksii II to visit the monastery, and he also transmitted the relics of seven of the *starcy* into one of monastic churches (Aleksakhina and Bogatyreva, 2003, p. 41).[21] The canonization was confirmed at the national level in 2000, when 1,097 persons were canonized.[22] Another three monks of Optina Pustyn' were added to the list of national Russian martyrs between the two canonizations of 2005 and December 27, 2007.[23] As the process of canonization continued during the second decade of 2000, the total number of nationally recognized new martyrs grew to 1,776 (Christensen, 2018, pp. 1, 5).

In the case of Kaluga, two institutional units are locally involved in the process of canonizing new martyrs and confessors. They function independently of each other in the district of Kaluga, an important particularity of the local context. The first of them is located in Optina Hermitage (Pustyn'). There, several monks have specialized in investigating testimonies and documents regarding the sanctity of their own predecessors, before and during the monastery's closure from 1918 to 1922. A member of the Kaluga Eparchial Commission of Canonization, a colleague to these monks, testified to their activities as follows:

> *They operate their own commission* [of canonization] *there in Optina Pustyn'. The monk Platon, the hieromonk Joseph, and the hieromonk Methodius are* [involved] *there. They work only on Optina monks; they bring fame to those who suffered and* [after the closure of the monastery] *served in different locations.*[24]

Optina Hermitage [Pustyn'] has the status of a *stavropigial'nyi* monastery (Aleksakhina and Bogatyreva, 2003, p. 38), which means that it enjoys autonomy, and it is subordinated directly and solely to the Patriarch who carries the title of its archimandrite. This explains the independent work of the Optina clergy regarding the canonization of its own predecessors. The monastery keeps a publishing house of its own (Nizovskii, 2000, p. 231),[25] which further allows it to "bring fame" to martyrs by publishing works on their lives and related documents (see for instance Zhizneopisanie, 2003).

Another Commission of Canonization of Saints, which was under the auspice of the Eparchy of Kaluga, was established in 2005. During the short period of its existence until 2007, it selected around 35 candidates to be "celebrated" as locally venerated martyrs and confessors. Father Andrei Bezborodov, an influential priest, historian, and lecturer in the Seminary of Kaluga, was the president of the commission of ten members. My information about the activity of the commission is based on interviews with two of its members. The data is rather limited, since written documents concerning the commission are not accessible; moreover, canonization is an ongoing process. During the time of my fieldwork, the proposals of the commission were still just proposals, and apart from a few exceptions, they have not yet been examined by the Metropolitan. Aleksii Kurovskii, the late priest of the village of Kurovskoe (located about 20 kilometers from Kaluga), was already recognized as a "locally venerated" martyr. According to the interviews, proposals for canonization concern mostly representatives of the clergy: priests, monks, and nuns. For example, all the monks from St. Trinity Liutikov monastery [*Sviato-Troickii Liutikov monastyr*] near the village of Peremyšl' were shot in 1918 together with eight villagers, who had helped the monks protect the monastery from the attacks of (initially) deserters and against the regular army (later on). Yet only the monks have been listed in the proposal for canonization. Why not the eight villagers too? We can presume that, at the very least, there was a lack of information concerning their biographies.

After all, the Commission of Canonization carefully evaluates the candidate's moral dignity during each period of his life. The lack of information is a serious obstacle to that evaluation in almost all cases (Rock, 2011, n.p.). But there are additional reasons that representatives of the clergy prevail among the new martyrs. Since the clergy has been particularly affected by repressions during different periods of the Soviet epoch, the aspirations for its moral rehabilitation in post-socialist times is an understandable reaction and purposeful politics of memory implemented by the present-day clergy.[26] Striving for the reinstatement of the clergy as a prestigious social group is another motivation here, as much as in other spheres of the religious life in Kaluga.[27] It would be helpful here to remember the interrelatedness between the politics of memory and the repressions in the past (Barahona de Brito, Gonzales-Enriquez and Aguilar, 2001, p. 11).

At first glance, the activity of the Eparchial Commission of Canonization of Kaluga looks like an intellectual task, motivated by specific moral models aimed at the rebuilding of religious institutions. This is a process, however, inevitably including more than one aspect. To the compulsory creation of *passio* detailing the sufferings of the new martyrs and icons – holy images – one should add the establishment of both new "places of memory" and rituals connected to them. I will focus here on the construction of new sacred "places of memory" and on the rituals giving them sacredness.

The simplest forms of new sacred "places of memory" are the crosses which mark the locations of abandoned or destroyed churches. One should also mention that the names of the priests of the diocese of Kaluga who were subject to Soviet repressions have been written on a memorial cross raised in 2005 in the churchyard of the St. George cathedral.

The creation of a new memorial center in Kaluga – Chapel of the New Martyrs and Confessors [*časovnia novomučenikov i ispovednikov*] – in an area that never accommodated a church, is an initiative implemented at the local level. The completion of the project reveals the social fabric that stands behind the politics of memory. The project for building the memorial center dates back to around late 2005, when the first symbolic actions of its inauguration took place. The initiator of the project was one of my interlocutors. The very choice of the locality for the center is loaded with symbolism. It is near the village of Kurovskoe,[28] where Aleksii Kurovskii (Gorbačev), canonized as martyr,[29] spent part of his life. At the same time, this is (approximately) the location where the Great Stand on the Ugra River took place (Makarova and Kalašnikova, 2006, pp. 340–356).

Apparently, the location of the memorial center was a deliberate choice aiming to accumulate and combine multiple symbolic characteristics. This becomes clear from the interview with Ostap Kirillovič, the initiator, who is also a lay member of the Eparchial Commission of Canonization:

> *This is the place of the Great Stand of 1480. It is located on the bank of Ugra River, where Khan Akhmat led his troops into battle.* [. . .] *And the locality: as I said, it is also a historic place. The bell tower of the Uspenskii Cathedral of Tikhonova Pustyn' Monastery can be seen from there. On the other side is located, you see, the Spaso-Vorotynskii Convent on the Ugra. It is a very sacred place, blessed by God. That is, we think, also blessed by the Holy Mother. And actually, the help of the Holy Mother can be felt here; and the prayer of the new martyrs can be felt.*[30]

National and local symbolism overlap, secular and religious values merge, the locality makes the symbolic contact possible between the holy places emblematic for Kaluga (Tikhonova Hermitage [Pustyn'] Monastery, Spaso-Vorotinskii Convent). According to the project, the accumulation of sacred meanings will continue by symbolic actions aiming at the further integration of national and local sanctuaries. For example, it was planned to immure a capsule with soil from two other localities where hundreds of clerics were shot (Butovo Polygon and the Prison of Sukhiniči). The integrative meaning of the memorial was emphasized by adding the names of the Optina Hermitage *starcy* (the already canonized monastics of Optina Hermitage) to the list of martyrs of Kaluga.

According to the project, the memorial was going to consist of a large chapel [*časovnia*], a cross to bow in front of, and a *kupal'nia*. A *kupal'nia* is a covered pool of a medicinal spring or holy water where people bathe to receive blessing and improve their health, traditionally located near monastic buildings or other sacred places. The one at the memorial center was meant to use the spring water near the house of St. Aleksii Kurovskii – evidencing another layer of combining sacralizing and memorializing projects because a local priest had earlier proposed to consecrate that spring, and this led to the idea to build a memorial. Ostap Kirillovič, the member of the Diocesan Commission of Canonization, accepted and supported the idea. The spring was consecrated on November 23, 2005 (St. Aleksii's Day) with a litany procession [*krestnyi khod*] from the village of Koslovo (presently at the outskirts of Kaluga) to the spring in Kurovskoe (see Kizjaev, 2006, p. 22). Blessing the idea to put a memorial by the spring of Kurovskoe, the Metropolitan signed the document for the construction of the chapel. An initiative, initially a modest one, developed into a project that changed the ecclesiastic geography of Kaluga lands. The chapel was finally built in 2014.[31]

Although "shrines associated with the 'new martyrs' of the Soviet period do not seem to resonate with the Orthodox faithful" and "the vast mass of new martyrs remain unvenerated" (unlike the "flourishing" of the major pre-revolutionary shrines – Rock, 2011, n.p.), the new Kaluga ritual has found good reception among representatives of the clergy and was accepted by the local believers. This support was evident from the participation of seven priests and a large crowd during the second performance of the procession on November 23, 2006. This fact confirms the observation that the veneration of the new martyrs is rather "local veneration, despite the status of the new martyrs as national saints" (Christensen, 2018, p. 187). The ritual marked a new sacred itinerary in Kaluga and the nearby villages. On its way, the procession featured intermediary "stations" to honor the memory of a priest who served more than 60 years in one of the local churches. Actually, another interlocutor of mine also participated a couple of times in this newly initiated pilgrimage, altogether with other members of the St. Elisaveta Fëdorovna Orthodox Sisterhood.[32] The representatives of the local Cossacks organization led the procession in 2006, and their presence emphasizes warrior-like features of both the event and the place (which obtains this characteristic also from its link to the historic military actions of 1480). Thus, the locality near Kurovskoe was marked as a culmination and final destination of the ritual action.

The creation of sacred "places of memory" demands and generates a ritual, and this ritual itself has become a stage of sacralization of the place. From the interviews, I derived useful information concerning the social interactions through which events had been accomplished. The project of the memorial chapel and the creation of the ritual connected to it was a result of the work of different levels of church institutions. Although local in its character, the project was still constructed "top-down". That is, it became possible through the interaction between an ordinary priest, an influential layman, and the Metropolitan.[33] The position of the layman playing the role of intermediary between the law and the higher level of the church hierarchy is of key significance.

Moreover, the layman's role in the practical implementation of the initiative to build the memorial was decisive. He organized the litany processions on St. Aleksii Kurovskii's Day. What is more important, he coordinated the construction of the memorial center: The Chapel of the New Martyrs and Confessors. One should stress that this specific social actor's activities are not limited to the initiative for the memorial center (and ritual events connected to it). He regularly publishes articles dedicated to specific new martyrs of Kaluga in local Orthodox periodicals. Some of his publications are simply entitled "The Life of Saint X". The articles do not intend to popularize the Eparchial Commission of Canonization or its activities. Published biographical stories about new martyrs[34] actually aim to construct their memory, at least at the regional and local level. Obviously, the orally transmitted memory concerning people who accepted martyrdom decades earlier (in certain cases more than 80 years previously), pale substantially and may be limited to the circles of immediate family or estate. At best, remembrance is concentrated in the settlements where they lived. Published narratives put an end to the anonymity of these martyrs and overcome (to a certain extent) their oblivion. Nonetheless, the audience of the local church press is rather limited and consists only of the active parishioners.

One should address here the question of how the local community accepts the veneration of new martyrs, especially in comparison to its worship of well-established and popular saints. Interviews, as well as observations, demonstrate that the saints – both old and new – are rather accepted depending on the contexts of the holy places. New martyrs connected to Optina Pustyn' – a "magnet" for pilgrims from all over Russia – attract veneration and draw somewhat on the aura of the shrine. Even people largely indifferent to religion visit Optina Hermitage and honor old and new saints while following common pilgrimage itineraries. In contrast, the new martyrs whose veneration is connected to less popular places tend to attract the attention of only the most committed believers and church activists.

Back to the author of biographies of martyrs, one can draw the conclusion that he, as a member of the Commission of Canonization, fulfilled the function of "impresario" of the cult of the martyrs (Brown, 2002 [1981], pp. 73, 64–65), which is an invariable part of the support for this cult since late Antiquity onwards. Of course, Ostap Kirillovič was not the only one active in this area. Some local journalists, guides organizing pilgrimage travels, church *kraevedy*, etc. play similar roles depending on their access to economic, social, or cultural resources. Their integration into church activities is a kind of semi-professionalization.

The role Ostap Kirillovič plays could be defined by the synonymous (but not identical) term of "religious entrepreneur", normally applied to clerics or laymen performing an intermediary function between society and religious experts (see Christian, 1996, chapters 3–5). In this case, religious "entrepreneurship" includes the construction of the memorial center: collecting funds through donations; negotiating between local authorities and the church in the struggle of the latter to get legal ownership of the land on which the memorial was to be built; providing construction materials; organizing the actual construction. All this became possible due to the influential positions of the mentioned person in the economic and social life of Kaluga. In other words, my interlocutor invests his personal social capital in his activities in the religious sphere. In doing so, he enhances his prestige among the community of the most devoted believers in both the city and the district.

The intellectual work that provides the background for the process of canonization brings together controversial and allegedly irreconcilable legacies. In fact, the archives of the KGB are the main and only trustworthy source of information regarding political persecutions, arrests, trials, and imprisonments (Rock, 2011, n.p.; Fedor, 2014, p. 124; Christensen, 2018, pp. 47–78). Moreover, the people entitled to carry out research in these archives sometimes could not be defined as "unrelated" to the repressive state apparatus of the past (Fedor, 2014, pp. 123–125).[35] Due to the distance in time, it is now the heirs of the former tormentors (institutionally speaking) who are personally involved in the current symbolic rehabilitation of their victims as martyrs. Two of my interlocutors match this description. Both manifest sincere personal and professional transformation towards a positive recognition of religion.

Some of the interviews provide evidence that this controversial strategy for reconciliation of seemingly irreconcilable memories finds supporters among some of the most active believers. They express restrained concern about atheist repressions and about the "godless life" under socialism, but emphasize the "constellations of martyrs shined up".[36] This type of forgetting (Connerton, 2008, pp. 62–64) evinces how the new Russian political identity, in which Orthodoxy plays prominent role, is formed together with continued positive images of the Soviet past. I will come back to this matter later on. As researchers note, the ROC avoids addressing the responsibility of once tormentors and executioners, due to recently growing loyalty to the Soviet legacy and even "Sovietophile" sentiments (Kormina, 2013a, p. 420; Torbakov, 2014, p. 163).

The process of reconstruction of sacred buildings (churches, monasteries, etc.) also brings with it the necessity to handle dead bodies, not just symbolically, but in a very immediate and physical way. Under socialism, many of the cemeteries located in church and monastic yards were destroyed, while all monastic and most church buildings in the district of Kaluga were used for secular purposes. In the context of post-Soviet religious revivalism, there are different ways to approach the re-sacralization of places and bodies. For instance, a large-scale identification of the graves and genetic identification of the remains was applied in Optina Pustyn'. It is not just about the restoration of historical justice, as it is the case for politically colored reburials (see Verdery, 1999, pp. 4–23). Bringing back the past pre-revolutionary fame of the monastery is another important motivation. One should point out the special role played in this initiative by the monk F., an ex-academic scholar in biology.[37] Both the identified and recovered graves in the yard of Optina Hermitage and the relics of the new martyrs are nowadays objects of veneration by pilgrims. The plausibility of identification is not a matter of discussion. On the contrary, the physical aspect of venerating the dead contributes to the strengthening of the symbolic meaning of the cemetery and its transformation into a highly valued object of pilgrimage.

In other words, the sacred status of the cemetery has been reformulated and reinforced. It is also an aspect of the struggle for symbolic and social capital in

Figure 4.1 Reburial of the anonymous dead in a churchyard. Kaluga, August 8, 2007.
Source: Photo: Milena Benovska

the competition between the religious communities identifying themselves with the sacred places. The more sacred a place is, the more prestige and respect its associated religious community receives.

Actually, the work of the Eparchial Commission of Canonization is in close parallel and even overlaps to a certain extent with the functions of the lay Commission for Reconstruction of Memory [*Komissiia po Vosstanovleniiu Pamiati*] led by the governor of the Kaluga district. Some of the church *kraevedy* are involved in both the Eparchial Commission of Canonization and the *secular* commission belonging to the institutions of local authorities. Vitalii Legostaev, the most prominent church *kraeved* of Kaluga, participated in both commissions. While working in the secular Commission for Reconstruction of Memory, one of his tasks was to take pictures of thousands of graves in different cemeteries of Kaluga in order to save the names of the dead from oblivion (i.e. to help preserve memory).

The long-term politics of suppressing memory during the Soviet period (Adler, 2001, p. 275) is sometimes reflected in the frustrating challenges of postsocialist times. In reconstructing and rebuilding churches, one tackles not just "the very special dead", but also the nameless and anonymous dead. Unlike the cases of (ex) Yugoslav or Serbian reburials of the nameless victims of mass murders wherein "entire social groups are repositioned" (Verdery, 1999, pp. 20–23) and serious political claims are raised, bones found in a church yard in Kaluga have turned into a source of frustration. The Soviet "politics of forgetting" (Adler, 2001, p. 275) are the reason for a complete oblivion and a lack of knowledge regarding certain bodies. In July 2007, I noticed a modest grave in a church yard with no name on the cross and asked to whom it belonged. Bones had been found repeatedly during construction works around the church, and the priests had reburied them. When I asked about the origin of these bones, one of the parishioners told me that no one knew whether the bones were from soldiers of the Second World War, and if so, which soldiers died here, Soviets or Germans. Telling me this, the woman whispered and asked me not to mention the matter to *matuška*. My astonishment became even stronger when I noticed a bag of bones left among construction materials waiting for the next reburial. Obviously, the presence of anonymous dead had caused serious confusion because anonymity did not allow even proper treatment of the dead. The "special dead" bring fame to a shrine; anonymous dead are a source of disorder and a potential threat to the sacred aura of a church.

The parallels between secular and religious manifestations of the politics of memory could be extended. The activities for the identification of graves, the relics of the "special dead", and the reburial of anonymous dead strikingly correspond to a large-scale secular initiative named *poiskovoe dvzhenie* [Movement of Explorers]. This one aims at the identification of mass graves of Soviet soldiers killed in the Second World War. Although the long-term initiative is being carried out in all of the Russian Federation (and across the former Soviet Union), citizens of Kaluga claim the city is prominent in its history. The organized movement was inaugurated namely in Kaluga, in 1988.[38] At present, the Movement of Explorers is a centralized organization combining participation of mainly young volunteers (mostly students) and financial support of different sources, including regular state finance. According to the Internet site of the movement, "it unites at present more than 42,000 explorers of all ages comprising 1,428 explorers' squads".[39]

In particular, the local Kaluga teams of explorers [*poiskovye otriady*] have searched the location called "The Valley of Death" in the district of Kaluga for 30 years. By 2007, the remains of approximately 5,500 Soviet soldiers had been found and reburied, accompanied by great efforts at personal identification of the remains. Due to the lack of physical evidence, however, personal identification was not always possible. On June 22, 2007, a similar ceremony took place in the village of Barsuki, where 145 soldiers were reburied (V "doline smerti", 2007, p. 23). Family members, heirs, and relatives of those whose remains had been positively identified were contacted and took part in the ceremony (ibid). For example, one of my interlocutors was included in the ritual part of the initiative. Her mother received a letter announcing that the place of death (during the Second World War) of her grandfather had been found near Kaluga. Both the mother and the daughter (my interlocutor) were invited to participate in the ceremony of his reburial, and for that purpose they travelled the tremendous distance from their place of residence, Komsomol'sk na Amur in the far east of Russia, to Kaluga.

Remembrances of the Second World War are not the central topic of everyday communication in Kaluga, unlike other places in Russia where social memory of the war is still very strong, as Tocheva (2007) reports concerning her field site. In fact, initiatives such as the one I mentioned, are mounted so as not to allow the memory of war to be transformed into history.[40] Who are the social actors behind this initiative? Why is it so important more than 70 years after the end of the war? It is no surprise that specific social groups stand behind this initiative, and at the local level, these are the Patriotic Union of Teams of Explorers named *Pamiat'* (Memory) and the city and district Committees of the Veterans of War and Military Service (Gorolevich, 2006, p. 31). In other words, the military professional community and societal circles connected to it are important driving forces of the initiative. School and university students are actively involved in it. The Movement of Explorers receives financial support from authorities, both central (Ministry of Defense) and local (regional administration).

A published interview of a representative of the mentioned community sheds some light on its motives. It confirms the observation that "social memory has been linked with the creation of 'imagined communities' and with a construction of moral order" (Barahona de Brito, Gonzales-Enriquez and Aguilar, 2001, p. 38). Deep social differentiation in present-day Russian society engenders feelings of a shortage of justice projected over history:

> White spots in our history turn to be a national disgrace, against the general background of the plunder of the people's property and of Russia's natural resources, the creation of absurd fortunes of native billionaires, the dire straits of the majority of the population [. . .], and the rise of criminality.
>
> (Gorolevich, 2006, p. 31)

The symbolic gesture of reburial also aims at symbolically overcoming unfairness:

> According to estimates of the District Committee of the Veterans of War and Military Service, there are more than 100,000 perished defenders of the Fatherland left without proper burial on the territory of the district of Kaluga. [. . .] Their relatives have suffered famine and deprivations and have not

> received any compensation for the loss of the bread giver; no postwar privileges have been established [for them]. Unwillingly, one raises the question: "What for have these people, full of vital energy, given their lives, if for sixty years so far we have not been able to rehabilitate their honest names and to give to the earth their remains according to Christian customs?"
>
> (Gorolevich, 2006, p. 31)

As I have noticed, anonymous dead are a source of frustration. Identification (i.e. personalization) and reburial change the symbolic status of the nameless dead soldiers. Here, already, an entire social group is being repositioned, similar to the victims of communist repressions; religious connotation is also being presented (Verdery, 1999, p. 20). Thus, anonymous dead are transformed into heroes via personalization and "proper burial".

It would not be difficult to find similarities between the images of the new martyrs and the heroes, constituted through the politics of memory. Images of the heroes are overshadowed by the connotation of martyrdom through the discourse of "victimization", as one can see from the aforementioned quotation. On the other hand, some of the martyrs acquire heroic features in the narratives created or popularized by the local church press. According to these narratives, a monk from St. Trinity-Liutikov monastery demonstrated supernatural strength of the spirit in 1918:

> *Gunmen [came to] the monastery; [they] demanded the handover of [monastic] horses. The abbot of the monastery refused to give them horses. So, the gunmen started to threaten the monks. They sounded alarm by ringing the bells; then peasants came and chased the gunmen away. At the end of the day, regular troops came from Kaluga and, you see, they imposed revolutionary order. They shot all the monks and eight other people, peasants.* [. . .]
>
> *This was in the middle of [nineteen] eighteen. [People remember] that when they were shot, they had to stand at the edge of a [grave] hole. [The soldiers] did not succeed in killing one of the monks. They shot him over and over again.* [. . .] *The soldiers were already afraid, and they wanted to run away. But the monk said: "Well, what's the matter! Go ahead, do your job!" He gave his blessing, and only then were they able to kill him. He must have been a very devotional monk!*[41]

The similarity with widespread (and stereotyped) literary and cinema plots, connected to the mythology of revolutionary struggles and partisan wars is obvious.

Although the images of new martyrs belong to the religious sphere and the images of war heroes are of secular character, one finds points of contact between them. This analogy is far from surprising, if we remember that the images of the martyr and the hero have been closely related since early Christian times. Extraordinary sufferings that have been experienced by the martyrs are a kind of miracle and sign for divine presence. "The heroism of the martyrs has always been treated as a form of possession, strictly dissociated from normal human courage" (Brown, 2002 [1981], p. 79).

In this particular case, heroization contributes to a new elaboration and reformulation of the memory: atrocities committed by the tormentors remain in the background, while the attention is focused on the valor of a martyr as chosen by God. This is the way to achieve symbolic reconciliation of allegedly irreconcilable fragments of the social memory. The narrative of martyrdom is implemented as a tool to positively perceive traumatic experiences from the past. Actually, both the secular project and the Orthodox project successfully transform and reformulate collective memory by constructing a positive vision of the past. This narrative strategy seems to give expression to a more general trend. Certain authors (Rousselet, 2007, p. 74; Christensen, 2018, pp. 198–206) noted the reluctance to judge perpetrators of atrocities. They remain in the shadow, even through iconography. Certainly, the Orthodox community avoids dividing Russian society into "victims" and "tormentors".

It is useful to remember the cross-culturally valid observation that:

> Historical memories and collective remembrances can be instruments to legitimate discourse, create loyalties, and justify political options. Thus, control over the narrative of the past means control over the construction of narratives for an imagined future. Memory is a struggle over power and who gets to decide the future. What and how societies choose to remember and forget largely determines their future options. Indeed, memories are constantly revised to suit current identities.
>
> (Barahona de Brito, Gonzales-Enriquez and Aguilar, 2001, p. 38)

I have addressed the *kraevedenie* and the cult of the "special dead" – martyrs and heroes – as two specific manifestations of the politics of memory. Exploring them in the local context of Kaluga allows for gaining an insight into the fabric of social life behind empirical evidence and summarizing answers to the initial research questions.

Although the interest in local history and local cultural heritage existed in pre-revolutionary Russia, *kraevedenie* was firmly conceptualized during the Soviet epoch as a distinct mode for the production of knowledge. Church *kraevedenie* is, on the other hand, a product of postsocialism and has gained momentum after 2000 and after President Putin took office. The expansion of church *kraevedenie* could be explained by the aspiration to strengthen national-affirmative views in Russian society. However, church *kraevedenie* is also an aspect of the return to Orthodoxy as an (historic) identification after the loss of Soviet political identity. Thus, *kraevedenie* has been transformed from a peripheral project into a socially significant one. Furthermore, church *kraevedenie* is a result of both politics from top-down and initiatives from bottom-up. In other words, strategies of the central power are supported by initiatives from below. *Kraevedy* are the social actors playing the role of the motor in this process; they are also the intermediaries passing important messages between distinct social groups of local society.

Church *kraevedenie* develops mostly in the secular milieu, although in close cooperation with local clergy. *Kraevedy* play a significant role in the process of religious revivalism, investing efforts to discover the locations of destroyed temples and monasteries and to revive remembrance of clerics of the past. *Kraevedy* are in synergy with the local professional community of clerics and contribute to strengthening their prestige and position in the social hierarchy. Church *kraevedy* contribute to the sacralization of both local and national history, popularizing half-forgotten legends and interpreting fateful historical events. *Kraevedy* of Kaluga are less interested in promoting local specificity and "uniqueness" than in constructing a nationally affirmative narrative and contributing to the "patriotic turn" in contemporary Russian society.

The active politics of memory is a strategy for reconciling irreconcilable historical legacies that are specific for Russia. The narrative of martyrdom is implemented as a tool to positively reformulate traumatic experiences of the past. In doing so, the Orthodox project of constructing memory successfully contributes to the larger societal project of elaborating a pacified version of memory and history.

Pursued in these forms, the politics of memory provide a symbolic means to overcome the historical ruptures of local and national, religious and secular, and past and present identities. In doing so, it gives a sense of continuity at the collective and personal levels. Together, clerics and secular authorities equally participate in the struggle for control over memory, which is actually a struggle for power. Both politics of memory and religious revivalism are involved in the construction of a new Russian identity, being parts of the large nationally affirmative narrative of post-Soviet Russia.

Notes

1 Certain parts of an earlier version of the chapter 4 are published as articles: 'Church kraevedenie: the politics of memory and religious revival in post-soviet Russia', *Narodna umjetnost*, 46 (1), 2009, pp. 121–132; and 'Martyrs and heroes: The religious and secular worship of the dead in post-Soviet Russia', *Ethnologia Europaea*, 2010, 40 (1), pp. 42–57. I thank both journals for their permission to publish this material in chapter 4 of the present book.

2 *Kraevedenie* is derived from the Russian '*kraj*' – region, area.

3 During the last decade, the history of Soviet *kraevedenie* has attracted significant interest among Russian historians. For an overview and references see: Mel'nikova (2012, 2013).

4 Eidson refers here to several of his previous articles on the matter. For bibliographical references see Eidson (2004, pp. 86–91).

5 See the official Internet site of the Eparchy of Kaluga: www.kaluga-eparhia.ru/abbats_churchs/mon_opt.htm.

6

> *Kraevedenie stalo modoj posle togo, kak prezident [Putin] skazal, chto detej nado vospityvat' patriotičeski i v školy vveli predmet "Krayevedenija". Nikto ran'še i ne znal, čto eto za predmet. Nikto na kraevedy ne obraščal vnimanija, oni pisali, no ikh ne pečatali. A sejčas oni pečatajutsia, stali organizovat' konferencii, pečatat' knigi. A delo i v tom, čto sredi kraevedov mnogo skazočnikov. Poetomu i na konferencii oni mezhdu soboj ssoriatsia. V sentiabre ili oktiabre [2006] mnogo takikh konferencij.*
>
> – Interview with Nina Viktorovna, 32, university education, bibliographer. 21.09.2006, Kaluga.

7 For similar observations concerning the practices of commemoration of World War I in Argonne (France), see Filippucci (2004, p. 46).
8 Since 2013, it has been transformed into United Reserve-Museum of Kaluga [Kaluzhskii ob'edinënnyj muzej-zapovednik]. See http://kaluga.amr-musum.ru. Last accessed: 25.09.2018.
9 *Uezd* – Rus. county (during pre-revolutionary and early-Soviet time).
10 In Russian:

> *I vot ja s devianosto vtorogo goda rabotaju tam. . . . Etot Kaluzhskij uezd ja izučaju bol'še desiati let. Okolo šestidesiati khramov, tam perečen' est', reestr. Vpervye v eparkhii my postavili krest na meste razrušennogo khrama. Krest khorošij polučilsya, zhelezobetonnyj. Nu sootvetstvenno ja vse eti shest'desiat khramov ja posetil. T.e. nametil maršruty, na karte oboznačil, u menia karty est' i starinnyye karty, i takiye. T.e. ja stavil krestik, prokladyval tuda maršrut zimoj, a letom ekhal tuda. Vsë eto fiksiroval, snimal. Tak polučilos', chto prišlos' neskol'ko raz ezdit.*
>
> – Interview with Vitalii Legostaev, 59, secondary education, writer and photographer. 9.07.2007, Kaluga.

I quote the name of Mr. Legostaev unchanged because of his great popularity as an author. With his remarkable energy and hard work, he published 186 publications; 15 of them are books. The interest in him and his work is expressed also in interviews taken from him and published mostly in local press and media. He keeps a personal Internet site; in addition, Belinskii Scientific Library of Kaluga also developed an Internet page dedicated to him and his books: http://legostaev.kaluga.net/; belinkakaluga.ru/легостаев-виталий-васильевич. Last accessed: 25.07.2019.
11 On the financial support of Russian entrepreneurs in favor of Orthodox initiatives, see Köllner (2012).
12 The same mixed character of genres has been noted by Eidson (2004).
13 Makarova and Kalashnikova list 160 titles in their bibliography before 2006 (ibid., pp. 352–356).
14 In Russian:

> *Fotografiroval vezde, gde ja byl: na celine fotografiroval, v armii fotografiroval, v detstve fotografiroval i v Kalugu priekhal- vse eto fotografiroval. [I vot zdes' uzhe v Kaluge] – fotografij mnogo, ja ikh načal sortirovat'. Domašnie v domashnij al'bom, sluzhebnye . . .: priroda, etiudy, babochki, tam skvortsy . . ., pamyatniki i khramy. I vot v 84 godu u menia sokhranilsia al'bom, «Khramy goroda Kalugi». Černo-belyye, ja vsë, čto mog snial, pod nimi biročki gde pamyatnye doski byli, tozhe pomestil annotacii ob etom khrame. Gde net, pošël v biblioteku, stal interesovat'sia krayevedčeskoj literaturoj. Vot otsiuda pošlo . . . s etim al'bomom, rešil pokazat' komu-to. Nu prišël, skazali – korifei kraevedenija v to vremia byli Dneprovskij Aleksandr Sergeyevič i Morozova Genrietta Mikhajlovna. Nu ja vpervyye popal k Dneprovskomu. Eto klub «Dobraja volia», oni sobiralis' po sredam, čaj delali, pili čaj i svobodnaja beseda, obsuzhdenija tam, mnenija i t.d. i t.p. K Morozovoj prišël. Genrietta Mikhajlovna rabotala zdes' v bibliografičeskom otdele. «U, govorit, molodoy čelovek, Vam nado v arkhiv». V arkhiv bylo slozhno. Nado bylo pis'mo . . . «Ja vam sdelaju, budete rabotat'».*
>
> – Interview with Vitalii Legostaev, 59, secondary education, writer and photographer. 9.07.2007, Kaluga.

15 For extensive overview on canonization, see Christensen (2018, pp. 19–79).
16 Some new cases of canonization also fit the notion of "new martyrdom", although the death of the martyrs concerned occurred after the end of the Soviet era, for example the three monks of Optina Pustyn' who were murdered on Easter in 1993 (see Optinskaia Golgofa, 1994; Zhizneopisanie, 2003).

17 The Synodal Commission of Canonization of Saints has been defined then as a "research organ". See www.patriarchia.ru/db/text/65980.html. Last accessed: 30.03.2019.

18 It started working in 2005, according to the interview with Ostap Kirillovič. See also the official Internet site of Kaluga Eparchy: www.kaluga-eparhia.ru. Last accessed: 20.09.2018.

19 On the institutional structures engaged in canonization of the new martyrs, see Christensen (2018, pp. 47–50).

20 See www.fond.ru. Last accessed: 20.09.2018; see also Christensen (2018, pp. 34–36).

21 See also the official Internet site of the Kaluga Eparchy: www.kaluga-eparhia.ru/abbats_churchs/mon_opt.htm.

22 This took place in the year 2000 during the Bishop Council [*Arkhiiereiskii Sobor*], see www.patriarchia.ru/db/text/65980.html. Last accessed: 1.03.2020.

23 See reference 14.

24 In Russian:

> *Sejčas v Optinoj pustyni tam rabotaet svoja komissija, tam takoy monakh Platon, jeromonakh Josif, jeromonakh Mefodii. Kak raz rabotayut čisto Optinskimi monakhami proslavliajut, kotorye postradali takzhe, sluzhili gde to v raznykh mestakh.*
>
> – Interview with Ostap Kirillovič, 50, university education, Orthodox activist. 16.08.2007, Kaluga.

25 Similar to other most important monastic centres of national Russian significance, such as Troitse-Sergieva Lavra in Sergiev Posad, Diveevo monastery, etc., see Mitrokhin (2004, p. 110).

26 According to (approximate) statistics suggested by Christensen (2018, pp. 51–53), 81.8% of canonized new martyrs and confessors were among the priests, bishops, and deacons. The statistics reflect the fact that "the NKVD executed 80 percent of the priests they arrested during the Great Terror" (ibid., p. 52).

27 Numerous Orthodox educational institutions function in Kaluga aiming at the formation and strengthening of the clergy, see Aleksakhina and Bogatyreva (2003, pp. 24–31).

28 Presently, it is already a town attached the city of Kaluga in 2012. See: https://ru.wikipedia.org/. Lats accessed: 30.09.2018.

29 www.fond.ru. Last accessed: 20.09.2018.

30 In Russian:

> *Eto mesto Velikogo stoyanija v 1480 godu. Eto mesto na tom beregu Ugry, gde khan Akhmat i stoyal. . . . I mesto: ja govoriu, čto nakhoditsia na istoričeskom meste. S etogo mesta vidna kolokol'nia Uspenskogo sobora Tikhonovoj pustyni. S drugoj storony tam, znachit, Spasov monastyr' tam na Ugre. Dovol'no sviatoe mesto, oboznačennoe Bogom, t.e. sčitaetsia, Bogorodicey – na Ugre. I dejstvitel'no, pomošč' uzhe Bogorodicy zametno oščuščaetsia i molitva novomučenikov tozhe oščuščaetsia.*
>
> – Interview with Ostap Kirillovič, 50, university education, Orthodox activist. 16.08.2007, Kaluga.

31 See the picture of the chapel near Kurovskoe at: https://sobory.ru/photo/258905. Last accessed: 30.08.2019.

32 Interview with Zinaida Anatolievna, 66, university education, an engineer/pensioner. 2.08.2007, Kaluga.

33 It is important to note the agreement between the central policy of the Moscow Patriarchy to encourage veneration of the new martyrs and the local Kaluga initiative. See "On measures to preserve the memory of new martyrs, confessors and all those innocents who suffered under the opponents of God in the years of persecution", document approved by Bishop Council in 2011 (Rock, 2011, n.p.).

34 I would avoid calling these publications "lives of the saints", as far as they lack the officially codified hagiography by the church hierarchy.

35 On the transformation of former experts in "scientific atheism" into experts in teaching religions after the end of socialism, see Bourdeaux (2000, p. 10).

36 Interview with Ekaterina Viačeslavovna, 36, university education, teacher/religious activist. 12.07.2007, Kaluga.

37 Interview with Lidia Vassilievna, 66, university education, bibliographer. 26.09.2006, Kaluga.

38 The first general assembly of 106 leaders of explorers took place in Kaluga, on March 13, 1988 (Kalakin, 2018). The Explorers' activity is also regulated by Russian legislation (1993), including by a legislative act of the district of Kaluga (2000). – See www. http://рф-поиск.рф/documents/54/. Last accessed: 1.09.2019.

39 See the official Internet site of the movement: http://rf-poisk.ru/page/230/. Last accessed: 1.09.2019.

40 Concerning similar reminders but about the First World War in Argonne, France, see Filippucci (2004, pp. 44–46).

41 In Russian:

> *Liudi vooruzhennyye prišli v monastyr', trebovali, čtoby otdali im lošadej. Igumen monastyria zapretil otdavat'. Ugrozhali. Monakhi dali nabatnyj kolokol, prišli krest'jane i otognali ikh. I v konce koncov prišli vojska s Kalugi i značit, naveli poriadok revoliucionnyj. Rasstreliali vsekh monakhov i eščë vosem' čelovek krest'jan. Eto vosemnadcatyj god, seredina. [Vspominajut] čto kogda rasstrelivali etikh liudej, oni stojali, značit, u jamy. Odnogo monakha ne mogli ubit'. Streliali, streliali. . . . Potom uzhe soldaty ispugalis', khoteli ubezhat'. A on skazal: „Nu čto vy! Davajte, delajte svoë delo!" Blagoslovil, togda oni smogli yego ubit'. Vot takoy, naverno, byl monakh molitvennyj.*
>
> – Interview with Ostap Kirillovich, 50, university education, religious activist. 16.08.2007, Kaluga.

Conclusions

The rise of Orthodoxy, triggered in 1988 in the context of *perestroika*, is a process initiated from the "top-down", but enthusiastically embraced from the "bottom-up" of Russian society. This amazing awakening of Orthodox religiosity after seven long decades of aggressive atheism is also possible due to the persistence of a responsiveness to religion in the depths of Soviet society. Several factors account for this responsiveness. These include: the practice of Orthodox religiosity in remote rural areas during socialism; the "underground" survival and ministry of a small part of the clerics and the most loyal laymen; the legitimacy of religion as a source of national cultural heritage since the 1960s; and the activity and protest actions of the few religious dissidents. The decisive factor for the "resurgence" of Orthodoxy, however, is the survival of the specific community of the most zealous believers of the *pricerkovnyj krug*: From its formation in the first decades of the twentieth century through its underground existence during the Soviet period, and through to the present day. This minority, "invisible" under socialism, is a kind of "reservoir" of knowledge and a living memory of Orthodox traditions, which were passed on to Russian society after the end of atheistic politics, on the border between the end of the Soviet era and postsocialism.

Post-Soviet Russian Orthodox religiosity is characterized by massive restoration of religious institutions, state support for the Russian Orthodox Church, mass identification with Orthodoxy among Russians, and a relatively low level of actual participation in religious practices. The key to understanding the last two characteristics – often described as a paradox – is the concept of vicarious religion (Davie, 2007). In such a situation, a few people are practicing religion on behalf of everyone else. The Russian examples allow an adjustment of this concept. Without neglecting the role of the clergy, it is the circle of the most zealous believers – the "little flock" – that is the basis for vicarious religion. It is they who are reviving church life and legitimizing clerics and their policies to influence Russian public life. The interaction between the clerics and the comparatively limited circle of the "little flock" leaves a significant imprint on the agenda of society, including even the imposition of certain extreme conservative policies or anti-modern messages.

Two social profiles can be distinguished, though conditionally, among the "little flock". One group is that of the *vocerkovlënnye* (in the narrow sense) – these people are "enchurched" and practice regularly, but they have an autonomous professional and family life and evince successful socialization in society. The second group, the *pricerkovnyj krug*, is characterized by self-isolation, the renunciation of secular professions, and a specific, eschatologically colored ideology.

The role of the "little flock" in post-Soviet religious life has determined the rise of Orthodox Christianity in Russia as a "bottom-up" social movement, albeit with political support for Russian Orthodox Church from the ruling elite. When seen from their perspective, the religious rise can indeed be conceptualized as Orthodox revivalism. However, secularism continues to be a major feature of the dominant contemporary Russian culture. Despite the scope of religious revivalism, it is (still) unreasonable to speak of desecularization. Nor is it quite accurate to invoke Jürgen Habermas' vision of post-secularism. As in many (West European) societies, Russia is marked by late-modern religious landscapes, but the notion of post-secularism – thus far developed – does not cover the unusual complexity and heterogeneous nature of religious life in Russia.

The significant influence of the Russian Orthodox Church on Russian political and social life, and the unequivocal political support for the Church by the ruling elite determine today's state of Orthodoxy as public religion. Yet, taking into consideration the complex and often controversial character of the Russian Orthodox Church, it is hard to suggest an all-encompassing formulation for the essence of Orthodox religious revivalism. Rather, it is about the parallel existence of different strategies, oriented either to the predominantly secular value system or to life under God's laws. There are passages and overflows between these strategies. Hence, the attitude towards Orthodox Christianity does not follow one unitary pattern, but a plurality of patterns that are ultimately interconnected by focusing on national ideas. In turn, Orthodox Christianity meets multiple needs in society. The political elite and some parts of the economic elite may adopt Orthodoxy as a language of political correctness or even as sheer opportunism. For other segments of the Russian society, Orthodox Christianity is the main priority and moral guide.

With its enhanced public presence, the Russian Orthodox Church sets out its strategies for establishing itself as a "moral entrepreneur" and a moral mentor. It seeks to lead internationally in the religious opposition to certain human rights. In Russian society, it works in collaboration with the secular central government to invent new traditions, such as the National Day of the Family, aimed at consolidating a postsocialist society. Orthodox family values, the state's pro-natalist policy, and the construction of national identity are in synergy, forged through historical imagination. Through another "invented tradition" – the raising of monuments of saints in the urban environment – the tendency to transform public space by saturating it with religious symbolism becomes evident. It should be pointed out that the Church's very pursuit of public presence also takes it away from strict adherence to some of its own precepts and canons. Orthodoxy is being rediscovered and reinvented. It is not being "dug out of the ashes" intact, nor is it a faithful copy of past patterns.

Social practices from different spheres of public and private religious life are united by two concepts: power and national consolidation. Religious power is the foundation upon which heterogeneous ethical discourses, negative moralizing, and disciplinary practices unfold. The local manifestations of the "asymmetric symphony" – the cooperation between state power and church – are evidence that high clergy becomes a part of the Russian ruling elites.

The appeals from some of the clergy for obedience and humility as an aspect of Christian soteriology reflect the strong influence of monastic religiosity on the lay environment. These "archaisms" follow Orthodox dogmas about the incurably "fallen" human nature and original sin. In turn, the empowerment of women is an aspect within the struggle for power and discipline in modern Orthodox communities. Women are empowered through active participation in important liturgical and charitable practices. Nevertheless, because the modern gender statuses within Orthodoxy face inherited patriarchal patterns, change comes tacitly.

Under the conditions of continued social change, the aspirations of the clergy to impose unitary Orthodox morals are confronted with the reality of multiple moralities. These moralities are located between the poles of disciplinary practices and negative moralizing at one end, and the search for good on the other. The ethic of Orthodox virtue is interwoven with and disputed by the humanist ideas and principles inherited from socialism. However, striving for good is the main ethos, explicitly discussed and shared in religious communities. It is supported by the charisma (spiritual or personal) of the religious shepherds. Together with the principles of shared moral imperatives, these are the pillars around which the identity of Orthodox parishes is consolidated.

Autobiographical narratives of Russian believers reveal the links between conversion, moral imagination, and moral perceptions, on the one hand, and radical personal transformation, on the other. If conversion to Orthodoxy is based on "interrupted continuity", it also includes the perception of an intimate, personal relationship of an individual with Orthodoxy. Unlike the Protestant tradition, personal stories have no ritual function in Orthodox liturgical life. Hence, Russian conversion narratives can hardly be reduced to a common pattern: they follow multiple models and reflect several trajectories of conversion from non-belief to religiosity.

Conversion is a continuous and controversial process. One narrative type presents it as sudden, lightning event following St. Paul's model. Another type describes conversion in terms of pain and acute physical suffering. Such "moral torment" preceding conversion, and indeed continuing for so long as the believer seeks personal transformation away from a sinful past and self, prove that a model of "break" and "rupture" is neither exclusively Protestant nor Pentecostal. "Moral torment" in Orthodoxy is also associated with radical personal transformation, with millenarian expectations, and with anxiety about personal religious salvation. The condition of "moral torment" is a sign of high moral sensitivity among the most committed Russian believers.

The widespread distribution of conversion in Russia can be linked to postsocialist social and economic instability. For people who lost orientation, including cognitive, in the rapidly changing postsocialist world in the 1990s, faith turned out to be a "moral lazaret" in the quest for stability and a new moral identity.

Yet conversion is narratively constructed as a cognitive process. The "ethically saturated" world is governed by a specific "semiotic ideology". Things and events are recognized, collectively and individually, as signs of an inner, second plan of action. The narrator, as a believer, finds evidence for God's presence and grace beyond external events. Conversion narratives revealing such evidence, and – even more so, stories of miracles – are based on a shared intersubjective knowledge of Orthodoxy and its moral imagination. Stories of miracles and miracle-working icons are central to the construction of positive identity and the sacralization of religious communities. They take on meaning by contrasting with the secularized and pragmatic social environment.

Autobiographical narratives of conversion, including those about miracles, are important for answering one of the key questions asked at the beginning of the book: Is Orthodox revivalsim in modern Russia genuine or spurious? Stories show the deeply personal, intimate nature of the passage from non-belief to religious dedication. The emotional nature of conversion, described at one moment as strong excitement and "bliss", and at another as an intolerable physical or moral pain, leaves no doubt about the genuine nature of the Orthodox resurgence in the grassroots perspective and among Orthodox parishes in particular. Yet, the cases of using religious language among the Russian ruling elite as political hypocrisy or chameleonism is evidence of (a) heterogeneous character of the Orthodox practices and (b) the lasting effect of secularization achieved due to communist politics of atheism.

Beyond what they show of the deeply woven religious threads in Russian society, and of the sincerity of Russian believers, conversion stories also draw attention to the symbolic bridges between Russian Orthodox believers and other Christians (perhaps most prominently, Charismatic Christians). Across the globe, "moral torment" presses on those with some Christian knowledge to seek the good, to leave behind their disbelief or unbelief, and to abandon worldly sin. The parallels between worlds so initially dissimilar as urban Russia and the small Pacific group of Urapmin are a remarkable reminder of the unified character (despite many differences) of the three branches of Christianity based on the Word (i.e. the Holy Scriptures). It is also a reminder that the anthropology of Christianity will remain incomplete without the inclusion of Eastern Orthodox Christians in its horizons.

The uncompromising moral maximalism on a personal level presented in the narratives is in contrast to the selectivity of the "bricolage" techniques, through which the great historical narrative – the fruit of politics of memory – is overwhelmed. The politics of memory is particularly intense in a postsocialist context, although they are far from being a patent of postsocialism. The Russian experience, however, is unique in that the duration of the Soviet period, respectively, of atheistic repression unlocks symmetrical politics of memory, i.e. initiatives and practices (including on the grassroots level) aimed at restoring historical justice.

The diverse politics of memory are characterized by different levels of religious "coloring". The canonization of new martyrs is primarily a religious initiative, despite the inevitable political connotations. Religious practices have a parallel in civil and political action, such as the re-burying of the dead bodies of soldiers who died during the Second World War. The Church *kraevedenie* and the worship of the "special dead" – martyrs and heroes – are two specific forms of politics of memory interwoven in the Russian historical context.

Postsocialist Russian politics of memory are marked by the effort to reconcile seemingly irreconcilable historical heritages. One can observe this struggle even by visually scanning public space: monuments to Soviet leaders stand in the company of renovated temples and new places of religious memory. Narratives for martyrdom are a rhetorical means of positively reformulating the traumatic experience of the past. Thus, the Orthodox project of constructing social memory integrates into a wider societal project for forging a non-conflictual historical narrative. The Soviet past – atheist and brutally repressive of religion – is to be integrated with a strong national sound.

Observations on developments in contemporary Russian Orthodoxy have brought the researcher repeatedly back to the question of the relationship between continuity and social change. As a definition of conversions in post-Soviet conditions, the term "interrupted continuity" is perfectly suited to Orthodox Christianity in modern Russia. The pursuit of continuity with the inheritances of the past is a powerful impetus for today's Russian citizens, including Orthodox Christians. The 70-year duration of the socialist period and its associated atheistic policies, processes of de-Christianization, and the loss of cultural knowledge of religion are challenging in this respect. The restoration of the institutional life of the Russian Orthodox Church also relies heavily on the "pro-Orthodox consensus" in Russian society: the mass perceptions of Orthodoxy as a national domain and an indispensable part of Russian identity. This intimate connection between the ideas of Russianness and Orthodoxy is a stronger factor in the recovery and rise of Orthodox life than the challenges of the interrupted tradition.

The processes of post-Soviet social changes, particularly in the sphere of religious life, place the researcher in a unique laboratory. Here, she may find insight into the unprecedented search, across Russian society, for what Hervieu-Léger called "chains of memory". Here, too, are a wealth of traditions in the midst of invention. Behind the essence of religious phenomena, there are the strategies to be uncovered by which believers are constantly adapting the forms of belief to the conditions of historical acceleration and uncertainty in the modern world. Such adaptation allows the core of the transcendental messages to be preserved intact.

References

27th Congress (1986) *XXVII s'ezd Kommunističeskoi partii Sovetskogo soiuza. Stenografičeskii otchět*. Moskva: Politizdat.

Abashin, S. (2015) *Sovetskij kišlak: mezhdu kolonializmom i modernizaciej* [Soviet Kishlak: Between Colonialism and Modernization]. Moskva: NLO.

Adler, N. (2001) 'In search of identity: The collapse of the Soviet Union and the recreation of Russia', in Barahona de Brito, A., Gonzales-Enriquez, C. and Aguilar, P. (eds.) *The Politics of Memory: Transnational Justice in Democratizing Societies*. Oxford: Oxford University Press, pp. 275–302.

Agadjanian, A. (2001) 'Revising Pandora's gifts: Religious and national identity in the post-Soviet societal Fabric', *Europe-Asia Studies*, 53(3), pp. 473–488.

Agadjanian, A. (2003) 'Breakthrough to modernity, apologia for traditionalism: The Russian Orthodox view of society and culture in comparative perspective', *Religion, State and Society*, 31(4), pp. 327–346.

Agadjanian, A. (2006) 'The search for privacy and the return of a grand narrative: Religion in a post-communist society', *Social Compass*, 53(2), pp. 169–184.

Agadjanian, A. (2010) 'Liberal individual and Christian culture: Russian Orthodox teaching on human rights in social theory perspective', *Religion, State and Society*, 38(2), pp. 97–113.

Agadjanian, A. (2011a) 'Exploring Russian religiosity as a source of morality today', in Zigon, J. (ed.) *Multiple Moralities and Religions in Post-soviet Russia*. New York and Oxford: Berghahn Books, pp. 16–24.

Agadjanian, A. (2011b) 'Prikhod i obščina v russkom pravoslavii: sovremennyj process v russkom pravoslavii v retrospective poslednego stoletija' [The parish and community in the Russian Orthodoxy: Contemporary proces in Russian Orthodoxy in the context of the last century], in Agadjanian, A. and Rousselet, K. (eds.) *Prikhod i obshchina v sovremennom russkom pravoslavii. Kornevaya sistema rossiyskoy religioznosti*. Moskva: Ves' mir, pp. 15–16.

Agadjanian, A. (avril–juin 2013) 'Reform and revival in Moscow Orthodox communities. Two types of religious modernity', *Archives de sciences sociales des religions*, 162, pp. 75–94.

Agadjanian, A. (2017) 'Tradition, morality and community: Elaborating Orthodox identity in Putin's Russia', *Religion, State and Society*, 45(1), pp. 39–60.

Agadjanian, A. and Rousselet, K. (eds.) (2006) *Prikhod i obshchina v sovremennom russkom pravoslavii. Kornevaja sistema rossiyskoj religioznosti* [The Parish and Community in the Russian Orthodoxy. The Root System of Russian Religiosity]. Moskva: Ves' mir.

Ajvazova, S. G. (1999) 'Zhenskoe dvizhenie Rossii: opyt tipologičeskogo analiza' [Feminist movement in Russia: An attempt for typological analysis], in Aksianova, G. A. et al. (eds.) *Muščina i zhenščina v sovremennom mire: meniaiuščiesia roli i obrazy*, vol. 1. Moskva: Institut etnologii i antropologii RAN, pp. 29–37.

Akhmetova, M. V. (2004) 'Zhëltaja ugroza v predstavlenijakh sovremennoy pricerkovnoj sredy' [The yellow threat in the views of the modern around-church environment], *Antropologičeskij forum*, 1(1), pp. 238–249.

Akhmetova, M. V. (2006) 'Utopija preobrazhënnogo mira v sovremennykh eskhatologičeskikh predstavlenijakh (Beloe bratstvo, Bogorodičnyj centr, Cerkov' poslednego zaveta, pravoslavnye monarkhisty)' [Utopia of the transformed world in modern eschatological ideas (White Brotherhood, Mother of God Center, Church of the last testament, Orthodox monarchists)], in Kormina, Z., Panchenko, A. A. and Shtyrkov, S. A. (eds.) *Sny Bogorodicy. Issledovanija po antropologii religii*. Sankt-Peterburg: Izdatel'stvo Evropeyskogo universiteta v Sankt-Peterburge. *Studia Ethnologica*, 3, pp. 203–216.

Akhmetova, M. V. (2010) *Konec sveta v odnoj otdel'no vziatoj strane: Religioznyye soobščestva postsovetskoj Rossii i ikh eskhatologičeskij mif* [The end of the world in one particular country: Religious communities of post-Soviet Russia and their eschatological myth]. Moskva: OGI.

Aleksakhina, M. N. and Bogatyreva, N. V. (2003) *Kaluzhskaia zemlia – zemlia sviataia* [The land of Kaluga – sacred land]. Moskva: Olma-Press.

Alexii II, Patriarch (2005) '"V monastyr' ne ukhodiat – tuda prikhodiat". Predstoiatel' Russkoj pravoslavnoj cerkvi otvetil na voprosy zhurnala "Foma"' ["They don't go away from the monastery – They come there". The head of the Russian Orthodox Church answered the questions of Foma Magazine], *Foma*, № 7(30). Official Site of the Russian Orthodox Church. www.mospat.ru/index.php?page=27834.

Alexii II, Patriarch (2008) 'Etot prazdnik prizvan sodeistvovat' utverzhdeniju v Rossii vysokih nravstvennyh cennostei i ukrepleniju instituta sem'i' [This holiday is intended to promote the establishment of high moral values in Russia and the strengthening of the institution of the family]. *On the Day of Family, Love, and Faithfulness in All the Churches of the Russian Orthodox Church Will Be Held Celebratory Worship. Announcement of the Information Agency Russkaja Linja*, 8.07.2008. https://rusk.ru/st.php?idar=177565. Last accessed: 3.09.2018.

Ammerman, N. T. (2007) 'Studying everyday religion: Challenges for the future', in Ammerman, N. T. (ed.) *Everyday Religion: Observing Modern Religious Lives*. Oxford: Oxford University Press, pp. 219–238.

Ammerman, N. T. and Williams, R. A. (2012) 'Speaking of methods: Eliciting religious narratives through interviews, photos, and diaries', in Benzano, L. and Preben Riis, O. (eds.) *Annual Review of the Sociology of Religion*, vol. 3. New methods in the sociology of religion. Leiden, The Netherlands: Brill, pp. 117–134.

Anderson, J. (2007) 'Putin and the Russian Orthodox Church: Asymmetric symphonia', *Columbia Journal of International Affairs*, 61(1), pp. 185–201.

Andreeva, L. A. (2003) 'Process dekhristianizacii v Rossii i vozniknovenie kvazireligioznosti XX veka' [The process of de-Christianization in Russia and the emergence of quasi-religiosity of the 20th century], *Obščestvennye nauki i sovremennost'*, 1, pp. 90–100.

[Anonymous] (2003) 'Mučeničestvo bez prolitija krovi' [Martyrdom without bloodshed], in *Zhizneopisanie Optinskikh novomučenikov ieromonakha Vasiliia, inoka Feraponta, inoka Trofima. Blagoslovenno voinstvo* [Lives of the new martyrs of Optina: Hieromonk

Vasilii, Monk Therapont, Monk Trofim]. Optina Pustyn': Izdatel'stvo Sviato-Vvedenskoi Optinoi Pustyni, pp. 265–272.
Arsent'ev, D. (2007) 'S čego načinaetsia Rodina? Reportazh iz kaluzhskoj školy rodinovedenija' [From where does motherland begins? A report from a Kaluga school of the study of motherland], *Pravoslavnyj christianin*, 6, pp. 18–19.
Asad, T. (1993) *Genealogies of Religion: Discipline and Reasons of Power in Christianity and Islam*. Baltimore and London: The Johns Hopkins University Press.
Asad, T. (1996) 'Comments on conversion', in Van der Veer, P. (ed.) *Conversion to Modernities: The Globalization of Christianity*. New York: Routledge, pp. 263–274.
Austin-Broos, D. (2003) 'The anthropology of conversion: An introduction', in Buckser, A. and Glazer, S. D. (eds.) *The Anthropology of Religious Conversion*. Lanham, Boulder, New York, Toronto and Oxford: Rowman & Littlefield Publishers, Inc., pp. 1–12.
Avramenko, A. A. (2001) 'Religioznaja obstanovka v Kaluge' [Religious situation in Kaluga], *Sociologičeskie isledovanija*, 11, pp. 92–100.
Baer, M. D. (2014) 'History and religious conversion', in Rambo, L. R. and Farhadian, C. E. (eds.) *The Oxford Handbook of Religious Conversion*. Oxford: Oxford University Press, pp. 25–47.
Bailey, F. G. (2001 [1969]) *Stratagems and Spoils: A Social Anthropology of Politics*. New York and London: Routledge.
Bandak, A. (2014) 'Of refrains and rhythms in contemporary Damascus urban space and Christian-Muslim coexistence', *Current Anthropology*, 55(Supplement 10), pp. 248–261.
Barahona de Brito, A., Gonzales-Enriquez, C. and Aguilar, P. (2001) 'Introduction', in Barahona de Brito, A., Gonzales-Enriquez, C. and Aguilar, P. (eds.) *The Politics of Memory: Transnational Justice in Democratizing Societies*. Oxford: Oxford University Press, pp. 1–39.
Barker, J. (September 2008) 'Toward an anthropology of Christianity', *American Anthropologist*, 110(3), pp. 377–381.
Basinger, D. (2011) 'What is a miracle?', in Twelftree, G. H. (ed.) *The Cambridge Companion to Miracles*. Cambridge: Cambridge University Press, pp. 19–35.
Basinger, D. (2018) *Miracles*. Cambridge: Cambridge University Press.
Bauer, A. (2001) 'Ot cerkovnogo kraevedenija – k pravoslavnoj kul'ture' [From Church local history to Orthodox culture], *Znamia truda*, 15.05.2001.
Bendix, R. (1992) 'National sentiments in the enactment and discourse of Swiss political ritual', *American Ethnologist*, 19(4), pp. 768–790.
Benovska-Sabkova, M. (2007) 'Monuments, collective memory, social imagination and local identity in Bulgaria on the borderline between two centuries', in Hemme, D., Tauschek, M. and Bendix, R. (eds.) *Prädikat "Heritage". Wertschoepfungen aus kulturellen Ressourcen. Studien zur Kulturanthropologie/ Europaische Ethnologie*. Band 1. Berlin: LIT Verlag, pp. 277–296.
Benovska-Sabkova, M. (2010) 'Martyrs and heroes: The religious and secular worship of the dead in post-Soviet Russia', *Ethnologia Europea*, 40(1), pp. 42–57.
Benovska-Sabkova, M. et al. (February 2010) '"Spreading grace" in post-Soviet Russia', *Anthropology Today*, 26(1), pp. 16–21.
Berestov, A. (2003) 'L. N. Tolstoy. Optinskie vstreči' [Optina's meetings], in Berestov, A. and Mironovič, S. (eds.) *Ot našikh korneij. Kul'tura i iskusstvo Kaluzhskogo kraia v istorii Rossii*. Kaluga: Izdatel'stvo N. Bočkarevoi, pp. 290–325.
Berestov, A. and Mironovič, S. (eds.) (2003) *Ot našikh kornei. Kul'tura i iskusstvo Kaluzhskogo kraia v istorii Rossii* [From Our Roots: Culture and art of the land of Kaluga in the history of Russia]. Kaluga: Izdatel'stvo N. Bočkarevoi.

Berger, P. L. (1967) *The sacred canopy: Elements of a sociological theory of religion*. New York: Garden City.

Berger, P. L. (ed.) (1999) *The desecularization of the world: Resurgent religion and world politics*. Grand Rapids, MI: Eerdmans Publishing.

Bernard, R. H. (2006) *Research methods in anthropology: Fourth edition. Qualitative and quantitative approaches*. Lanham, New York, Torornto, Oxford: Altamira Press.

Bertaux, D. (juillet–décembre 1980) 'L'approche biographique: sa validité méthodologique, ses potentialités', *Cahiers internationaux de sociologie*, Nouvelle série, 69, pp. 197–225.

Bertaux, D. (1986 [1991]) 'Fonctions divers des récit de vie dans le processus de recherche', in Desmarais, D. and Grill, P. (eds.) *Les récit de vie. Théorie, méthode et trajectoires types*. Montréal: Éditions Saint-Martin. Quoted by Bulgarian translation in: *Sociologičeski problemi*, 1, pp. 134–141.

Bloch, M. (1989) 'The disconnection of power between power and rank as a process: An outline of the development of kingdoms in Central Madagascar', in *Ritual, History and Power: Selected Papers in Anthropology*. London: The Athlone Press, pp. 44–88.

Bodin, P.-A. (2014) 'The enthronement of Patriarch Kirill. A liturgical event', in Tolstaya, K. (ed.) *Orthodox paradoxes: Heterogeneities and complexities in contemporary Russian Orthodoxy*. Leiden and Boston: Brill, pp. 56–70.

Borneman, J. and Hammoudi, A. (2009) 'The fieldwork encounter, experience, and the making of truth: An introduction', in Borneman, J. and Hammoudi, A. (eds.) *Being there: The fieldwork encounter and the making of truth*. Berkeley and Los Angeles, CA: University of California Press, pp. 1–24.

Borowik, I. (2001) 'Where is Orthodoxy going? Sociological remarks on Orthodoxy and Orthodox churches in Eastern Europe after the collapse of communism', in Borowik, I. and Tomka, M. (eds.) *Religion and social change in post-communist Europe*. Krakow: Zaklad Wydawniczy "Nomos", pp. 43–56.

Borowik, I. and Tomka, M. (2001) 'Preface', in Borowik, I. and Tomka, M. (eds.) *Religion and social change in post-communist Europe*. Krakow: Zaklad Wydawniczy "Nomos", pp. 7–9.

Bourdeaux, M. (1999) 'The new Russian law on religion: A view from the regions', *De Paul Law Review*, 49(139), pp. 139–160.

Bourdeaux, M. (2000) 'Religion revives in all its variety: Russia's regions today', *Religion, State & Society*, 28(1), pp. 9–27.

Bourdieu, P. (2003) 'Participant objectivation', *Journal of Royal Anthropological Institute* (N.S.), 9, pp. 281–294.

Brown, P. (2002 [1981]) *The cult of the saints: Its rise and function in Latin Christianity*. Chicago: The University of Chicago Press.

Burdo, M. and Filatov, S. (1999) 'Novoe rozhdenie staroj idei: pravoslavie kak nacional'nyj simvol' [The new birth of the old idea: Orthodoxy as national symbol], *Polis*, № 3, pp. 138–149.

Buzalka, J. (2007) *Nation and religion: The politics of commemoration in Southeast Poland*. Berlin: LIT Verlag.

Caldwell, M. (2011) 'The politics of rightness: Social justice among Russia's Christian communities', in Zigon, J. (ed.) *Multiple moralities and religions in post-Soviet Russia*. New York and London: Berghahn Books, pp. 48–66.

Cannell, F. (ed.) (2006) *The anthropology of Christianity*. Durham and London: Duke University Press.

Casanova, J. (1994) *Public religions in the modern world*. Chicago: University of Chicago Press.

Chaikina, V. and Chaikin, E. (eds.) (2006) *1480 god v istorii Rossii* [The Year of 1480 in the History of Russia]. Kaluga: Poligraf-inform.

Chaplin, V. (1995) 'The Church and politics in contemporary Russia', in Bourdeaux, M. (ed.) *The politics of religion in Russia and the new states of Eurasia*. New York and London: M.E. Sharpe, Armonk, pp. 41–74.

Chernyshev, S. and Personal'nyj, S. K. (1992 [1912]) 'Geografičeskii očerk Kaluzhskoj gubernii' [Geographical sketch of the Kaluga province], in Malinin, D. I. (ed.) *Kaluga. Opyt istoričeskogo putevoditelia po Kaluge i glavnejšim centram gubernii*. Kaluga: Zolotaja alleja.

Chesnokova, V. F. (2005) *Tesnym putëm: Process vocerkovlenija naselenija Rossii v konce XX veka* [On narrow road: The process of enchurchment of the population of Russia at the end of 20th Century]. Moskva: Akademičeskij proekt, pp. 3–4.

Christensen, K. H. (2018) *The making of the new martyrs of Russia: Soviet repression in Orthodox memory*. London and New York: Routledge.

Christian, W. A. (1996) *Visionaries: The Spanish Republic and the reign of Christ*. Berkeley: University of California Press.

Chua, L. (2012) *The Christianity of culture: Conversion, ethnic citizenship, and the matter of religion in Malaysian Borneo*. New York: Palgrave McMillan.

Clifford, J. and Marcus, G. (eds.) (1986) *Writing culture: The poetics and politics of ethnography*. Berkeley, Los Angeles and London: University of California Press.

Coleman, S. (2000) *The globalization of Charismatic Christianity: Spreading the Gospel of prosperity*. Cambridge: Cambridge University Press.

Coleman, S. (2003) 'Continuous conversion? The rhetoric, practice and rhetorical practice of Charismatic Protestant conversion', Buckser, A. and Glazer, S. D. (eds.) *The anthropology of religious conversion*. Lanham, Boulder, New York, Toronto and Oxford: Rowman & Littlefield Publishers, Inc., pp. 15–28.

Coleman, S. (2017) 'Izučat' religiju i ne tol'ko' [Studying religion and more], *Antropologičeskij forum*, 34(1), pp. 87–93. Forum: Antropologija religii.

Coleman, S. and Hackett, R. I. J. (2015) 'Introduction: A new field?', in Coleman, S. and Hackett, R. I. J. (eds.) *The anthropology of global Pentecostalism and Evangelicalism*. New York and London: New York University Press, pp. 1–40.

Comaroff, J. (2010) 'The end of anthropology, again: On the future of an in/discipline', *American Anthropologist*, 112(4), pp. 524–538.

Comaroff, J. and Comaroff, J. L. (1991) *Of revelation and revolution: Christianity, colonialism and consciousness in South Africa*. Chicago and London: The University of Chicago Press.

Connerton, P. (2003 [1989]) *How societies remember*. Cambridge: Cambridge University Press.

Connerton, P. (2008) 'Seven types of forgetting', *Memory Studies*, 1(1), pp. 59–71.

Davie, G. (1999) 'Europe: The exception that proves the rule', in Berger, P. L. (ed.) *The desecularization of the world*. Grand Rapids, MI: William B. Eerdmans Publishing Company, pp. 65–85.

Davie, G. (2000) *Religion in modern Europe: A memory mutates*. Oxford: Oxford University Press.

Davie, G. (2007) 'Vicarious religion: A methodological challenge', in Ammerman, N. T. (ed.) *Everyday religion. Observing modern religious lives*. Oxford: Oxford University Press, pp. 21–37.

Davis, N. (1995) *A long walk to church: A contemporary history of Russian Orthodoxy*. Boulder, Colorado, San Francisco and Oxford: Westview Press.

Delamont, S. (2004) 'Ethnography and participant observation', in Seale, C. et al (eds.) *Qualitative research practice*. London, Thousand Oaks and New Delhi: Sage, pp. 217–230.

Delehaye, H. (1909) *Les légendes Grecques des Saints militaires*. Paris: Librairie Alfons Piccard et fils.

Dimitrov, D. (2016) 'Akrivia i ikonomia v pravilata na sv. Vasilii Veliki' [Akriveia and oikonomia in the rules of St. Basil the great], in Kokudev, S. and Osikovski, M. (eds.) *Christianitas, Historia, Metaphysica: Miscellany in Honor of Prof. Kalin Yanakiev*. Sofia: Communitas, pp. 59–70.

Divisenko, K. S. and Divisenko, O. V. (2016) 'Biografičeskoe issledovanie reinterpretacii ličnoj istorii u pravoslavnykh veruyuščikh' [Biographical study of the reinterpretation of personal history among Orthodox believers], *Zhurnal sociologii i social'noy antropologii*, 19(4), pp. 24–37.

Donovan, V. (2012) '"Idia nazad, šagaem vpered": kraevedčeskie muzej i sozdanie mestnoj pamiati v Severozapadnom regione. 1956–1981', *Antropologičeskii forum*, 16, pp. 379–402.

Dostoevskaja, A. G. (1981 [1871]) *Vospominanija* [Memories]. Moskva: Khudozhestvennaja literatura.

Douglas, M. (1966) *Purity and danger: An analysis of concept of pollution and taboo*. New York: Routledge & Kegan Paul.

Dubas, A. (2004) 'Religia – pamięć narodu. O roli prawosławia w kształtowaniu tożsamości narodowej kałuskiej inteligencji' [Religion – the memory of a nation. On the role of Orthodoxy in shaping the national identity of the Kaluga intelligentsia], in Mroz, L. (ed.) *Etnos przebudzony*. Warszawa: Wydawnictwo DIG, pp. 215–240.

Dubin, B. (2004) 'Massovaja religioznaja kul'tura v Rossii (tendencii i itogi 1990-kh godov)' [Mass religious culture in Russia (trends and outcomes of the 1990s)], *Vestnik obshchestvennogo mneniya: Dannyye. Analizy. Diskussii*, 71(3), pp. 35–44.

Dubin, B. (2006) '"Legkoe bremia": massovoe pravoslavie v Rossii 1990–2000 godakh' ["The light burden": Mass Orthodoxy in Russia 1990–2000], in Russelet, K. and Agadzjanian, A. (eds.) *Religioznye praktiki v sovremennoj Rossii*. Moskva: Novoe izdatel'stvo, pp. 69–88.

Dubovka, D. (2015a) 'Zabytoe vremia, ili praktiki samotransformacii v sovremennom pravoslavnom monastyre' [A forgotten time, or practice of self-transformation in a contemporary Orthodox monastery], *Gosudarstvo, religija, tserkov' v Rossii i za rubezhom*, 33(3), pp. 322–344.

Dubovka, D. (2015b) 'Poslušaniye kak fizičeskij trud i kak dobrodetel': semiotičeskoe nasyščenie proizvodstva v sovremennykh monastyriakh RPC' [Obedience as physical labor and as a virtue: Semiotic saturation of production in modern monasteries of the Russian Orthodox Church], in Kormina, Z. V., Panchenko, A. A. and Shtyrkov, S. A. (eds.) *Izobretenie religii: desekuliarizacija v postsovetskom obščestve*. Sankt-Peterburg: Izdatel'stvo Evropejskogo universiteta v Sankt-Peterburge, pp. 63–81.

Dubovka, D. (2017) 'Sila slova starca: mekhanizm osuščestvlenija kharizmatičeskoj vlasti' [The power of the word of a spiritual elder: A mechanism for exercising charismatic power], *Antropologičeskij forum*, 33, pp. 36–64.

Dubovka, D. (2018) 'Struggling bodies at the crossroads of economy and tradition: The case of contemporary Russian convents', in Luehrmann, S. (ed.) *Praying with the senses: Contemporary Orthodox Christian spirituality in practice*. Bloomington, IN: Indiana University Press, pp. 192–213.

Dudchenko, A. (2011) 'Soborovanie: tainstvo iscelenija duši i tela [Unction: The sacrament of healing the soul and body], 17.03.2011. www.pravmir.ru/soborovanie-tainstvo-isceleniya/. Last accessed: 18.05.2029.

Duncan, P. J. S. (2000) *Russian Messianism: Third Rome, revolution, communism and after*. London and New York: Routledge.

Eidson, J. (2004) 'From avoidance to engagement? Coming to terms with the Nazi past in a German home town', in Pine, F., Kaneff, D. and Haukaness, H. (eds.) *Memory, politics and religion*. Münster: LIT Verlag, pp. 59–92.

Ellis, J. (1996) *The Russian Orthodox Church: Triumphalism and defensiveness*. St. Antony's College, Oxford: Palgrave.

Engelhardt, J. (2005) *Singing in "transition": Musical practices and ideologies of renewal in the Orthodox church of Estonia*. PhD dissertation. Chicago, IL.

Engelhardt, J. (2010) 'The Acoustics of geopolitics of Orthodox practices in the Estonian-Russian border region', in Hann, C. and Goltz, H. (eds.) *Eastern Christians in anthropological perspective*. Berkeley, Los Angeles and London: University of California Press, pp. 101–127.

Engelhardt, J. (2018) 'Listening and the sacramental life: Degrees of mediation in Greek Orthodox Christianity', in Luehrmann, S. (ed.) *Praying with the senses: Contemporary Orthodox Christian spirituality in practice*. Bloomington, IN: Indiana University Press, pp. 58–81.

Engelke, M. (2012) 'Angels in Swindon: Public religion and ambient faith in England', *American Ethnologist*, 39(1), pp. 155–170.

Engelke, M. and Tomlinson, M. (eds.) (2006) *The limits of meaning: Case studies in the anthropology of Christianity*. Oxford: Berghahn.

Englund, H. (2007) 'Pentecostalism beyond belief: Trust and democracy in a Malawian township', *Africa*, 77(4), pp. 477–499.

Evgin, A. V. (2003) '"V načale bylo slovo . . ." (Optina pustyn' v zhizni N. V. Gogolia)' ["In the beginning was the word . . ." (Optina Hermitage in the life of N.V. Gogol)], in Berestov, A. D. and Mironovich, S. (eds.) *Ot našikh kornej. Kul'tura i iskusstvo Kaluzhskogo kraja v istorii Rossii*. Kaluga: Izdatel'stvo N. Bočkarevoj.

Fedor, J. (2014) 'Setting the Soviet past in stone: The iconography of the new martyrs of the Russian Orthodox church', *Australian Slavonic and East European Studies*, 28(1–2), pp. 121–153.

Filatov, S. (2007) 'Tradicionnye religii, „russkaja civilizacija" i suverennaja demokratija' [Traditional religions, "Russian civilization" and sovereign democracy], in Malashenko, A. and Filatov, S. (eds.) *Religija i konflikt*. Moskva: Moskovskij centr Karnegi, pp. 15–46.

Filatov, S. and Lunkin, R. (March 2006a) 'Statistics on religion in Russia: The reality behind the figures', *Religion, State & Society*, 34(1), pp. 33–49.

Filatov, S. and Lunkin, R. (2006b) 'Kaluzhskaja oblast' [Kaluga region], in Burdeaux, M. and Filatov, S. (eds.) *Atlas sovremennoj religioznoj zhizni Rossii*. Moskva-Sankt-Peterburg: Letnij sad, pp. 320–321.

Filičeva, O. N. (2006) 'Zapiski dlia Ksenii Blazhennoj: pozicii cerkovnosluzhitelej i narodnye obyčai' [Messages to Xenia the Blessed: The positions of clergy and the folk customs.], in Kormina, Z., Panchenko, A. A. and Shtyrkov, S. A. (eds.) Sny Bogorodicy. Issledovanija po antropologii religii. Sankt-Peterburg: Izdatel'stvo Evropeyskogo universiteta v Sankt-Peterburge. Studia Ethnologica, 3, pp. 171–183.

Filipova, E. (2001) 'Amvrosii [St. Ambrose]', in *Pravoslavnaja enciklopedija*, v. 2. Moskva: Cerkovno-naučnyj tsentr „Pravoslavnaja enciklopedija", pp. 135–137.

Filippucci, P. (2004) 'Memory and marginality: Remembrance of war in Argon (France)', in Pine, F., Kaneff, D. and Haukaness, H. (eds.) *Memory, politics and religion*. Münster: LIT Verlag, pp. 35–58.

Forbess, A. (2005) *Democracy and miracles: Political and religious agency in an Orthodox convent and village of South-Central Romania.* PhD dissertation. London: University of London.

Forbess, A. (2010) 'The Spirit and the letter: Monastic education in a Romanian Orthodox convent', in Hann, C. and Golz, H. (eds.) *Eastern Christians in anthropological perspective.* Berkeley, Los Angeles, and London: University of California Press, pp. 131–154.

Foucault, M. (1980) *Power/ knowledge: Selected interviews and other writings, 1972–1977*, ed. C. Gordon. New York: Pantheon Books.

Freeze, G. L. (1983) *The parish clergy in nineteenth-century Russia. Crisis, reform, counter reform.* Princeton, NJ: Princeton University Press.

Friedgel'm, E. (1998) *Kaluga i kaluzhane. Byt i nravy zhitelej gubernskogo goroda konca 19-togo – načala 20-togo veka* [Kaluga and Kaluga Citizens. Everyday Life and Mores of the Inhabitants of the Provincial Center in the Early 19th – Early Twentieth Century]. Kaluga: Zolotaja alleja.

Garadzha, V. I. (2005) *Sociologija religii* [Sociology of religion]. Moskva: INFRA-M.

Geertz, C. (1973) 'Religion as a cultural system', in *The Interpretation of Cultures.* New York: Basic Books, pp. 87–125.

Gibson, J. J. (1977) 'The theory of affordances', in Shaw, R. and Bransford, J. (eds.) *Perceiving, acting, and knowing: Toward an ecological psychology.* Hillsdale, NJ: Erlbaum, pp. 67–82.

Glanzer, P. L. (2005) 'Postsoviet moral education in Russia's state schools: God, country and controversy', *Religion, State and Society*, 33(3), pp. 207–221.

Goffman, E. (1961) 'Encounters', in *Two studies in the sociology of interaction.* Indianapolis, NY: Bobbs-Merrill company.

Gooren, H. (2014) 'Anthropology of religious conversion', in Rambo, L. R. and Farhadian, C. E. (eds.) *The Oxford handbook of religious Conversion.* Oxford: Oxford University Press, pp. 85–111.

Gorbacheva, N. B. (2006) *Optinskie startsy* [The Elders of Optina]. Moskva: Podvor'e Sviato-Troickoi Sergievoj Lavry.

Gorolevich, I. (2006) 'Natsional'noe i dukhovnoe edinenie. Interv'iu s direktorom nekommercheskogo partnerstva "Garal' Igorem Gorolevičem. Besedovala Nataliia Guščina' [National and spiritual unification. Interview with director of non-commercial association "Garal" Igor Gorolevič], *Pravoslavnyj khristianin*, 6, pp. 30–31.

Greeley, A. (1994) 'A religious revival in Russia?', *Journal for the Scientific Study of Religion*, 33(3), pp. 253–272.

Gromyko, M. M. and Buganov, A. V. (2000) *O vozzrenijakh russkogo naroda* [On the Views of the Russian People]. Moskva: Palomnik.

Grozovskii, V. (protopriest) (2006) *Kak vocerkovit' detej* [How to In-church Children]. Moskva: Satis.

Gubernatory (2015) 'Gubernatory Kaluzhskoy oblasti i YANAO vozglavili rejting effektivnosti' [Governors of the Kaluga Region and Yamalo-Nenets autonomous district topped the performance rating], *Kommersant Daily*, 9.06.2015.

Hammoudi, A. and Borneman, J. (2009) 'Afterthoughts: The experience and agony of fieldwork', in Borneman, J. and Hammoudi, A. (eds.) *Being there: The fieldwork encounter and the making of truth.* Berkeley and Los Angeles, CA: University of California Press, pp. 259–272.

Hanganu, G. (2010) 'Eastern Christians and religious objects: Personal and material biographies entangled', in Hann, C. and Golz, H. (eds.) *Eastern Christians in*

anthropological perspective. Berkeley, Los Angeles and London: University of California Press, pp. 33–55.
Hann, C. (2006a) 'Between East and West: Greek Catholic icons and cultural boundaries', in Olson, D. and Coleman, M. (eds.) *Technology, literacy and the evolution of society: Implications of the work of Jack Goody*. New York: Erlbaum, pp. 73–100.
Hann, C. (2006b) 'Introduction: Faith, power, and civility after socialism', in Hann, C. and Civil Religion Group (eds.) *The postsocialist religious question: Faith and power in Central Asia and East-Central Europe*. Berlin: LIT Verlag, pp. 1–26.
Hann, C. (2007) 'The anthropology of Christianity per se', *European Journal of Sociology/ Archives Européennes de Sociologie*, 48(3), pp. 383–410.
Hann, C. (2010) 'Broken chains and moral lazarets: the politicization, juridification and commodification of religion after socialism', in Hann, C. (ed.) *Religion, identity, postsocialism: The Halle Focus Group 2003–2010*. Halle/Saale: Max Planck Institute for Social Anthropology, pp. 3–21.
Hann, C. (December 2014) 'The heart of the matter. Christianity, materiality, and modernity', *Current Anthropology*, 55(Supplement 10), pp. 182–192.
Hann, C. and Goltz, H. (eds.) (2010a) *Eastern Christians in anthropological perspective*. Berkeley, Los Angeles and London: University of California Press.
Hann, C. and Golz, H. (2010b) 'Introduction: The other Christianity?', in Hann, C. and Golz, H. (eds.) *Eastern Christians in anthropological perspective*. Berkeley, Los Angeles and London: University of California Press, pp. 1–29.
Harris, O. (2006) 'The eternal return of conversion: Christianity as contested domain in Highland Bolivia', in Cannell, F. (ed.) *The Anthropology of Christianity*. Durham: Duke University Press, pp. 5–76.
Heino, H. (2000) 'What is unique in Russian religious life', in Kotiranta, M. (ed.) *Religious transition in Russia*. Helsinki: Kikimora Publications. Serries B, 15, pp. 288–304.
Heintz, M. (ed.) (2009a) *The anthropology of moralities*. New York and Oxford: Berghahn Books.
Heintz, M. (2009b) 'Introduction: Why there should be an anthropology of moralities', in Heintz, M. (ed.) *The anthropology of moralities*. New York and Oxford: Berghahn Books, pp. 1–19.
Heo, A. (2018) 'Imagining holy personhood: Anthropological thresholds of the icon', in Luehrmann, S. (ed.) *Praying with the senses: Contemporary Orthodox Christian spirituality in practice*. Bloomington, IN: Indiana University Press.
Hervieu-Léger, D. (1999a) *Religion as a Chain of Memory*. Cambridge: Polity Press.
Hervieu-Léger, D. (1999b) *La religion en mouvement. Le pèlerin et le converti. La religion en mouvement*. Paris: Flammarion.
Hindmarsch, B. (2014) 'Religious conversion as narrative and autobiography', in Rambo, L. R. and Farhadian, C. E. (eds.) *The Oxford handbook of religious conversion*. Oxford: Oxford University Press, pp. 343–369.
Howell, S. (ed.) (1997) *The ethnography of moralities*. London and New York: Routledge.
Ipatova, L. P. (2006) *Tipy religioznogo obraščenija v pravoslavie zhenščin v sovremennoj Rossii*. Avtoreferat dissertatsii na soiskanie uchennoy stepeni kandidat sotsiologicheskikh nauk. [Types of religious conversion to Orthodoxy of women in modern Russia. Abstract of Dissertation for the degree of PhD of Sociological Sciences], Moskva, 2006. www.isras.ru/files/File/Avtoreferat/avtoreferat_Ipatova.pdf. Last accessed: 2.05.2019.
Ivanov, V. (1994) 'Church and society in Russia today', in Nilesen, J. (ed.) *Christianity after communism: Social, political and cultural struggle in Russia*. Boulder, San Francisco and Oxford: Westview Press, pp. 29–39.

Ivkin, V. and Gusev, A. (2007) 'Russkij Fol'ksvagen v Kaluge prodavat' ne budut', *Kaluzhskij perekrëstok*, № 49, p. 2. www.kp40.ru/. Last accessed: 3.04.2019.

Johnson, E. D. (2006) *How St. Petersburg learned to study itself: The Russian idea of kraevedenie*. University Park, PA: Pennsylvania State University Press.

Johnson, M. (1997) *Moral imagination: Implications of cognitive science for ethics*. Chicago and London: The University of Chicago Press.

Kääriäinen, K. (1998) *Religion in Russia after the collapse of communism: Religious renaissance of secular state*. Lewinston, Queenstone and Lampeter: The Edwin Mellen Press.

Kääriäinen, K. (1999) 'Religiousness in Russia after the collapse of communism', *Social Compass*, 46(1), pp. 35–46.

Kääriäinen, K. and Furman, D. (2000) *Starye cerkvi, novye verujuščiye. Religia v massovom soznanii postsovetskoj Rossii* [Old churches, new believers. Religion in the mass consciousness of post-Soviet Russia]. Sankt-Peterburg: Letnij sad.

Kääriäinen, K. and Furman, D., eds. (2007) Novye cerkvi, starye verujuščie - starye cerkvi, novye verujuščiye. Religija v postsovetskoj Rossii [New churches – old believers - old churches, new believers. Religion post-Soviet Russia]. Moskva; Sankt-Peterburg: Letnii sad.

Kalakin, A. (2018) 'Prezident RF Vladimir Putin: poiskovaja rabota dostojna samogo glubokogo uvazhenija' [Russian President Vladimir Putin: The work of investigators deserves the deepest respect]. www.medyn.ru/prezident-rossii/prezident-rf-vladimir-putin-poiskovaya-rabota-dostoyna-samogo-glubokogo-uvazheniya.php?sphrase_id=4182. Last accessed: 10.02.2019.

Kaluzhskij kraj (1976) *Kaluzhskij kraj. Dokumenty i materialy. Kniga pervaja* [Kaluga Region. Documents and Materials. Book One]. Kaluga: Gosudarstvennyj arkhiv Kaluzhskoj oblasti.

Karpov, V. (2013) 'The social dynamics of Russia's desecularization: A comparative and theoretical perspective', *Religion, State and Society*, 41(3), pp. 254–283.

Kaufmann, E. (2010) *Shall the religious inherit the world? Demography and politics in the twenty-first century*. London: Profile Books.

Kazancev, G. (2006) 'Mërtvye duši' [Dead souls], *Pravoslavnyj khristianin*, № 8, pp. 9–12.

Keane, W. (2014) 'Rotting bodies. The clash of stances toward materiality and its ethical affordances', *Current Anthropology*, 55(S10), pp. 312–321. The Anthropology of Christianity: Unity, Diversity, New Directions (December 2014).

Keane, W. (2016) *Ethical life: Its natural and social histories*. Princeton and Oxford: Princeton University Press.

Kearl, M. C. and Rinaldi, A. (1983) 'The political uses of the dead as symbols in contemporary civil religions', *Social Forces*, 61(3), pp. 693–708.

Kennworthy, S. M. (2008) 'To save the world or to renounce it: Modes of moral action in Russian Orthodoxy', in Steinberg, M. D. and Wanner, C. (eds.) *Religion, morality, and community in post-Soviet societies*. Washington, DC: Woodrow Wilson Press and Bloomington, IN: Indiana University Press, pp. 21–54.

KEV – *Kaluzhskie eparkhial'nye vedomosti* [Kaluga Diocesan Herald], Kaluga: 1862–1907. www. pravoslavnoe-duhovenstvo.ru/library/material/4714/. Last accessed: 01.12.2019.

KEV. (1863) № 13 [Anonymous] 'Skazanie o javlenii i čudesakh Kaluzhskoj ikony Bozh'jej materi' [The story of the apparition and miracles of the Kaluga icon of the Mother of God], *Kaluzhskie eparkhial'nye vedomosti*, № 13, pp. 223–234.

KEV (1863) № 18 [Anonymous] 'Skazanie o čudotvornoy ikone Bozhi'ej materi Kazanskoj, čhto v gorode Kaluge, v Preobrazhenskoj, pod goroju cerkvi' [Story of the miraculous icon of the Mother of God of Kazan, in the city of Kaluga, in the transfiguration, under the Mountain Church], *Kaluzhskie eparkhial'nye vedomosti*, № 18, pp. 309–317.

KEV (1864a) № 22 [Anonymous] 'Ustav prikhodskogo v gorode Kaluge sv. Velikomučenika Georgia za verkhom bratstva' [Statute of the Brotherhood of the parish beyond the hill in Kaluga, St. Great Martyr George], *Kaluzhskie eparkhial'nye vedomosti*, № 22, pp. 170–174.

KEV (1864b) № 22 Izvekov, I. 'Otčet v upotreblenii pozhertvovanij prihodskim bednym pri grado-Kaluzskoj Georgievskoj za verhom cerkvi, s marta 1862 po mart 1964' [Report on the utilization of offerings to the parish's poor at the Kaluga city church St. George beyond the hill, from March 1862 to March 1864], *Kaluzhskie eparkhial'nye vedomosti*, № 22, pp. 406–411.

KEV (1866) № 2 [Anonymous] 'Otčet o dejatel'nosti Georgievskogo za verkhom, bratstva, za 1865 god' [Report of the activities of the Brotherhood at St. George beyond the hill, for 1865], *Kaluzhskie eparkhial'nye vedomosti*, № 2, pp. 37–50.

KEV (1866) № 21 [Anonymous] 'Godovščina bratstva sviatitelia Nikolaja (12 oktiabria)' [Anniversary of St. Nocolas Brotherhood, on October 12], *Kaluzhskie eparkhial'nye vedomosti*, № 21, pp. 650–653.

KEV (1867) № 7 [Anonymous] 'Kratkij otčet o dejatel'nosti Georgievskogo, za verkhom, bratstva za 1866 god' [A short report of the activities of the Brotherhood at St. George beyond the hill, for 1866], *Kaluzhskie eparkhial'nye vedomosti*, № 7, pp. 197–200.

KEV (1867) № 19 [Anonymous] 'Skazanie o javlenii čudotvornogo obraza Uspenija presviatoj vladyčicy našey Bogorodicej devy Marii, s dvanadesiatymi prazdnikami, čto v sele Ryškove, Borovskogo uezda, Kaluzhskoj gubernii' [The legend of the apparition of the miracle-working image of the Assumption of the Blessed Mother of God, our Virgin Mary, with the twelfth holidays, which is in the village of Ryškov, Borovskij district, Kaluga province], *Kaluzhskie eparkhial'nye vedomosti*, № 19, pp. 457–466.

KEV (1868) № 5 [Anonymous] 'Ob učrezhdenii pri zhenskikh monastyriakh učebnykh zavedenii dlia devic' [Concerning the establishment of educational institutions for madens at the convents], *Kaluzhskie eparkhial'nye vedomosti*, № 5, pp. 48–49.

KEV (1870) № 2 [Anonymous] 'Skazanie o čudesakh, byvšikh v nedavnee vremia ot ikony Kazanskoy Bogomateri, v g. Kaluge, v Kazanskoj, pod goroyu, cerkvi' [The legend of miracles, which recently occurred from the icon of the Kazan Mother of God, in the city of Kaluga, in Kazan, under the hill, the church], *Kaluzhskie eparkhial'nye vedomosti*, № 2, p. 263.

KEV (1870) № 5 [Anonymous] 'Kratkij otčet o dejatel'nosti Georgievskogo, za verkhom, bratstva za 1869 god' [A short report of the activities of the Brotherhood at St. George beyond the hill, for 1869], *Kaluzhskie eparkhial'nye vedomosti*, № 5, p. 153.

KEV (1870) № 20 Ugorskij, A. I. 'Skazanie o spiske čudotvornoj ikony Petrovskoj Bozh'ej Materi, nakhodiaščemsia v grado-kaluzhskoj Pokrovskoj, na rvu, cerkvi' [The story of the copy of the miracle-working icon of the Mother of God, located in the City of Kaluga church, on the moat], *Kaluzhskie eparkhial'nye vedomosti*, № 20, pp. 571–574.

KEV (1871) № 12 'Otkrytie zhenskikh učilišč pri zhenskikh monastyriakh raznykh eparkhii i prijutov dlia bednykh dukhovnogo zvanija' [Opening of female schools at the convents of various dioceses and shelters for the poor of spiritual ranks], *Kaluzhskie eparkhial'nye vedomosti*, № 12, p. 288.

Kizjaev, O. (2006) 'V den' pamiati kaluzhskikh novomučenikov' [On the day of memory of the Kaluga new martyrs], *Pravoslavnyj khristianin*, № 1.

Kliment, M. (2005) 'Kaluga – drevnij gorod' [Kaluga: An ancient city], in Korobtsov, S. (ed.) *Khramy zemli Kaluzhskoy. Nabor iz 45 otkrytok* [Temples of the Land of Kaluga. Set of 45 Postcards]. Fotografii: tekst i oformleniye S. Korobtsov.

Klimova, S. G. (2005) 'Predislovie' [Introduction], in Chesnokova, V. F. (ed.) *Tesnym putem: Process vocerkovlenija naselenija Rossii v kontse XX veka*. Moskva: Akademičeskij proekt, pp. 3–4.

Knore, B. (2014) 'Rossjyskoe pravoslavie. Postsekulyarnaja institucionalizatsija v prostranstve vlasti, politiki i prava' [Russian Orthodoxy. Postsecular institutionalization in the space of power, politics and law], in Malashenko, A. and Filatov, S. (eds.) *Montazh i demontazh sekuryarnogo mira*. Moskva: ROSSPEN, pp. 42–103.

Knorre, B. K. (2011) 'Kategorii "viny" i "smirenija" v sisteme cennostej cerkovno-prikhodskoy subkul'tury' [Parishes and communities in contemporary Russian Orthodoxy. The root system of Russian religiosity], in Agadjanian, A. and Rousselet, K. (eds.) *Prikhody i obščiny v sovremennom russkom pravoslavii. Kornevaja sistema rossijskjy religioznosti*. Moskva: Ves' Mir.

Knox, Z. K. (2004) *Russian Orthodoxy, religion, and society: After communism*. New York: Routledge Curzon.

Köllner, T. (2011) 'Build with gold or tears? Moral discourses on church construction and the role of entrepreneurial donations', in Zigon, J. (ed.) *Multiple moralities and religions in post-Soviet Russia*. New York and Oxford: Berghahn Books, pp. 191–213.

Köllner, T. (2012) *Practicing without belonging? Entrepreneurship, morality, and religion in contemporary Russia*. Berlin: LIT Verlag.

Köllner, T. (2016) 'Patriotism, Orthodox religion and education: Empirical findings from contemporary Russia', *Religion, State & Society*, 44(4), pp. 366–386.

Köllner, T. (2018) 'On the restitution of property and the making of "authentic" landscapes in contemporary Russia', *Europe-Asia Studies*, 70(7), 1083–1102.

Köllner, T. (2020, forthcoming) *Religion and politics in contemporary Russia: Beyond the binary of power and authority*. London and New York: Routledge.

[Kologrivov], Ioan, hieromonk, D.K. (2010) 'Serafim Sarovskii' [Seraphim of Sarov], in Platonov, O.A. (ed.) *Russkie sviatye i podvizhniki pravoslaviya. Istoričeskaja enciklopedija*. Moskva: Institut russkoj civilizacii, pp. 683–690.

Komáromi, T. (2010) 'Religious and secular concepts of evil in contemporary Russia', in Hann, C. (ed.) *Religion, identity, postsocialism: The Halle Focus Group 2003–2010*. Halle/Saale: Max Planck Institute for Social Anthropology. Department II, pp. 103–106.

Komáromi, T. (2011) 'In search of moral balance: Conversion and church adherence in the Russian Orthodox Church during the post-Soviet period', *Acta Ethnographica Hungarica*, 56(1), pp. 93–108.

Komáromi, T. (2017) 'Possession and conversion: The influence of Russian Orthodox exorcists', *Orma. Revista de studii istorico-religioase. Journal of Religious-Historical Studies /Rites of Passage*, pp. 47–61.

Kormina, J. (2004) 'Pilgrims, priest and local religion in contemporary Russia: Contested religious discourses', *Folklore*, 28, pp. 25–40.

Kormina, J. (2010) 'Avtobusniki: Russian Orthodox pilgrims longing for authenticity', in Hann, C. and Goltz, H. (eds.) *Eastern Christians in anthropological perspective*. Berkeley, CA: University of California Press, pp. 240–266.

Kormina, J. (2013a) 'Canonizing Soviet pasts in contemporary Russia: The case of Saint Matrona of Moscow', in Body, J. and Lambeck, M. (eds.) *A Companion to the anthropology of religion*. Wiley Blackwell, pp. 409–421.

Kormina, J. (2013b) 'La langue des pèlerins orthodoxes: "l'énergie sacrale d'un lieu chargé de prière"', *Slavica occitana*, № 36, pp. 201–218.

Kormina, J. (2018) 'Inhabiting Orthodox Russia: Religious nomadism and the puzzle of belonging', in Luermann, S. (ed.) *Praying with the Senses: Contemporary Orthodox Spirituality in Practice*. Bloomington, Indiana: Indiana University Press, pp. 143–162.

Kormina, Z. V. (2010) 'Politicheskie personazhi v sovremennoj agiografii: kak Matrona Stalina blagoslovliala' [Political characters in contemporary hagiography: How Matrona blessed Stalin], *Antropologičeskij forum Online*, 12, pp. 1–29.

Kormina, Z. V. (2011) 'Rezhimy pravoslavnoj social'nosti v sovremennoj Rossii: prikhozhane, palomniki, seteviki (na primere o. Zalita)' [Regimes of Orthodox sociality in contemporary Russia: Parishioners, pilgrims, networkers (on the example of Island of Zalita)], in Agadjanian, A. and Rousselet, K. (eds.) *Prikhody i obščiny v sovremennom russkom pravoslavii. Kornevaja sistema rossijskjy religioznosti*. Moskva: Ves' Mir, pp. 189–211.

Kormina, Z. V. (2012) 'Nomadičeskoye pravoslavie: O novykh formakh religioznoy zhizni v sovremennoy Rossii' [Nomadic Orthodoxy: On the new forms of religious life in contemporary Russia], *Ab Imperio*, № 2, pp. 195–227.

Kormina, Z. V., Panchenko, A. A. and Shtyrkov, S. A. (eds.) (2015) *Izobretenie religii. Desekuliarizacija v postsovetskom kontekste* [*The invention of religion: Desecularization in the post-Soviet contexts*]. Sankt-Peterburg: Izdatel'stvo Evropejskogo univeriteta v Sankt-Peterburge.

Kormina, Z. V., Panchenko, A. A. and Shtyrkov, S. A. (2017) 'Social'nye isssledovanija religii: teorija, metody, opyt' [Social studies of religion: Theory, methods, experience], *Antropologičeskij forum*, 35, pp. 127–166.

Kormina, J. and Shtyrkov, S. (2011) 'St. Xenia as a patron of female social suffering: An essay on Anthropological Hagiology', in Zigon, J. (ed.) *Multiple moralities and religions in post-Soviet Russia*. New York and Oxford: Berghahn Books, pp. 160–190.

Kormina, Z. V. and Shtyrkov, S. A. (2008) 'Pis'ma verujuščikh kak reklama: "vsenarodnaja priemnaja" sviatoj Ksenii Peterburgskoy' [Letters of believers as an advertisement: "nationwide reception room" of St. Xenia of Petersburg], *Antropologičeskij forum*, 9, pp. 154–184.

Kormina, Z. V. and Shtyrkov, S. A. (2015) '"Eto nashe iskonno russkoe, i nikuda nam ot etogo ne det'sia": predystoriya postsovetskoj desekuliarizacii' ["This is ours, primordially Russian, and we can't get anywhere else from it": The pre-history of post-Soviet desecularization], in Kormina, Z. V., Panchenko, A. A. and Shtyrkov, S. A. (eds.) *Izobretenie religii: desekuliarizatsija v postsovetskom kontekste*. Sankt Peterburg: Izdatel'stvo Evropeyskogo universiteta v Sankt-Peterburge, pp. 7–45.

Krasilin, M. M. (1996) 'Ikonografičeskij arkhetip i narodnoe počitaniye čudotvornykh obrazov' [Iconographic archetype and popular veneration of miraculous images], in Lidov, A. M. (eds.) *Čudotvornaja ikona v Vizantii i Drevnej Rusi*. Moskva: Martis, pp. 392–398.

Krogius, V. R. (2009) *Istoričeskie goroda Rossii kak fenomen eë kul'turnogo nasledija* [The Historical Cities of Russia as a Phenomenon for Her Cultural Heritage]. Moskva: Progress-Tradicija.

Kuchumov, V. A. (2002) 'Russkoe starčestvo' [The Russian spiritual eldership], in Sinicyna, N. V. (ed.) *Monashestvo i monastyri v Rossii XIX-XX veka*. Moskva: Nauka, pp. 223–244.

Kvale, S. (2007) *Doing interviews*. Los Angeles and London: SAGE.

Kyrlezhev, A. (2008) 'The postsecular age: religion and culture today', *Religion, State and Society*, 36(1), pp. 21–31.

Kyrlezhev, A. (2014) 'A postsecular conceptualization of religion: Defining the question?' *State, Religion and Church*, 1(1), pp. 7–22.

Ładykowska, A. (2011) 'Post-soviet Orthodoxy in the making: Strategies for continuity thinking among Russian middle-aged school teachers', in Zigon, J. (ed.) *Multiple moralities and religions in post-Soviet Russia*. New York and Oxford: Berghahn Books, pp. 27–47.

Ładykowska, A. (2018) 'The changing scope of religious authority and reconfigurations of social status in post-socialist Russia', *Religion, State & Society*, 46(2), pp. 96–107.

Ładykowska, A. and Tocheva, D. (2013) 'Women teachers of religion in Russia: Gendered authority in the Orthodox Church', *Archives de Sciences Sociales des Religions*, 162, pp. 55–74.

Law No 327 (2010) 'O peredače religioznym organizacijam imuščestva religioznogo naznačenija, nahodiaščegosia v gosudarstvennoi ili municipal'noi sobstvennosti' [On the transfer to religious organizations of religious property being in state or municipal ownership], *Rossijskaja gazeta* [Russian Newspaper], 3.12.2010. *Federal'nyi vypusk* [Federal Issue] № 5353 (274). www.rg.ru/2010/12/03/tserkovnoedobro-dok.html. Last accessed: 30.08.2018.

Legostaev, V. V. (2000a) '*Letopis' tserkvi sela Kaluzhka*' [Chronicle of the village of Kaluzhka]. Kaluga: Izdatel'stvo N. Bočkarevoj.

Legostaev, V. V. (2000b) '*Letopis' tserkvi sela Bobrovo*' [Chronicle of the Church in the village of Bobrovo]. Kaluga.

Legostaev, V. V. (2000c) '*Letopis' cerkvi sela Pokrov na Kaluzhke*' [Chronicle of the village of Pokrov on the river Kaluzhka]. Kaluga: Letnij sad.

Legostaev, V. V. (2001) '*Khramy Kaluzhskogo uezda*' [The temples of Kaluga County]. Kaluga: Grif.

Legostaev, V. V. (2003) '*Khramy Kalugi. Nabor tsvetnykh otkrytok*' [Temples of Kaluga: Set of Color Cards]. Kaluga: Fest.

Legostaev, V. V. and Pautova, L. (2004) '*Letopis' Il'inskoj cerkvi na Nikizme*' [Chronicle of St. Elias church on the river Nikizma]. Kaluga: Izdatel'stvo "Fridgel'm".

Lestvica (1862) *Prepodobnogo otca našego Ionna Sinajskoj gory Lestvica* [The Ladder, by Our Reverent Father John of Mount Sinai]. Moskva: Tipografija V. Got'e.

Lidov, A. M. (ed.) (1996a) *Čudotvornaja ikona v Vizantii i Drevnej Rusi* [The miracle-working icon in Byzantium and ancient Russia]. Moskva: Martis.

Lidov, A. M. (1996b) 'Ot redaktora' [From the Editor], in Lidov, A. M. (ed.) *Čudotvornaja ikona v Vizantii i Drevnej Rusi*. Moskva: Martis, pp. 5–10.

Likhachev, D. S. (1987) 'Velikoe nasledie' [The great heritage], in Likhachev, D. S. (ed.) *Izbrannyye raboty v trekh tomakh*, vol. 2. Leningrad: Khudozhestvennaja literatura, pp. 273–277.

Lindekinde, L. and Kühle, L. (2015) 'Religious revivalism and social movements', in Dellaporta, D. and Diani, M. (eds.) *The Oxford handbook of social movements*. Oxford: Oxford University Press, pp. 173–183.

Linquist, G. (2006) *Conjuring hope: Magic and healing in contemporary Russia*. New York and Oxford: Berghahn Books.

Luckmann, T. (2002) 'Moral communication in modern societies', *Human Studies*, 25, pp. 19–32.

Luehrmann, S. (2010) 'A dual quarrel of images on the Middle Volga: Icon veneration in the face of Protestant and pagan critique', in Hann, C. and Golz, H. (eds.) *Eastern*

Christians in anthropological perspective. Berkeley, Los Angeles and London: University of California Press, pp. 36–78.

Luehrmann, S. (2017) 'Dilemmy priznanija' [Dilemmas of recognition], *Antropologičeskij forum*, № 35, pp. 25–32.

Luehrmann, S. (ed.) (2018) *Praying with the senses: Contemporary Orthodox Christian spirituality in practice*. Bloomington, IN: Indiana University Press.

Mahieu, S. (2010) 'Icons and/or statues? The Greek Catholic divine liturgy in Hungary and Romania, between renewal and purification', Hann, C. and Golz, H. (eds.) *Eastern Christians in anthropological perspective*. Berkeley, Los Angeles and London: University of California Press, pp. 79–100.

Mahieu, S. and Naumescu, V. (eds.) (2008) *Churches in-between: Greek Catholic churches in postsocialist Europe*. Berlin: LIT Verlag.

Makarova, N. and Kalašnikova, L. (2006) 'Velikoe stoianie na Ugre. 1480 god: Bibiliograficheskii ukazatel' [The great stand on the Ugra River. 1480: Bibliographic index], in Chaikina, V. and Chaikin, E. (eds.) *1480 god v istorii Rossii* [The Year 1480 in the History of Russia]. Kaluga: Poligraf- inform, pp. 340–356.

Makrides, V. N. (2004) '"L'autre" orthodoxies: Courant du rigorisme orthododx grec', *Social Compass*, 54(4), pp. 511–521.

Malinin, D. I. (1992 [1912]). *Kaluga. Opyt istoricheskogo putevoditelia po Kaluge i glavneishim centram gubernii*. Kaluga: Zolotaja aleja.

Manchester, L. (2008) *Holy fathers, secular sons: Clergy, intelligentia, and the modern self in revolutionary Russia*. DeKalb, IL: Northern Illinois University Press.

Mango, E. (1977) 'Historical introduction', in Bryer, A. and Herrin, J. (eds.) *Iconoclasm*. Birmingham: Centre for Byzantine Studies, University of Birmingham.

Marcus, E. G. and Fischer, M. M. J. (1986) *Anthropology as cultural critique: An experimental moment in the human sciences*. Chicago: University of California Press.

Medvedeva, K. S. (2016a) 'Polevaja rabota v monastyre: osobennosti vkliučennogo nabliudenija' [Fieldwork in a convent: Particularities of the participant observation], *Zhurnal sociologii i social'noj antroppologii*, 19(1) [84], pp. 59–72.

Medvedeva, K. S. (2016b) 'Labour discipline in a Christian Orthodox sisterhood in Russia', *Culture and Religion*, 17(1), pp. 92–108.

Mel'nikova, E. A. (2012) '„Sblizhalis' narody kraja, predstavitelem kotorogo javlyayus' ja": krayevedčeskoe dvizhenie 1920–1930-kh godov i sovetskaja nacional'njya politika' [The peoples of the region, of which I am a representative, came closer": The local history movement of the 1920s and 1930s and Soviet national politics], *Ab Imperio*, № 5, pp. 209–240.

Mel'nikova, E. A. (2013) 'Centrobezhnaja sila: Kraevedenie na okrainakh Leningrada v 1920–1930-e gody' [Centrifugal force: Local history on the Outskirts of leningrad in the 1920s and 1930s], *Rossijskaja istoria*, № 5, pp. 43–58.

Mitrokhin, N. (2004) *Russkaia pravoslavnaia tserkov': sovremennoe sostoianie i aktual'nye problem* [The Russian Orthodox Church: Contemporary Situation and Actual Problems]. Moskva: Novoe literaturnoe obozrenie.

Molendijk, A. L. (2015) 'In pursuit of the postsecular', *International Journal of Philosophy and Theology*, 76(2), pp. 100–115.

A Monument (2018) 'A monument to Sts. Pётr and Fevronia will be mounted in Yaroslavl', *Announcement of the Information Agency Russkaja Linija*, 30.05.2009. https://rusk.ru/newsdata.php?idar=183110. Last accessed: 3.09.2018.

Morozova, G. M. (1993) *Kaluga: Progulki po staroi Kaluge* [Promenades on the Old Kaluga]. Kaluga: Zolotaia aleia.

Morris, J. (2016) 'Not soft power, but speaking softly. "Everyday diplomacy" in field relations during the Russia-Ukraine conflict', *The Cambridge Journal of Anthropology*, 34(2), pp. 110–126.

Morris, J. (2017) 'From betrayal to resistance: Working-class voices in Russia today', *Journal of Working-Class Studies*, 2(1), pp. 45–57.

Mulders, J. (2008) 'The debate on religion and secularization in Russia today: Comments on Kyrlezhev and Morozov, with focus on education', *Religion, State & Society*, 36(1), pp. 5–20.

Mullin, R. B. (1996) *Miracles and the Modern Religious Imagination*. New Haven and London: Yale University Press.

Naletova, I. (2010) 'Pilgrimages beyond the walls of the church', in Hann, C. and Goltz, H. (eds.) *Eastern Christians in anthropological perspective*. Berkeley, Los Angeles and London: University of California Press, pp. 240–266.

Naumescu, V. (2007) *Modes of religiosity in Eastern Christianity: Religious processes and social change in Ukraine*. Berlin: LIT Verlag.

Naumescu, V. (2010) 'Exorcising demons in post-Soviet Ukraine. A monastic community and its imaginative practice', in Hann, C. and Golz, H. (eds.) *Eastern Christians in anthropological perspective*. Berkeley, Los Angeles and London: University of California Press, pp. 155–176.

Naumescu, V. (2018) 'Becoming Orthodox: The mystery and mastery of a Christian tradition', in Luehrmann, S. (ed.) *Praying with the senses: Contemporary Orthodox Christian spirituality in practice*. Bloomington, IN: Indiana University Press, pp. 29–54.

NEWSru. (2006) 'Internet edition NEWSru.com'. www.newsru.com/religy/19sep2006/orthopiket.html. Last accessed: 13.08.2015.

Nizovskii, A. U. (2000) *Samye znamenitye monastyri i hramy Rossii* [The most famous monasteries and temples of Russia]. Moskva: Veče.

Nocks, A. D. (1933) *The old and new in religion from Alexander the Great to Augustine of Hippo*. New York: Oxford University Press.

Novosti eparkhii (2014) 'Novosti eparkhii' [News of the eparchy], *Pravoslavnyj khristianin*, 5, p. 2.

Novosti eparkhii (2015) 'Novosti eparkhii' [News of the eparchy], *Pravoslavnyj khristianin*, 8, p. 2.

Optinskaia Golgofa (1994) *Optinskaia Golgofa. K ubiistvu inokov na Sviatuiu Paskhu* [The Golgotha of Optina. On the murder of coenobits on the Saint Easter]. Moskva: Pravoslavnyi palomnik.

[Orlovskii], Damascin (1992), (1996), (1999), (2000), (2001), (2002a), (2002b) *Mučeniki, ispovedniki i podvizhniki blagočestija Rossijskoj Pravoslavnoj Tserkvi XX stoletija. Zhizneopisanija i materialy k nim* [Martyrs, Confessors and Ascetics of Piety of the Russian Orthodox Church in 20th Century. Lives and Materials Concerning Them]. Vol. 1–7. Tver': Bulat.

[Orlovskii], Damascin (2014) *Zhitijaa mučenikov i ispovednikov Optinoj Pustyni. Pis'ma prepodobnogo Rafaila ispovednika* [Lives of the Martyrs and Confessors of the Optina Hermitage. The Letters of the Reverent Confessor Rafail]. Kozel'sk: Vvedenskii muzhskoj monastyr' Optina Pustyn'.

Orsi, R. A. (2017) [no title] *Forum: Antropologija religii* (2), *Antropologičeskij forum*, № 35, pp. 55–66.

Paert, I. (2010) *Spiritual elders: Charisma and tradition in Russian Orthodoxy*. DeKalb: Northern Illinois University Press.

Pamiatniki (1880) *Pamiatniki drevnerusskogo kanoničeskogo prava* [Monuments of Old Russian Canon Law], Part 1. Sankt-Peterburg: Imperial Archaeographic Commission, pp. 136–140.

Panchenko, A. A. (1998) *Issledovanija v oblasti narodnogo pravoslavija. Derevenskie svyatyni Severo-Zapada Rossii* [Research in the field of popular Orthodoxy. Village shrines of the North-West of Russia]. Sankt-Peterburg: "Alejteja".

Panchenko, A. A. (1999) 'Religioznye praktiki: k izučeniju "narodnoj religii"' [Religious practices: Toward the study of the "popular religion"], in *Mifologija i povsednevnost'*, vol. 2. Materialy naučnoj konferencii 26–26 fevralia 1999 goda. Sankt-Peterburg, pp. 198–218.

Panchenko, A. A. (2001) 'Eschatological expectations in a changing world: Narratives about the end of the world in present day Russian folk culture', *SEEFA Journal*, 6(1), pp. 10–25.

Panchenko, A. A. (2004 [2002]) *Khristovstvo i skopchestvo: fol'klor i traditsionnaya kul'tura russkikh mističeskikh sekt* [Khristovstvo and skopčestvo: Folklore and traditional culture of Russian mystical sects]. Moskva: OGI.

Panchenko, A. A. (2006a) 'Ivan i Jakov – strannye sviatye iz bolotnogo kraja (religioznye praktiki sovremennoj novgorodskoj derevni)' [Ivan and Jakov: Strange saints from the swamp land (religious practices of the modern Novgorod village)], in Rousselet, K. and Agadjanian, A. (eds.) *Religioznye praktiki v sovremennoj Rossii: sbornik statej* [Religious Practices in the Contemporary Russia: Collection of Articles]. Moskva: Novoe izdatel'stvo, pp. 211–236.

Panchenko, A. A. (2006b) 'Historical anthropology and the study of popular religion: Recent research works in Russia', *Sanctorum*, № 3, pp. 189–193.

Panchenko, A. A. (2011) 'Morality, utopia, discipline. New religious movements and Soviet culture', in Zigon, J. (ed.) *Multiple Moralities and Religions in Post-Soviet Russia*. New York and Oxford: Berghahn Books, pp. 119–145.

Panchenko, A. A. (2012) 'Popular Orthodoxy' and identity in Soviet and post-Soviet Russia', in Bassin, M. and Kelly, C. (eds.) *Soviet and Post-Soviet Identities*. Cambridge: Cambridge University Press, pp. 321–340.

Papkova, I. (2011) *The Orthodox Church and Russian Politics*. New York: Oxford University Press.

Papkova, I. (2013) 'The contemporary study of religion, society and politics in Russia: A scholar's reflections', *Religion, State and Society*, 41(3), pp. 244–253.

Pavlovich, N. (1980) 'Optina Pustyn'. Počemu tuda ezdili velikie?' [Optina hermitage: Why did great people traveled there?], in *Istoriko-biograficheskii al'manakh*, vol. 12. Moskva: Prometei, p. 88.

Pelkmans, M. (2009) 'Introduction: Post-Soviet space and the unexpected turns of religious life', in Pelkmans, M. (ed.) *Conversion after socialism: Disruptions, modernisms and technologies of faith in the former Soviet Union*. New York and Oxford: Berghahn Books, pp. 1–16.

Pelkmans, M. (2010) 'Religious crossings and conversions on the Muslim – Christian frontier in Georgia and Kyrgyzstan', *Anthropological Journal of European Cultures*, 19(2), pp. 109–128.

Pelkmans, M. (2015) 'Mediating miracle truth: Permanent struggle and fragile conviction in Kyrgyzstan', in Coleman, S. and Hackett, R. I. J. (eds.) *The anthropology of global Pentecostalism and Evangelicalism*. New York and London: New York University Press, pp. 177–196.

Pesmen, D. (2000) *Russia and the Soul*. Ithaca: Cornell University Press.

Pestova, N. (2008) 'Nariadnyj, kak škatuločka' [Beautiful, as a Jewelry Box], *Znamia*. Kaluga: Setevoe informacionnoe izdanie Kaluzhskogo regiona. https://znamkaluga.ru/index.php/75-14/6243-19. Last accessed: 1.09.2019.

Petrovskii, A. (1902) 'Vocerkovlenie' [Enchurchment], *Pravoslavnaja bogoslovskaja ennciklopedija*, 3, column 1020. Izdaniye Petrograd. Prilozhenie k dukhovnomu zhurnalu „Strannik".

Pine, F., Kaneff, D. and Haukanes, H. (2004) 'Introduction: Memory, politics and religion – A perspective on Europe', in Pine, F., Kaneff, D. and Haukaness, H. (eds.) *Memory, politics and religion: The past meets the present in Europe*. Münster: LIT Verlag, pp. 1–33.

Pitirimov, S. (2002) 'V kaluzhskom khrame sviatitelia Nikolaja zamirotočila ikona Serafima Sarovskogo' [In the Kaluga church of St. Nicholas, the icon of St. Seraphim of Sarov was streaming chrism], *Kaluzhskij perekrestok*, № 45(255), 14.11.2002.

Popkov, V. (2004) 'Die Wahrnehmung der Arbeitsbeziungen in einem sozialistischem Betrieb in der UdSSR', in Roth, K. (Hg.) *Arbeit im Sozialismus – Arbeit im Postsozialismus: Erkunden Zum Arbeitsleben im östlichen Europa*. Münster: LIT Verlag, pp. 167–178.

Pospielovsky, D. (1995) The Russian Orthodox Church in the postcommunist CIS, in Bourdeaux, M. (ed.) *The politics of religion in Russia and the new states of Eurasia*. Armonk, New York; London: M.E. Sharpe, pp. 45–46.

Poujeau, A. (2010) 'Monasteries, politics and social memory: The revival of the Greek Orthodox Church of Antioch in Syria during the twentieth century, in Hann, C. and Golz, H. (eds.) *Eastern Christians in anthropological perspective*. Berkeley, Los Angeles, London: University of California Press, pp. 177–192.

Powell, D. E. (1991) 'The revival of religion', *Current History*, 90(558), pp. 328–332.

Rambo, L. R. and Farhadian, C. E. (2014) 'Introduction. Conversion and global transformation,' in Rambo, L. R. and Farhadian, C. E. (eds.) *The Oxford handbook of religious conversion*. Oxford: Oxford University Press, pp. 1–22.

Razumovskaja, E. V. (2002) 'Liubov' k otečeskim grobam' [Love for Fatherly Tombs]. *Pravoslavnyj khristianin*, № 3, pp. 12–13.

Ricoeur, P. (1992) *Oneself as another*. Chicago: University of Chicago Press.

Ries, N. (1997) *Russian Talk: Culture and Conversation During Perestroika*. Ithaca and London: Cornell University Press.

Robbins, J. (ed.) (2003) 'The anthropology of Christianity', Special Issue, *Religion*, 33, p. 3.

Robbins, J. (2004) *Becoming sinners: Christianity and moral torment in a Papua New Guinea society*. Berkeley: University of California Press.

Robbins, J. (2007) 'Continuity thinking and the problem of Christian culture: Belief, time, and the anthropology of Christianity', *Current Anthropology*, 48(1), pp. 5–38.

Robbins, J. (2009) 'Value, structure, and the range of possibilities: A response to Zigon', *Ethnos*, 74(2), pp. 277–285.

Robbins, J. (2013) 'Beyond the suffering subject: Toward of an anthropology of the good', *Journal of the Royal Anthropological Institute* (N.S.), 19, pp. 447–462.

Robbins, J. (2014) 'The anthropology of Christianity: Unity, diversity, new directions', *Current Anthropology*, 55(Supplement 10), pp. 157–171.

Rock, S. (2011) 'Russia new saints and the challenges of memory', *Open Democracy*. www.opendemocracy.net/en/odr/russias-new-saints-and-challenges-of-memory/. Last accessed: 29.12.2019.

Rogers, D. (2005) 'Introductory essay: The anthropology of religion after socialism', Special Issue, *Religion, State & Society*, 33(1), pp. 5–18.

Rogers, D. (2009) *The old faith and the Russian land: A historical ethnography of ethics on the Urals*. Ithaca: Cornell University Press.

Rosenthal, G. (2004) 'Biographical research', in Seale, C. at al. (eds.) *Qualitative research practice*. London, Thousand Oaks and New Delhi: Sage, pp. 48–64.

Rossijane (2010) 'Rossijane b'jut rekordy po obraščeniju v pravoslavie, no ne spešat čitat' Bibliju – opros' [Russians break records for conversion to Orthodoxy, but are in no hurry to read the Bible – A survey], *Interfaks*, 30.03.2010. www.interfax-religion.ru/?act=news&div=34881. Last accessed: 24.08.2018.

Rossijskaja gazeta (2009) 'Rasporiazheniee pravitel'stva Rossijskoj Federcii ot 29 oktiabria 2009 g., № 1578-r g. Moskva, 11.11.2009' [Order of the government of the Russian Federation of October 29, 2009, No. 1578-r, Moscow, 11.11.2009], *Rossijskaja gazeta*. www.rg.ru/2009/11/11/obr-doc.html.

Rousselet, K. (2007) 'Butovo: la creation d'un lieu de pèlerinages sur une terre de massacres', *Politix*, 77, pp. 55–78.

Rousselet, K. (2011a) 'Constructing moralities around the Tsarist family', in Zigon, J. (ed.) *Multiple moralities and religions in post-Soviet Russia*. New York and Oxford: Berghahn Books, pp. 146–167.

Rousselet, K. (2011b) 'Ob otnošenijakh mezhdu sviaščennikami i mirianami: poslušanie i blagoslovenie' [On the relations between priests and laity: Obedience and blessing], in Agadjanian, A. and Rousselet, K. (eds.) *Prikhod i obshchina v sovremennom russkom pravoslavii. Kornevaja sistema rossijskoj religioznosti*. Moskva: Ves' mir, pp. 298–316.

Schroeder, R. L. and Karpov, V. (2013) 'The crimes and punishment of the "enemies" of the Church and the nature of Russia's desecularizing regime', *Religion, State and Society*, 41(3), pp. 284–311.

Seale, C. (1999) *The quality of qualitative research*. London: Sage.

Seliverstova, N. G. and Zaharova, L. V. (eds.) (2019) *Kaluzhskaja oblast' v cifrakh 2012–2018 g.g. Statistieskii sbornik* [Kaluga Region in Numbers 2012–2018. Statistical Digest]. Kaluga: Kalugastat.

Sergazina, K. (2006) 'Dinamika vozrozhdenija russkoy religioznoj kul'tury', in Rousselet, K. and Agadjanian, A. (eds.) *Religioznye praktiki v sovremennoj Rossii: sbornik statej*. Moskva: Novoe izdatel'stvo, pp. 106–125.

Sergazina, K. (2015) 'Zaščita čuvstv veruyuščikh v Rossii: ot "Pussyriot" do "Tangeyzera"' [Protection of the feelings of believers: from "Pussyriot" to "Tangeyzer"], paper at the conference *Svetskost' gosudarstva i realizatsija prav verujuščikh*, 20.04.2015, Sankt – Peterburg. www.religiopolis.org/documents/8982-zashchita-chuvstv-veruyushchikh-v-rossii-ot-pussyriot-do-tangejzera-doklad-k-sergazinoj-k-s-svetskost-gosudarstva-i-realizatsiya-prav-veruyushchikh-20-04-2015-spb.html. Last accessed: 30.08.2018.

Shamordino (2006 [1908]) '*Kazanskaja Amvrosievskaja zhenskaja pustyn' i eë osnovatel' Optinskii starec ieroskhimonakh Amvrosii*' [Kazan's women's hermitage of Ambrose and its founder the elder hieromonk Ambrose]. Printed according to the edition of 1908: Shamordino.

Shevchenko, E. V. (2015) 'Kaluzhskaja ikona Bozh'ej materi' [Kaluga icon of God's mother], *Pravoslavnaja enciklopedia* (*electronic version*), 29, pp. 628–634.

Shevzov, V. (1999) 'Miracle-working icons, laity, and authority in the Russian Orthodox Church, 1861–1917', *Russian Review*, 58(1), pp. 26–48.

Shevzov, V. (2007) 'Scripting the gaze: Liturgy, homilies and the Kazan icon of the Mother of God in late Imperial Russia,' in Steinberg, M. D. and Coleman, H. J. (ed.) *Sacred stories. Religion and spirituality in modern Russia*. Bloomington, IN: Indiana University Press, pp. 61–92.

Shnirelman, V. (2011) 'V poiskah samobytnosti: u istokov sovetskogo mul'tikul'turalizma' [In search of uniqueness: To the origins of Soviet multiculturalism], *Neprikosnovennyi zapas*, 78(4).

Shtyrkov, S. A. (2001) '„Sviatye bez zhitii" i zabuduščie roditeli: cerkovnaja kanonizacija i narodnaja tradicija' ["Saints without lives" and forgotten parents: Church canonization and popular tradition], in Belova, O. (ed.) *Koncept čuda v slavianskoj i evrejskoj tradicii*, vol. 7. Moskva: Akademicheskaja serija, pp. 130–155.

Shtyrkov, S. A. (2006) 'Posle „narodnoj religioznosti"' [After "popular religiosity"], in Kormina, Z. V., Panchenko, A. A. and Shtyrkov, S. A. (eds.) *Sny Bogorodicy. Issledovanija po antropologii religii*. Sankt-Peterburg: Izdatel'stvo Evropejskogo universiteta v Sankt-Peterburge. Studia Ethnologica, 3, pp. 7–18.

Shtyrkov, S. A. (2011a) 'Religious nationalism in contemporary Russia: The case of the Ossetian ethnic religious project', in Alapuro, R., Mustajoki, A. and Pesonen, P. (eds.) *Understanding Russianness (Routledge Advances in Sociology)*. London and New York: Routledge, pp. 232–244.

Shtyrkov, S. A. (2011b) 'The unmerry widow: The blessed Kseniia of Petersburg in hagiography and hymnography', in Hunt, P. and Kobets, S. (eds.) *Holy foolishness in Russia: New perspectives*. Bloomington, IN: Slavica Publishers, pp. 281–304.

Sinelina, J. J. (2001) 'O kriterijakh religioznosti naselenija' [On the criteria of religiosity of the population], *Sociologicheskie issledovanija*, № 7, pp. 89–96.

Sinelina, J. J. (2003) 'O ciklakh izmenenija religioznosti obrazovannoj chast'ju rossijskogo obščestva (načalo XVIII – 1917)' [On the cycles of change in the religiousness of educated part of Russian society (beginning of the 18th – 1917)], *Sociologičeskie issledovanija*, № 10, pp. 88–96.

Sinelina, J. J. (2006) 'Dinamika processa vocerkovlenija pravoslavnykh' [Dynamics of the process of the churching of the Orthodox Christians], *Sociologičeskie issledovaniya*, № 11, pp. 89–97.

Skripil', M. O. (1949) *Povest' o Petre i Fevronii Muromskikh v eë otnošenii k russkoj skazke* [Novelette on Petr and Fevronia from Murom in its concern towards Russian fairytale], vol. 7. Moskva: Trudy otdela drevne-russkoj literatury Instituta russkoj literatury, pp. 131–167.

Slabova, S. (2010) '„Budeš', budeš', poydeš', poydëš'" ["You will, you will, you will go, you will go"], *Vera molodykh*, № 3, no page.

Smirnov, M. (2008) 'Reformator v kresle činovnika. Konstantin Kharchev: Sovet po delam religii byl posrednikom mezhdu verujiuščimii pravitel'stvom' [Reformer in the chair of a clerk. Konstantin Kharchev: The council of religious affairs used to be a mediator between believers and the government], *Nezavisimaja gazeta*, 17.09.2088, p. 1.

Sokolov, V. (2018) *Mladostarčestvo i pravoslavnaja tradicija* [New-eldership and the Orthodox Tradition]. Moskva: Pravoslavnaja enciklopedija, Azbuka very.

Solov'ëv, A. (1899 [2005]) *Starčestvo po učeniju sviatykh otcov i asketov* [Spiritual eldership according to the teachings of the holy fathers and ascetics]. [SergievPosad]: Svyato-Troickaja Sergieva Lavra.

Spilka, B., Hood, R. W. Jr., Hunsberger, B. and Gorsuch, R. (2003) *The psychology of religion. An empirical approach* (3rd edn). New York: The Guilford Press.

Stark, Rodney and Bainbridge, W. S. (1996). *A theory of religion*. New Brunswick, NJ: Rutgers University Press. Stark, R. and Bainbridge, W. S. (1996) *A theory of religion*. New Brunswick, NJ: Rutgers University Press,

Stefanovič, P. S. (2002) *Prikhod i prikhodskoe dukhovenstvo v Rosssii XVI-XVII vekakh*. Moskva: Indrik.

Steinberg, M. D. and Wanner, C. (eds.) (2008) *Religion, morality, and community in post-Soviet societies*. Washington, DC: Woodrow Wilson Press and Bloomington, IN: Indiana University Press.
Stevenson, L. (2009) 'The suicidal wound and fieldwork among Canadian Inuit', in Borneman, J. and Hammoudi, A. (eds.) *Being there: The fieldwork encounter and the making of truth*. Berkeley, CA: University of California Press, pp. 55–76.
Stoeckl, K. (2016) 'The Russian Orthodox Church as moral norm entrepreneur', *Religion, State & Society*, 44(2), pp. 132–151.
Stromberg, P. G. (2008) *Language and self-transformation: A study of the Christian conversion narrative*. Cambridge: Cambridge University Press.
Stromberg, P. G. (2014) 'The role of language in religious conversion', in Rambo, L. and Farhadian, C. E. (eds.) *Oxford handbook of religious conversion*. Oxford: Oxford University Press, pp. 117–139.
Sveshnikova, O. and Puchkova, I. (2011) 'Portret odnogo molodezhnogo prikhoda pri universitete: khram Sviatoj muchenicy Tatiany goroda Omska' [Portrait of a youth parish at the University: Church of the holy Martyr Tatiana of Omsk], in Agadjanian, A. and Rousselet, K. (eds.) *Prikhod i obshchina v sovremennom russkom pravoslavii. Kornevaja sistema rossijskoy religioznosti*. Moskva: Ves' mir, pp. 98–118.
Tarabukina, A. V. (2000) *Fol'klor i kul'tura pricerkovnogo kruga* [Folklore and the culture of the around-church circle]. Sankt-Peterburg: Dissertacija na soiskanie učenoj stepeni kandidata filologičeskikh nauk. www.krotov.info/history/20/tarabuk/tar01.html. Last accesed: 29.08.2018.
Tocheva, D. (2007) 'Renewed Orthodoxy in Northwest Russia and its effects on local social life and integration', Paper presented on October 29, 2007, MPI for Social Anthropology, Halle/Saale.
Tocheva, D. (2011) 'An ethos of relatedness: foreign aid and grassroots charities in two Orthodox parishes in North-Western Russia', in Zigon, J. (ed.) *Multiple moralities and religions in post-Soviet Russia*. New York and Oxford: Berghahn Books, pp. 67–91.
Tocheva, D. (2017) *Intimate divisions: Street-level Orthodoxy in post-Soviet Russia*. Berlin: LIT Verlag.
Tomka, M. (2001) 'Religious change in East-Central Europe', in Borowik, I. and Tomka, M. (eds.) *Religion and social change in post-communist Europe*. Krakow: Zaklad Wydawniczy "Nomos", pp. 43–56.
Tomlinson, M. and Engelke, M. (2006) 'Meaning, anthropology, Christianity', in Engelke, M. and Tomlinson, M. (eds.) *The limits of meaning: Case studies in the anthropology of Christianity*. Oxford: Berghahn, pp. 1–38.
Torbakov, I. (2014) 'The Russian Orthodox Church and contestation over history in contemporary Russia', *Demokratizatsiya*, 22(1), pp. 145–170, Washington.
Torik, A. (2007) '*Vocerkovlenie dlia načinajuščikh cerkovnuju zhizn*' [Enchurchment for beginners in the church life]. Moskva: Sibirskaja Blagozvonnica.
Tsekhanskaya, K. V. (2004) *Ikonopočitanie v russkoj tradicionnoj kul'ture* [The veneration of icons in the Russian traditional culture]. PhD Dissertation. Moskva.
Tsekhanskaia, K. V. (2015) 'Russia: Trends in Orthodox religiosity in the twentieth century (Statistics and reality)', in Mandelstam-Balzer, M. (ed.) *Religion and politics in Russia: A reader*. New York: Routledge.
Tsypin, V. (2012) *Istorija russkoj pravoslavnoj cerkvi. Sinoda'nyj i novejšie periody 1700–2005* [History of the Russian Orthodox Church. The synodal and newest periods of 1700–2005]. Izdatel'stvo: Izdatel'stvo Sretenskij monastyr', pp. 547–563.

Tul'ceva, L. A. (2002) 'Tajnaja milostynia' [The secret almsgiving], in Kirichenko, O. V. and Poplavskaja, Ch. V. (eds.) *Pravoslavnaja vera i tradicii pravoslavija u russkikh v XVIII-XX vekakh. Etnografičeskie issledovanija I materialy* [the orthodox faith and Traditions of Orthodoxy Among Russians. Ethnographic Studies and Materials]. Moskva: Nauka, 90–100.

Tupakhina, Ol'ga V. (2012) Religioznaja biografija kak forma narrativizacii zhiznennogo mira verujuščikh (na primere pravoslavnykh khristian) [The religious biography as a form of narratization of the life-world of believers (on the Example of Orthodox Christians)]. *Zhurnal sociologii i social'noj antropologii*, 15, № 1, 185–197.

Utiatnikova, O. (2019) 'V Kaluge otkrylsia pravoslavnyj blagotvoritel'nyj centr' [Orthodox charitable center had been open in Kaluga], *NIKA TV*, 25.10.2019. https://nikatv.ru/news/obshestvo/vkaluge-otkrylsya-pravoslavnyy-blagotvoritelnyy-centr'.

Uzlaner, D. (2014) 'The Pussy Riot case and the peculiarities of Russian post-secularism', *State, Religion and Church*, 1(1), pp. 23–58.

Valchinova, G. (2003) 'Bona Velinova, edno predizvikatelstvo pred balgarskata etnologija (Belezhki i razmisli varkhu istorijata i etnografijata na pravoslavnata religioznost v period na kriza)' [Bona Velinova, a challenge to Bulgarian ethnology (Notes and Reflections on the history and ethnography of Orthodox Religion during the Crisis]. *Balgarska etnologia*, № 2–3, pp. 149–162.

Vallikivi, L. (2009) 'Christianization of words and selves: Nenets reindeer herders joining the state through conversion', in Pelkmans, M. (ed.) *Conversion after socialism: Disruptions, modernisms and technologies of faith in the former Soviet Union*. New York and Oxford: Berghahn Books, pp. 59–83.

V "doline smerti" (2007) [Anonymous] 'V "doline smerti" nashli ostanki razvedčikov specotriada NKVD' [The remains of intelligence officers from the special detachment of NKVD have been found in the "Valley of the Dead"], *Kaluzhskaia nedelia*, 28, 28.06.2007–04.07.2007.

Verdery, K. (1999) *The political lives of the dead bodies: Reburial and postsocialist change*. New York: Columbia University Press.

Verkhovsky, A. (2003) *Političeskoe pravoslavie. Russkie pravoslavnye nacionalisty i fundamentalisty 1995–2001* [Political Orthodoxy. Russian Orthodox nationalists and fundamentalists]. Moskva: Centr „Sova".

Vorontsova, L. M., Filatov, S. B. and Furman, D. E. (1995) 'Religija v sovremennom massovom soznanii' [Religion in the contemporary mass consciousness], *Sociologičeskie issledovanija*, 11, pp. 81–91.

Vulchinova, G. (1999) *Znepolski pokhvali. Lokalna religia i identičnost v Zapadna Balgaria* [The praises of Znepole. Local religion and identity in Western Bulgaria]. Sofia: Akademično izdatelstvo „Prof. Marin Drinov".

Vusheva, M. (2009) *Počitanieto na čudotvorni bogorodični ikoni – tradicii i savremenni praktiki* [Veneration of the miracle-working icons of the Virgin – traditions and modern practices]. PhD Dissertation. Sofia, Nov balgarski universitet.

Wagner, W. G. (2007) '"Orthodox domesticity": Creating a social role for women', in Steinberg, M. D. (ed.) *Sacred Stories*. Bloomington, IN: Indiana University Press, pp. 119–145.

Wallace, A. F. C. (1956) 'Revitalization movements', *American Anthropologist*, New Series, 58(2), pp. 264–281.

Walters, P. (1994) 'Current developments in Russia and the response of the Russian Orthodox', in Nilesen, J. (ed.) *Christianity after communism: Social, political and cultural struggle in Russia*. Boulder, San Francisco and Oxford: Westview Press, pp. 85–102.

Wanner, C. (2009) 'Conversion and the mobile self: Evangelism as "travelling culture"', in Pelkmans, M. (ed.) *Conversion after socialism: Disruptions, modernisms and technologies of faith in the former Soviet Union.* New York and Oxford: Berghahn Books, pp. 163–182.

Wanner, C. (2011) 'Afterword. Multiple moralities, multiple secularisms', in Zigon, J. (ed.) *Multiple moralities and religions in post-Soviet Russia.* New York and Oxford: Berghahn Books, pp. 214–225.

Wanner, C. (2013) 'The city as promised land: moral reasoning, evil and the dark side of capitalism in Ukraine', *Religion*, 43(3), pp. 365–384.

Wanner, C. (2018) 'Public religions after socialism: Redefining norms of difference', *Religion, State & Society*, 46(2), pp. 88–95.

Wanner, C., and Steinberg, M. D. (2008) 'Introduction: Reclaiming the sacred', in Steinberg, M. D. and Wanner, C. (eds.) *Religion, morality, and community in post-Soviet Societies.* Washington, DC: Woodrow Wilson Press and Bloomington, IN: Indiana University Press, pp. 1–20.

Warner, S. R. (1991) 'Oenology: The making of the new wine', in Feagin, J. R., Orum, A. M. and Sjoberg, G. (eds.) *A Case for the case study.* Chapel Hill, NC: University of North Carolina Press, pp. 174–199.

Weber, M. (2002) *Wirtschaft und Gesellschaft: Grundis der verstehende Soziologie* [5th edition]. Tübingen: J. C. B. Mohr (Paul Siebeck).

Willems, J. (2006) 'The religio-political strategies of the Russian Orthodox Church as a "politics of discourse"', *Religion, State and Society*, 34(3), pp. 287–298.

Worobec, C. D. (2007) 'Miraculous healings', in Steinberg, M. D. and Coleman, H. J. (eds.) *Sacred stories: Religion and spirituality in modern Russia.* Bloomington and Indianapolis: Indiana University Press, pp. 22–43.

Wynot, J. J. (2004) *Keeping the faith: Russian Orthodox monasticism in the Soviet Union, 1917–1939.* College Station: Texas A & M University Press.

Yushina, N. (2007) 'V Nikol'skom khrame mirotočili ikony', *Kaluzhskii perekrëstok*, quoted after the Internet edition of the newspaper: https://old.kp40.ru/index.php?cid=600&nid=130. Last accessed: 10.02.2019.

Zabaev, I. (2007a) 'Osnovnye kategorii khoziajstvennoj etiki sovremennogo russkogo pravoslavija' [The basic categories of economic ethics of contemporary Russian Orthodoxy], *Social'naya real'nost'*, № 9(21), pp. 5–26.

Zabaev, I. (2007b) 'Osnovnye kategorii khoziajstvennoj etiki sovremennogo russkogo pravoslavija' [The basic categories of economic ethics of contemporary Russian Orthodoxy], *Social'naya real'nost'*, №10(22), pp. 36–46.

Zernov, N. (1963) *The Russian religious renaissance of the twentieth century.* London: Darton.

Zhizneopisanie. (2003) *Optinskikh novomučenikov ieromonakha Vasilija, inoka Feraponta, inoka Trofima. Blagoslovenno voinstvo* [Lives of the new martyrs of Optina: Hieromonk Vasilii, monk Therapont, monk Trofim]. Optina Pustyn': Izdatel'stvo Sviato-Vvedenskoi Optinoi Pustyni.

Zigon, J. (2006) '"You should reform yourself not other people": The ethics of hope in contemporary Moscow', *Working Paper* 88, Max Planck Institute for Social Anthropology, Halle/Saale, pp. 1–20.

Zigon, J. (2008a) *Morality: An anthropological perspective.* Oxford: Berg.

Zigon, J. (2008b) 'Aleksandra Vladimirovna: Moral narratives of a Russian Orthodox woman', in Steinberg, M. D. and Wanner, C. (eds.) *Religion, morality, and community in post-Soviet societies*. Washington, DC: Woodrow Wilson Press and Bloomington, IN: Indiana University Press, pp. 85–114.

Zigon, J. (2010) *Making the new post-Soviet person: Moral experiences in contemporary Moscow*. Leiden: Brill.

Zigon, J. (2011a) 'Multiple moralities: Discourses, practices, and breakdowns in post-Soviet Russia', in Zigon, J. (ed.) *Multiple moralities and religions in post-Soviet Russia*. New York and Oxford: Berghahn Books, pp. 3–15.

Zigon, J. (ed.) (2011b) *Multiple moralities and religions in post-Soviet Russia*. New York and Oxford: Berghahn Books.

Zigon, J. (2011c) *HIV is God's blessing: Rehabilitating morality in neoliberal Russia*. Berkeley, CA: University of California Press.

Znamia. (2020) 'Vladislav Shapsha naznačen vrio gubernatora Kaluzhskoj oblasti' [Vladislav Shapsha is appointed as governor of the Kaluga region], *Znamia. Kaluga dayly*, 13.02.2020. Quoted following the Internet edition. https://znamiakaluga.ru/2020/02/13. Last accessed: 1.03.2020.

Zyrianov, P. N. (1999) 'Russkie monastyri i monašestvo v XIX – načale XX veka' [Russian monasteries and monasticism in the 19th – early 20th centuries], in Sinitsyna, N. V. (ed.) *Monašestvo i monastyri v Rossii XIX-XX veka*. Moskva: Nauka, pp. 302–331.

Sources from the Internet

http://drevo-info.ru/articles/4966.html

http://eparhia-kaluga.ru/periodika.html.

http://eparhia-kaluga.ru/periodika/gazeta-nasha-vera.html. Last accessed: 23.07.2018.

http://kaluga.amr-musum.ru. Last accessed: 25.09.2018.

http://Kaluga-poisk.ru/ Новости-Калуга/Новости-Калуга-Благоустройство/В-Калуге-построят-третий-мост-через-Оку-и-новую-окружную-дорогу.

http://kaluga-pokrov.cerkov.ru/voskresnaya-shkola. Last accessed: 23.07.2018.

http://kalugastat.gks.ru/wps/wcm/connect/rosstat_ts/kalugastat/resources/.

http://legostaev.kaluga.net/. Last accessed: 25.07.2019.

http://petripavel.tomsk.ru/openArticle.php?number=96. Last accessed: 25.09.2018.

http://rf-poisk.ru/page/230/. Last accessed: 1.09.2019.

http://social.diaconia.ru/search?eparchy_id=56. Last accessed: 18.09.2019.

http://tv-soyuz.ru/peredachi/lektsii-professora-a-i-osipova). Last accessed: 1.09.2018.

http://volvotrucks.com/trucks/russia-market/ru-ru/kaluga_factory/Pages/firstpage.aspx. Last accessed: 5.08.2018.

https://airkaluga.ru.

https://antimodern.ru/. Last accessed: 24.09.2018.

https://dvagrada.ru/wiki/Заглавная_страница. Last accessed: 24.09.2018.

https://eu.spb.ru/car/about. Internet page of the Center for Anthropology of Religion. Last accessed: 5.08.2018.

https://kaluga.ru/infor/.

https://ok.ru/lektsiipr. Last accessed: 1.09.2018.

https://sobory.ru/photo/258905. Last accessed: 30.08.2019.

Optina Hermitage Monastery site: www.optina.ru/rites/about/. Last accessed: 28.08.2018.

Soiuz slavianskikh obščin slavianskoj rodnoj very'. – www.rodnovery.ru; www.rodnoverie.org. Last accessed: 17.08.2018

www. belinkakaluga.ru/легостаев-виталий-васильевич. Last accessed: 25.07.2019.

www.fond.ru. Last accessed: 20.09.2018
www.hristianstvo.ru.
www.investkaluga.com.
www.kaluga-eparhia.ru/eparh.htm (Official website of the Kaluga diocese of the Russian Orthodox Church)
www.kdi40.ru.
www.molitvoslov.com/content/molitva-Chestnomu-Krestu. Last accessed: 14.09.2018.
www.parad-nevest.ru. Last accessed: 14.09.2018.
www.patriarchia.ru/db/text/5072750.html.
www.volklswagengrouprus.ru.
www.volvotrucks.com/trucks/russia-market/ru-ru/kaluga_factory/Pages/firstpage.aspx.
Zakon Russkoj Federacii (1993) O prave grazhdan Rossijskj Federacii na svobodu peredvizhenija, vybor mesta prebyvanija i zhitel'stva v predelakh Russkoj Federacii" [On the right of citizens of the Russian Federation to freedom of movement, choice of place of residence and residence within the Russian Federation" dated 06.06.1993 N 5242–1 (latest edition)], 25.06.1993, № 5242–1]. – www.consultant.ru/document/cons_doc_LAW_2255/. Last accessed: 1.12.2019.
Znamia Daily. Kaluga.

Appendix

Overview of interviews[1]

2006

(1) 21.09.2006: Nina Victorovna, 31, university education, a bibliographer/ social worker
(2) 22.09.2006: Father E. Č., 54, university education, a teacher/ priest
(3) 24.09.2006: Ul'jana Vladimirovna, 25, university education, a teacher
(4) 26.09.2006: Lidia Vasilievna, 67, university education, a bibliographer

2007

(5) 30.06.2007: Nadezhda Sidorovna, 32, university education, a housewife
(6) 4.07.2007: Nadezhda Sidorovna
(7) 30.06.2007: Father E. K., 34, university education, an engineer/ priest
(8) 5.07.2007: Father A. B., 36, university education, a priest and writer
(9) 9.07.2007: Vitalij Legostaev, 59, secondary technical education, a writer and photographer
(10) 11.07.2007: Maksim Andreevič, 22, secondary education, a student
(11) 12.07.2007: Ekaterina Viačeslavovna, 36, university education, a teacher/ religious activist
(12) 17.07.2007: Ekaterina Vasilievna, 60, university education, a bibliographer
(13) 30.07.2007: Victorija Leontievna, 51, university education, a bibliographer
(14) 13.07.2007: NN, 52, university education, an author
(15) 17.07.2007: Tamara Kirillovna, 46, secondary education, an administrative position
(16) 17.07.2007: Evgenija Afanasievna, 32, university education, a bibliographer
(17) 18.07.2007: Zinaida Anatolievna, 66, university education, an engineer/ pensioner

23.07.2007: Zinaida Anatolievna
2.08.2007: Zinaida Anatolievna

(18) 18.07.2007: Tamara Fëdorovna, 56, university education, a doctor/ pensioner
(19) 24.07.2007: Zinaida Makarovna, 45, university education, a teacher/ religious activist
(20) 24.07.2007: Elizaveta Mikhajlovna, 31, secondary education, a paramedic
(21) 30.07.2007: Valerija Pavlovna, 54, secondary education, a librarian
(22) 30.07.2007: Ivan Ignat'evič, 19, student, an IT specialist
(23) 1.08.2007: Sviatoslav Denisovič, 52, university education, an engineer/ manager
(24) 1.08.2007: Vera Gavrilovna, 37, university education, a bibliographer
(25) 4.08.2007: Larissa Makarovna, 50, secondary education, a paramedic
(26) 4.08.2007: Andrej Mikhajlovič, 32, secondary education, a religious activist
(27) 9.08.2007: Vadim Nikityč, 41, university education, a doctor
(28) 12.08.2007: Father I. K., 30, university education, a lawyer/ deacon
(29) 13.08.2007: Valerij Matveevič, 68, elementary education (middle school), a skilled worker
(30) 16.08.2007: Ostap Kirillovič, 50, university education, an administrative position
(31) 18.08.2007: Father V. K., 34, university education, a priest
(32) 19.08.2007: Natalia Emelianovna, 55, secondary education, a housewife

Note

1 All interviews have been recorded and are in the author's possession. The names of the interlocutors are fictitious, in order to keep their anonymity. Their age, education, and occupation correspond to the time of fieldwork (2006–2007). In cases when an interview is of sensitive character, no name is referred to. I use initials for the names of the priests as far as they are public figures; a prolific and known author (Vitalij Legostaev) is mentioned by his real name.

Summary

The proposed book explores driving forces of the socio-cultural change in contemporary Russia associated with the resumption of Orthodox life after 1988. The book addresses the main challenge of religious resurgence: the paradox of high-level Orthodox identification while having an actually low level of church attendance. This study is based on the methods, both theoretical and empirical, of socio-cultural anthropology.

Existing research rarely addresses the perspective of ordinary believers: it more often focuses on church-state relations or the political aspects of religion. Unlike that approach, proposed book explores one of the main social actors on the Russian Orthodox stage: the most devoted believers, the "little flock" that makes contemporary Orthodox revivalism possible, and their moral convictions. Research focus on this community as social background and vehicle of the Russian religious revivalism allows revisiting of the concept of "vicarious religion". By drawing a portrait of the "little flock", the book allows insight into the fabric of the religious life. Complex moral beliefs of the faithful have larger resonance on the agenda of Russian society and, respectively, the book gives them special attention. Value preferences and "ethical reasoning" among believers bring about the strong will to achieve moral perfection in religious terms. The study of the narratives of conversion shed additional light on Orthodoxy as a source of radical personal transformation (not that different from Pentecostalism). While the narratives of conversion reveal personal moral trajectories, the manifestations of the politics of memory show collective ideas marked by religious nationalism and by synergy between the secular and the religious. More broadly, the book contributes to the understanding of Orthodoxy as an important element of the "alchemy of power" in Russian political life.

Milena Benovska

Index